A Renaissance of Violence

Based on a close examination of more than 700 homicide trials, *A Renaissance of Violence* exposes the deep social instability at the core of the early modern states of North Italy. Following a series of crises in the early seventeenth century, interpersonal violence in the region grew to frightening levels, despite the efforts of courts and governments to reduce social conflict. In this detailed study of violence in early modern Europe, Colin Rose shows how major crises, such as the plague of 1630, reduced the strength of social bonds among both elite and ordinary Italians. As a result, incidents of homicidal violence exploded – in small rural communities, in the crowded urban center and within tightly knit families. Combining statistical analysis and close reading of homicide patterns, Rose demonstrates how the social contexts of violence, as much as the growth of state power, can contribute to explaining how and why interpersonal violence grew so rapidly in North Italy in the seventeenth century.

COLIN ROSE is Assistant Professor of European and Digital History at Brock University, St. Catharines, Canada. He has held fellowships with the Harry Frank Guggenheim Foundation, the Centre for Criminology and Criminological Studies at the University of Toronto and the Academy for the Advanced Study of the Renaissance. He is co-editor of *Mapping Space, Sense and Movement in Florence: Historical GIS and the Early Modern City* (2016) with Nicholas Terpstra, and co-director of the innovative DECIMA web-GIS of Renaissance Florence (www.decima-map.net).

A Renaissance of Violence

Homicide in Early Modern Italy

Colin Rose

Brock University

CAMBRIDGE
UNIVERSITY PRESS

CAMBRIDGE
UNIVERSITY PRESS

University Printing House, Cambridge CB2 8BS, United Kingdom

One Liberty Plaza, 20th Floor, New York, NY 10006, USA

477 Williamstown Road, Port Melbourne, VIC 3207, Australia

314-321, 3rd Floor, Plot 3, Splendor Forum, Jasola District Centre, New Delhi - 110025, India

79 Anson Road, #06-04/06, Singapore 079906

Cambridge University Press is part of the University of Cambridge.

It furthers the University's mission by disseminating knowledge in the pursuit of education, learning and research at the highest international levels of excellence.

www.cambridge.org
Information on this title: www.cambridge.org/9781108726924
DOI: 10.1017/9781108627948

© Colin Rose 2019

First published 2019
First paperback edition 2021

A catalogue record for this publication is available from the British Library

ISBN 978-1-108-49806-7 Hardback
ISBN 978-1-108-72692-4 Paperback

To Sarah Blanshei, *Maestra in Archivio*

Pieter Spierenburg, whose influence on my work is deep and abiding, unfortunately passed away during the production of this work. Though I met him only once, I will remember his kindness to me as a graduate student challenging his research. I regret that he will not be able to review this book. I hope it can stand as a testament to his foundational research into the problems of early modern violence, upon which a large community of scholars has depended for many years.

Contents

Illustrations

FIGURES

MAPS

Acknowledgments

I would like to thank the many people who aided and abetted the writing of this book, from its beginnings as my PhD dissertation at the University of Toronto through to its present form.

The research for this project was funded by the Social Sciences and Humanities Research Council of Canada, the Harry Frank Guggenheim Foundation and the Andrew W. Mellon Foundation via a Distinguished Achievement Award to Edward Muir in 2010. Both the University of Toronto and Brock University contributed money for trips to the archives. I am grateful for the support of these organizations.

While working in the very pleasant archives in Bologna, I was privileged to work with the archivists and staff of the *Archivio di Stato di Bologna* and the *Biblioteca dell'Archiginnasio*. Many thanks in particular to Giancarlo and Laborio at the ASBo. Long may North Americans receive such kind welcomes in your care. Grazie anche a Prof. Giancarlo Angelozzi.

Thanks indeed to my colleagues at Brock University for welcoming me to faculty life and providing mentorship and advice as I have begun my teaching career.

Thanks to the community of *bolognisti* whom I have encountered along the way, and who have always been generous with ideas and friendship.

Many, many thanks to Dr. Edward Muir and Dr. Regina Schwartz, along with the entire membership of the Academy for the Advanced Study of the Renaissance, 2014 edition, for their friendship, generosity and critical readings of various stages of this work.

To many colleagues and friends at the University of Toronto, especially fellow Italianists Vanessa McCarthy and John Christopoulos, and dissertation committee members Paul Cohen and Mark Meyerson, and my "Internal External" examiner Ken Bartlett: thank you all for supporting this project at an early phase.

Thanks to the scholars at the Centre for Reformation and Renaissance Studies in Toronto, especially Amyrose McCue-Gill and Natalie Oeltjen, for providing a welcome home away from home to this day.

Thanks to all of the historians of violence who have contributed ideas and explanations over the years, in particular my External dissertation examiner Stuart Carroll for his insightful comments on early stages of the manuscript.

To the two anonymous reviewers of Cambridge University Press, especially Reader #2, without whose trenchant comments you would all be subject to thirty-five pages of historiography in Chapter 1. The work is stronger for their helpful suggestions, though of course, any and all errors or sloppy prose remain mine and mine alone.

Thanks to Jovi the Shar-Pei, who supervised the writing of the first draft but who is no longer with us to see the final product.

Thanks to Dr. Gregory Hanlon, who deserves much credit for pushing me toward this project in the first place, and for first teaching me the skills and habits of an effective archival historian.

Thanks to Dr. Nicholas Terpstra, who has been a mentor for fourteen years and a friend for many of those, and a collaborator for many more to come. I have benefitted immensely from his patience and wisdom, and his academic and professional advice.

Thanks to Dr. Sarah Blanshei, to whom I dedicate this work. Sarah has been a mentor and a friend and she deserves more gratitude than can be offered here. I am utterly in her debt for the kindness she has shown me since we first met in 2011.

Thanks to my partner Madison, whose suggestions I have learned to take the first time offered.

Thanks to Arthur and Henry, my little guys. Maybe you can read the next one, not about murder ... love, Daddy.

1 Introduction

Bartholomeo Minconi did not have the profitable day he hoped for in the market outside Medicina. The forty-year-old salt smuggler came to the large town directly east of Bologna, from his hometown of Lugo in the Romagna, in April of 1670. A notary from Bologna's criminal court, the *Tribunale del Torrone*, recorded his brother's testimony the next day, itself informed by the gossip of "many and diverse persons": Bartholomeo attempted to break up a fight between two of his fellow townsmen and smugglers, Francesco Zanconi and Baldissera Vetria. The pair argued over "a certain wagon of grain," which, presumably, was stuffed with their contraband. When harsh words left them "injured, both of them brought themselves forward with their guns in hand," and the men squared off to fight. Francesco pulled the trigger first, but his weapon jammed. Because all involved were neighbours, Bartholomeo Minconi tried to intervene in this brewing duel; he died in the ensuing crossfire. According to his brother, Bartholomeo was a peaceful citizen who had offered to settle the debt between Zanconi and Vetria out of his own funds.[1] The smugglers' conflict, rooted in their illegal trade, arose from their familiarity with each other and might have been quelled by its virtues. That conflict came to violence in Medicina and occurred in the bright market day in a crowded square, where onlookers hid in doorways but still watched with fascination. A dispute over an unspecified debt between men, who otherwise cooperated in their illegal trade, left a third man, another smuggler, dead in the square, turning an argument into a homicide. Bartholomeo paid for his peacefulness with his life – one of

---

[1] Archivio di Stato di Bologna (hereafter ASBo), *Tribunale del Torrone, Atti e Processi* (hereafter *Torrone*), 6954/1, *in fine*. The brother's account paints Bartholomeo as a peacemaker, and at least one witness agreed that he was well known and respected in Medicina's market, unlike the two who came to violence. But Francesco Mingoni finished his statement with a list of Bartolomeo's goods that he now wanted to retrieve, in particular a horse that had been seized on a surety he could not afford, and he himself named the witness who spoke glowingly of Bartholomeo.

sixty-one people in this North Italian province of some 225,000 to die violently in Bolognese lands in that late-century year.

The figure of sixty-one homicides in 1670 translates to a "homicide rate," expressed as the number of people killed by others per 100,000 population, of about 27. Out of context, that rate may not alarm readers unfamiliar with homicide statistics, but it is frighteningly high in modern terms. Developed nations in the modern West – outside the United States – generally have homicide rates below 5 per 100,000 and strive to reach "intentional" homicide rates of less than 1 per 100,000.[2] That a largely agrarian society of three centuries past was more violent than our contemporary urban societies is perhaps not surprising, but the snapshot of a homicide rate in 1670 is only the prelude to the larger story told in this book. Over the course of the first seven decades of the seventeenth century, in Bologna and other parts of Northern Italy, homicide rates rose precipitously before falling off to similar levels as in 1600 by century's end. That dramatic rise and fall of fatal violence, in an economically robust, politically developed area of Catholic Europe, has much to tell us about the reasons why homicide rates rise in areas where society seems otherwise stable.

In North Italy, a resurgence of frequent revenge and political homicides reflects the dissolution of socioeconomic stability amid a series of crises that engulfed the region in the seventeenth century.[3] Regional patterns of homicide challenge models hitherto used to explain the decline of violence in the West and the role of elite populations in effecting that change. Qualitative analysis of a large body of homicide trials from Bologna demonstrates how environmental, political and economic crises broke a fragile peace established between the Papacy and various groups of elite nobility in the sixteenth century. The crumbling of that peace engendered a decades-long outburst of violence and

---

[2] For comparison, Italy had a homicide rate of ~1 per 100,000 in 2014, and ~2 per 100,000 in 1995. Honduras, the most homicidal country in the world in 2014, had a homicide rate of ~75 per 100,000. *The World Bank: Intentional Homicides (per 100,000 people)*, http:// data.worldbank.org/indicator/VC.IHR.PSRC.P5?year_high_desc=false, accessed December 7, 2017.

[3] For an overview of recent Anglo-American and Italian scholarship on seventeenth-century Italy, cf. Edward Muir, "Italy in the No Longer Forgotten Centuries," *I Tatti Studies in the Italian Renaissance* 16, nos. 1–2 (September 1, 2013): 5–11; Gregory Hanlon, *Early Modern Italy, 1550–1800: Three Seasons in European History* (New York: St. Martin's Press, 2000). Domenico Sella's survey of the period provides the best introduction to local Italian histories of seventeenth-century Italy, though Bologna receives scant attention. Cf. Domenico Sella, *Italy in the Seventeenth Century* (London: Longman, 1997).

necessitated the reestablishment, on new terms, of the sociopolitical equilibrium that might reduce elite and ordinary violence.[4]

That process is significant because the major cities of North Italy, of which Bologna was foremost, were perhaps archetypal examples of Norbert Elias's "civilizing process," a theory that looms large over the history of violence and its decline in the West.[5] That theory, which holds (among other things) that over the late medieval and early modern period the centralization of local and regional government subdued the violent passions of elite and ordinary people and subjected those people to the authority of laws and courts, has gripped both academic and popular literature on violence.[6] However, the experience of Northern Italy demonstrates how fragile could be the peaceful society brought about by administrative and judicial centralization, steep hierarchical order, and attempts to institute the rule of law. When it failed to mitigate the impact of warfare, economic stagnation, famine and plague in the 1620s and 1630s, the papal government of Bologna witnessed a sharp increase in interpersonal homicides across society. When it sought to curb the violence of regional elites, the criminal court of Bologna became party to the revival of vendetta violence between urban nobles seeking the reestablishment of feudal privileges in their rural lands. When authorities sought to punish and reduce violence, they found themselves confronted by the norms of a society that valued reciprocity and restitution over lawful redress, which preferred that the debts of violence be composed with blood money or with blood in kind.

Throughout the period under consideration, ordinary *bolognesi* killed each other in conflicts that are sometimes very familiar to modern readers

---

[4] This negotiated peace was established following decades of conflict between papal legates, republican factions of the nobility who sought to advance their positions through governance in the Senate and other institutions, and vestiges of the Bentivoglio oligarchy. In this long struggle, the criminal court became an active agent in the pacification of the violent sectors of each set of noble factions. Andrea Gardi, "Lineamenti della storia politica di Bologna: da Giulio II a Innocenzo X," in A. Prosperi, ed., *Storia di Bologna* (Bologna: Bononia University Press, 2005–2008), 3–60; M. Cavina, "I luoghi della giustizia," in ibid., 368–73; Giancarlo Angelozzi and Cesarina Casanova, *La nobiltà disciplinata: violenza nobiliare, procedure di giustizia e scienza cavalleresca a Bologna nel 17. secolo* (Bologna: CLUEB, 2003).

[5] Norbert Elias, *The Civilizing Process* (New York: Pantheon Books, 1978).

[6] The academic debate on violence in the early modern West is largely defined by the work of Pieter Spierenburg, the early proponent of Eliasian theories of violence. See, for instance, P. Spierenburg, *The Spectacle of Suffering: Executions and the Evolution of Repression: From a Preindustrial Metropolis to the European Experience* (New York: Cambridge University Press, 1984). In popular literature, Harvard linguist and sociologist Steven Pinker has melded Eliasian thinking with evolutionary psychology to create a rosy view of an inexorable decline in violence across time. Steven Pinker, *The Better Angels of Our Nature: Why Violence Has Declined* (New York: Viking, 2011).

and sometimes seem quite alien. They killed for love or lust, for financial gain or to prevent financial ruin, to avenge a wrong or to shame an enemy. They killed in tightly knit, face-to-face communities and neighbourhoods, which were themselves deeply concerned with the amount of violence they suffered, and which possessed formal and informal means to resolve violent conflicts. Taking place in a society that deeply valued personal honour and maintained a deeply rooted culture of affront, violence in early modern Italy always had the potential to become cyclical; as such, the importance of peacemaking institutions cannot be overstated.[7] Fortunately for the communities suffering crisis and violence, the ordinary people of Bologna and its environs found a powerful agent of peace in the *Tribunale del Torrone*, a criminal court whose functional purpose was not punishment but the prevention of cyclical violence. Here peasants and artisans found, if not neutral justice, at least a mediating justice largely divorced from the rivalries and local politics of rural communities and urban neighbourhoods. The *Torrone*'s notaries offered better arbitration and mediation of disputes, through a system of exile, reconciliation and pardon, than did the patronage of biased noble landlords and employers. However, it would still be a mistake to place significant causative power onto the imposition of centralized justice: when violence declined among North Italian communities, it did so because of increased opportunities for non-violence to effectively resolve conflicts, and because violence ceased to be an effective means of pursuing social, economic and political advantage.

This book argues, using the example of North Italy in the seventeenth century, that the imposition of centralized legal and political institutions has a limited effect on the level and character of violence in a given society. It is true, as the example of the *Tribunale del Torrone* shows, that broad swathes of a population will prefer the mediation and resolution of their conflicts under the umbrella of some legal authority and will happily pursue this option when it is available. Simply put, most people do not like violence and avoid its use if possible. That preference lurks beneath the surface of many peace accords, petitions and pardon letters bringing judicial processes to a close, and is sometimes expressed quite clearly by petitioners who happily offloaded the responsibilities of revenge onto institutional powers.[8] However, the reduction of violence to levels

---

[7] Stuart Carroll, "Revenge and Reconciliation in Early Modern Italy," *Past & Present* 233, no. 1 (November 1, 2016): 101–42.

[8] Colin Rose, "'To Be Remedied of Any Vendetta': Petitions and the Avoidance of Violence in Early Modern Parma," *Crime, Histoire & Sociétés/Crime, History & Societies*, no. 2 (2012): 23–25.

desired by modern states in the West – ideally, homicide rates below 1 per 100,000 and not more than 3 per 100,000 – requires more than the strong arm of the law. The institutions that seek to reduce violence – or to increase control, depending on one's perspective – must also achieve a wide degree of legitimacy that binds members of society across economic and social bounds.[9] When one or more elements of society reject the legitimacy of social and legal institutions, when those institutions fail to address the needs and concerns of particular groups in society, those groups have good reasons not to participate in the social contract proposed by those institutions. The history that unfolds in this book is a history in which the fragile legitimacy of institutions crumbles under the weight of a series of societal crises. In response to that disintegration of legitimacy, both elite and ordinary groups of people turned to violence, enthusiastically or not, to solve the problems wrought by crisis.

In the pre-industrial context of seventeenth-century North Italy, socio-economic and environmental crises, and how institutions responded to them, had a profound impact on the amount and character of fatal violence in the region. The seventeenth century in Italy was long considered by many historians to be a period of economic, industrial and social stagnation, at least in comparison to the dynamic city-states of the fifteenth and sixteenth centuries, the height of the European "Renaissance."[10] Though recent work has revived interest in the seventeenth century and attempted to rehabilitate the reputation of its princely states, the seventeenth century was difficult for much of Italy.[11] At the root of that difficulty, and at the root of the frightening increase in homicidal violence that this book reveals, was a series of social, economic and environmental crises. Spanish and French armies fought in the Po Valley and Lombard Plain during the Thirty Years' War, and Italian princes had to muster their own armies and respond to growing numbers of deserting and delisted soldiers.[12] The industries that had sustained Italian cities in earlier centuries declined in European and global

---

[9] This is the idea at the core of Randolph Roth's counter to the idea of the civilizing process, using the example of American homicide rates since the colonial period. Cf. Randolph Roth, *American Homicide* (Cambridge, MA: Belknap Press of Harvard University Press, 2009). My thinking on violence and the factors influencing it is deeply informed by Roth's work.

[10] Three survey texts from around the turn of the twenty-first century rely on this point as the central plank for understanding Italian society in the *seicento*. Hanlon, *Early Modern Italy, 1550–1800*; Sella, *Italy in the Seventeenth Century*; Christopher F. Black, *Early Modern Italy: A Social History* (London: Routledge, 2001).

[11] See the above-cited review of recent work on Italy in the seventeenth century. Muir, "Italy in the No Longer Forgotten Centuries."

[12] Gregory Hanlon, *Italy 1636: Cemetery of Armies* (Oxford University Press, 2015).

importance. Climate change, in the form of an ongoing "Little Ice Age," rendered the harvests of the early seventeenth century extremely unpredictable: a series of famines in the 1620s created hunger and disarray in much of the Lombard Plain and Po Valley, the traditional breadbasket of Italy and much of Europe.[13] Following those famines, a terrible epidemic in 1630 resulted in the deaths of thousands, killing as much as 50% of the already-weakened population in cities such as Parma, Padua and Venice.[14] The death of so many people – elites, urban artisans and rural labourers – shook the institutions of North Italian states to their core, and despite well-rehearsed plans for quarantining their cities against the plague, governors proved unable to protect their populations from sickness. In the uncertainty that followed the environmental crises of the 1620s and the 1630 plague, recourse to violence became more common in the pursuit of resources, romance and revenge.

The institutions of North Italy suffered a serious blow to their legitimacy. Critical to the project of consolidating centralized ducal and princely states in the region – as were established in the sixteenth century in Parma and Piacenza, Bologna, Ferrara (the Este moved from there to Modena in 1598), Mantua, Florence, and elsewhere – was the transformation of local elite groups to a form of service nobility, or the courtiers made famous by Baldassare Castiglione. Following 1630 those elite groups turned again on the representatives of centralized government, which in Bologna meant the papal legate appointed by the pontiff in Rome to govern his northern capital, reviving a class-based practice of revenge violence that had never fully died away. In the wake of the epidemic of 1630, interpersonal violence among all classes surged over the next thirty years, culminating in what can best be described as an urban civil war in Bologna in the 1650s and 1660s, when homicide rates reached levels hitherto undocumented in Europe. The belligerents of this civil war were those elements of society that rejected the legitimacy of centralized judicial institutions. North Italy thereby offers an

---

[13] Robin D. Greene, "Mountain Peasants in an Age of Global Cooling" (MA thesis, Dalhousie University, 2010); Andrew B. Appleby, "Epidemics and Famine in the Little Ice Age," *The Journal of Interdisciplinary History* 10, no. 4 (April 1, 1980): 643–63; Brian M. Fagan, *The Little Ice Age: How Climate Made History, 1300–1850* (New York: Basic Books, 2000).

[14] Guido Alfani and Marco Percoco, "Plague and Long-Term Development: The Lasting Effects of the 1629–30 Epidemic on the Italian Cities," Working Paper (IGIER [Innocenzo Gasparini Institute for Economic Research], Bocconi University, 2014), http://ideas.repec.org/p/igi/igierp/508.html; Samuel K. Cohn Jr. and Guido Alfani, "Households and Plague in Early Modern Italy," *The Journal of Interdisciplinary History* 38, no. 2 (October 1, 2007): 177–205; Carlo M. Cipolla, *Fighting the Plague in Seventeenth-Century Italy* (Madison: University of Wisconsin Press, 1981).

illuminating case study of the effects of socioeconomic and environmental stressors on the stability of a society, and the violent consequences of a failure to maintain institutional legitimacy among broad swathes of the population.

The framework of this argument draws on more than thirty years of accumulated studies of homicide and non-fatal violence in Europe and the Americas. Several perspectives come together here to make the case that the history of violence in the West is not a progressive history of societies becoming more peaceful. Rather, as North Italy shows, reductions in violence are contingent on the maintenance of the conditions that brought them about. In the right circumstances, most people generally prefer to abjure personal violence. But absent the conditions that make non-violence a viable option to bring about socioeconomic success, violence will become more prevalent and homicide rates will rise. I am not the first to make this argument, which appears in various forms outlined below. But this is the first attempt to make that argument legible in a long-term analysis of homicidal violence in North Italy, an important region of early modern Europe where practices of elite violence had a significant impact on the social, political and economic development of several major states and the lives of more than one million people residing in the Lombard Plain and Po Valley.

The Scene of the Crime: Seventeenth-Century Bologna

Bologna enjoyed, or perhaps suffered, a unique physical, political and social environment amid the seventeenth-century Italian states (see Map 1.1). The political, social and economic processes engendered by these characteristics significantly impacted the patterns and prosecutions of fatal violence within Bologna's borders. Like many Italian states of the period, it had a political history of oligarchic domination by a few powerful local families, whose descendants remained deeply involved in Bolognese politics under the reasserted papal regime of the sixteenth and seventeenth centuries. Bologna's political flavour proved decisive in its history of violence: during the period of "absolutist" government, Bologna's nobility remained riven by the violent factional rivalries that had dominated the late communal period. The conflicts that emerged from these rifts triangulated powers in Bologna: republican (or *anti-Bentivoleschi*) noble factions of the late medieval and early modern period, which included branches of the Pepoli and Paleotti families, worked to advance their family interests and power through the newly established papal government, by participating in the reformed Senate

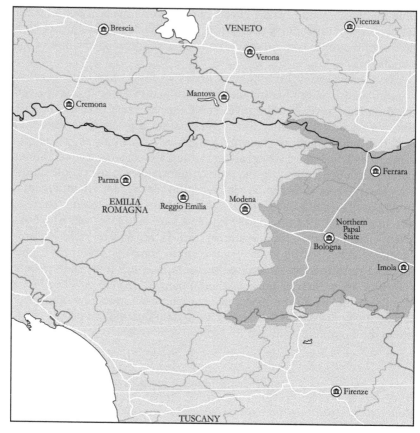

Map 1.1 The major cities of North Italy, showing the borders of the papal state north of Tuscany.
Map by author and Cox Cartographic Ltd. Basemap data provided by ESRI and OpenStreetMap.

and proposing grand civic gestures, such as the "Pious Heap of Mercy" dreamed up by Giovanni Pepoli.[15]

The vestigial supporters of the Bentivoglio oligarchy that dominated fifteenth-century Bologna, the *Bentivoleschi* nobles which included families such as the Malvezzi and Barbazza, antagonized both those nobles who accommodated papal power as well as the papal government itself.

---

[15] Nicholas Terpstra, "Republicanism, Public Welfare and Civil Society in Early Modern Bologna," in N. Terpstra, A. de Benedictis and G. Anselmi, eds., *Bologna: Cultural Crossroads from the Medieval to the Baroque: Recent Anglo-American Scholarship* (Bologna: Bononia University Press, 2013), 205–7.

The government of Bologna – led by a papal legate, or ambassador/ governor – faced the difficult task of identifying the members of each faction from among a deeply intertwined population of nobility whose networks of family power stretched over much of North and Central Italy.[16] This multivalent struggle for primacy cast its shadow over much of the social conflict and interpersonal violence of Bologna's nobility and urban artisan communities. Moreover, its physical position on the Peninsula made it an important and highly trafficked centre of trade and transit, giving it a cosmopolitan population and, at any given time, a large body of itinerant travellers spending limited time in the city. A series of crises over the seventeenth century exacerbated the already unstable political and social orders of Bologna. Other Emilian states confronted the same challenges from noble and artisan populations, and the ways in which Bologna endured these trials help us to understand the complicated regional history of interpersonal violence.

Much of the troubled history of the seventeenth century in Bologna had its roots in the violent factionalism that characterized the medieval commune and oligarchy. From the medieval period, Bolognese politics and civil society were highly unstable, and frequent, violent changes of regime were the norm during the thirteenth to fifteenth centuries.[17] In this crucible, the major noble lineages of Bologna honed their practice of revenge-as-politics, blending personal rivalry and affront with membership in city bodies such as the *Senato* to advance family fortunes through a combination of private warfare and political action. During this period, urban power was very much rooted in rural land: the leading noble families of the oligarchic period (Pepoli, Bentivoglio, Lambertazzi) possessed large feudal domains bequeathed by emperors and popes, whence they launched attacks against other nobles, and whose tenants provided manpower for their urban retinues. Homicide and violence were regular aspects of the struggle for political power, and civil and criminal justice in Bologna developed in the realities of that unstable situation.

Justice, and the right to dispense it, was a critical privilege of the medieval oligarchs. In their rural holdings, they possessed the authority to arbitrate and punish civil and criminal disputes among their serfs.[18]

---

[16] M. Carboni, *Il debito della città: mercato del credito, fisco e società a Bologna fra cinque e seicento* (Bologna: Il mulino, 1995); M. Carboni, "Public Debt, Guarantees and Local Elites in the Papal States (XVI–XVIII Centuries)," *The Journal of European Economic History* 38, no. 1 (Spring 2009): 149–74.

[17] Sarah R. Blanshei, *Politics and Justice in Late Medieval Bologna* (Boston: Brill, 2010), 313–497.

[18] The rise of the *Torrone* from this system was first documented by Tiziana Di Zio, "Il Tribunale del Torrone," *Atti E Memorie (Romagna)* 43 (1992): 333–48.

Magnates – the elite among oligarchic nobility – used this power as a means of dispensing favours and raising funds through fines and fees.[19] Rural justice was beholden to the capricious favouritism of a violent local elite, and it made an effective tool for factional nobility to grow their manpower and revenue. In short, justice was partial: the ability for *bolognesi* to receive redress for wrongs done against them depended on the strategic goodwill of a violent elite, whose judgment might be swayed by money, material goods or promises of loyalty and service. Bolognese peasants lived under the shadow of these magnate lineages, whose factional battles for control of the urban core were fought largely by retainers raised from rural landholdings. The retinues of fighting men of each faction often found themselves in the sway of magnates through the magnate's skilled manipulation of justice and the right to arbitrate conflicts.

In each change of regime, civil society was rebuilt by the recent victorious faction. Within the city, justice was officially the jurisdiction of the *Podestà*, a foreign judge employed on limited terms and therefore, in theory, an impartial judge unbeholden to powerful local interests. However, the ability of the *podestà* to dispense impartial justice was compromised by the use of accusatory procedure, which placed the burden of cost onto a complainant in either a civil or criminal denunciation.[20] Better justice therefore was available to those who could afford these costs or secure the sponsorship of those who could. Magnates and their followers also intimidated and assaulted those who might bring complaints against them.[21] As in Florence, the magnate lineages of Medieval Bologna were defined less by economic power than by lifestyle and shared cultural and military interests. Alliances shifted constantly, and each new regime change brought the threat that displaced rulers might find themselves proscribed, their families banished or confined, and all decrees, concords and criminal sentences published under the previous regime cancelled.

The sixteenth-century popes took a much harsher approach to the governance of Bologna than had earlier pontiffs, who had been unable to govern effectively in the face of the Bentivoglio oligarchy. Julius II was unwilling to tolerate local resistance, and when the Bentivoglii revolted

---

[19] On definitions and characteristics of magnates in Medieval Italy, cf. C. Lansing, *The Florentine Magnates: Lineage and Faction in a Medieval Commune* (Princeton, NJ: Princeton University Press, 1991); Blanshei, *Politics and Justice in Late Medieval Bologna*, 183–210.

[20] Blanshei, *Politics and Justice in Late Medieval Bologna*, 337–65.

[21] Lansing, *The Florentine Magnates*; Blanshei, *Politics and Justice in Late Medieval Bologna*, 216–60.

against emboldened papal rule in 1509, he expelled them and razed their urban palace, replacing it with a sporting field for university students – a significant act, given that exile was usually understood to be temporary. During the next thirty years, factional strife dominated Bologna's streets and canals, and the papal legates took hard stances against noble agitation, hanging dozens of leading oligarchs.[22] Judicial privilege among the nobility became a focus of sixteenth-century papal government in Bologna: Julius II vowed to strip the nobility of the right to adjudicate conflicts in their territories, and he and his successors further subjected them to papal courts and, eventually, the *Tribunale del Torrone*.[23]

Sixteenth-century legates also worked to accommodate noble ambitions, albeit without the concessions given out in the fifteenth century. A series of land grants made in the mid-century to minor oligarchs of the *Bentivoleschi* party, such as the Barbazza and Malvezzi, allowed them to grow their power from a rural land base. This transfer of urban social power to a grounded, resource-based power in the *contado* allowed these families to grow in stature as the seventeenth century approached and to play a larger role in urban politics. Moreover, around 1586, the Senate of Forty was expanded to include fifty members of leading families, including some branches of *Bentivoleschi* families recently enticed into the papal fold with rural lands.[24] The legates wanted to reduce the levels of anti-papal tension present among sectors of the nobility by providing them with useful civil service through which they could advance their families' fortunes. Many noble houses effectively followed this path and, through membership in the Senate and in various government boards, gained access to the wider network of Italian elite families that bound the centralizing governments of the Italian peninsula through elite social ties.[25]

During this same period and extending into the seventeenth century, economic stagnation and regional politics affected Bologna's civil society in significant ways. The textile industries that had borne Bologna

---

[22] N. Terpstra, "Theory into Practice," in N. Terpstra, ed., *The Art of Executing Well: Rituals of Execution in Renaissance Italy* (Kirksville, MO: Truman State University Press, 2008), 121–24, 130–32.

[23] Giancarlo Angelozzi and Cesarina Casanova, *La giustizia criminale in una città di antico regime: il tribunale del Torrone di Bologna, secc. XVI–XVII* (Bologna: CLUEB, 2008), 20–30.

[24] Gardi, "Lineamenti," 30–35.

[25] J. deSilva, "Ecclesiastical Dynamicism in Early Modern Bologna: The Canonical Chapters of San Pietro and San Petronio," in Terpstra et al., eds., *Bologna: Cultural Crossroads*, 173–92.

through the medieval period declined here as elsewhere in Italy.[26] Nevertheless, a series of regulatory and institutional choices made by legatine governments allowed Bologna to emerge from this decline toward the end of the seventeenth century, renewing its economy as a north Italian industrial centre.[27] This general decline in Italy was blamed either on the domination of the Peninsula by French and Spanish interests or on the decadence of the merchant class that had animated its economic growth in earlier centuries; neither of these explanations is quite satisfactory. The participation of the Italian economy in a broader, highly volatile European and global marketplace is more likely the culprit, though that was surely cold comfort to early modern *bolognesi*.[28] Moreover, in the 1620s both regional and international warfare erupted, and North Italy suffered both conflict and crisis during the Thirty Years' War. From 1627 to 1629, and again in 1636, French and Imperial armies fought in the Lombard valleys, while in 1641 the first Castro War inflicted serious damage on the areas around Bologna and Ferrara.[29] The 1620s revival of pro-French sentiment in places such as Ferrara and Modena threatened the stability of the papal state in Bologna, such that there was no easy transition from the turbulent process of papal consolidation. These processes deeply shaped the experience of Bologna's civil society and had reverberating effects through the seventeenth century.

By 1600, then, Bologna had endured more than two centuries of regional instability, rapid regime change and violent domination by entrenched factional nobility. These nobles exercised power over the urban core of the province by drawing on men and resources from their rural landholdings. Moreover, they claimed the right of justice for themselves, adjudicating conflicts among their serfs and tenants in the countryside and exempting themselves from podestarial jurisdiction. With each regime change came a period of violence and instability, followed by a limited accommodation and an attenuation of violence as one faction slowly dominated the other. The instability of Bolognese politics appears as a generational phenomenon, with each new generation fighting among themselves to reestablish hegemony over Bologna. The addition of the Papacy to this volatile sociopolitics made the factionalism of Bologna a murky, multivalent affair. The Papacy's nascent rule was

---

[26] Domenico Sella, *Italy in the Seventeenth Century* (London: Longman, 1997), 29–32; Christopher F. Black, *Early Modern Italy: A Social History* (London: Routledge, 2001), 23; Brian S. Pullan, *Crisis and Change in the Venetian Economy in the Sixteenth and Seventeenth Centuries* (London: Methuen, 1968), 132.

[27] A. Guenzi, "Politica ed Economica," in Prosperi, ed., *Storia di Bologna*, 335–40, Vol. 3, part 1.

[28] Sella, *Italy in the Seventeenth Century*, 33–35.   [29] Ibid., 7–11.

challenged initially by members of both republican and oligarchic factions, with elements of those factions accommodating papal rule in the latter half of the sixteenth-century in exchange for land and membership on various councils and administrative bodies. The major families on either side of the republican–oligarch divide (the Pepoli and Paleotti, the Barbazza and Malvezzi) variously participated in government and frequently stymied the efforts of legates to reform councils from within.[30] This environment of deep factional instability remained a powerful social force in early seventeenth-century Bologna, which should be considered a period of accommodation and quiescence as outlined above. The seventeenth century, then, witnessed the failure of the Bolognese legation as a state project. A failure to achieve a functional civil society in which conditions of social trust were strong and reliable is the hallmark of papal governance in Bologna, and the evidence of that weak state lies in its inability to restrain homicidal violence across the seventeenth century.

Interpreting Early Modern Violence

Violence is a highly flexible concept open to interpretation through many different methodologies, theoretical lenses and explanatory frameworks. Until recently it was largely relegated to the edges of political histories of Renaissance and early modern Europe. Famous incidents such as the Pazzi Conspiracy of 1478 attracted attention because of their relation to high politics and the severe repercussions they entailed; even then, the brutal murder of Giuliano de' Medici was considered an episode in the Florentine struggle for freedom and liberty.[31] Lauro Martines's early venture into the history of violence in the Italian communes did not attempt a comprehensive analysis of the place of violence in their streets, but instead focused on violent factional politics to lionize the republican interests of those cities' elites.[32] In many ways, the violence of Italian cities was incompatible with their projected identities as civic republics of *virtù*-ous men, and much of it was easily ignored by both contemporary and modern writers. Only recently, Trevor Dean and Kate Lowe edited a

---

[30] N. Terpstra, "Republicanism, Public Welfare, and Civil Society in Early Modern Bologna," 205–16.

[31] Harold Acton, *The Pazzi Conspiracy: The Plot against the Medici* (London: Thames and Hudson, 1979); Renee Watkins, ed., *Humanism and Liberty: Writings on Freedom from Fifteenth-Century Florence* (Columbia: University of South Carolina Press, 1978); Charles Lloyd, *The Conspiracy of the Pazzi* (Cambridge: Chadwyck-Healey, 1994); Lauro Martines, *April Blood: Florence and the Plot against the Medici* (London: Jonathan Cape, 2003).

[32] L. Martines, ed., *Violence and Civil Disorder in Italian Cities, 1200–1500*; L. Martines, *Power and Imagination: City-States in Renaissance Italy* (New York: Knopf, 1979).

collection of essays dedicated to the problem of murder in this period.[33] While these essays clarify the central role of homicidal violence in early modern Italian culture, we still lack rigorous analysis of violence for any Italian city-state, let alone a comprehensive national synthesis on the level that now exists for England, the Netherlands, much of Scandinavia and the United States.[34] The aggregation of reliable datasets from Italian city-states must start somewhere, though, and Bologna is an appropriate place given the richness and completeness of its judicial archive. This book interprets the first mining of north Italian archives for meaningful criminal figures on homicide in the early modern period.[35]

Ritual and Performance

The structures of control and limitation that seemed to govern much early modern violence attracted the interest of a generation of historians from the 1970s to 1990s, whose research remains influential today. Early modern Europe presented historians with a vibrant world of ritual activity. Inspired by Geertzian anthropology, social historians exploited rich Italian archives to create "thick descriptions" of the many forms of political, social and ludic ritual that seemed to characterize Italian city-states.[36] In the thirty-five years since Muir's *Civic Ritual in Renaissance Venice*, the "ritual turn" became a leading school of social history.[37] The trappings of civic pride, religious identity and personal relationships

---

[33] Trevor Dean and K. J. P. Lowe, eds., *Murder in Renaissance Italy* (Cambridge University Press, 2017).

[34] J. S. Cockburn, "Patterns of Violence in English Society: Homicide in Kent 1560–1985," *Past & Present*, no. 130 (February 1, 1991): 70–106; Spierenburg, "Faces of Violence"; Roth, *American Homicide*; E. Monkkonen and E. Johnson, eds., *The Civilization of Crime: Violence in Town and Country since the Middle Ages* (Urbana: University of Illinois Press, 1996).

[35] Italian and French scholars have been more freely exploring violence in Italian archives for some time, but Emilia has been left out so far. Cf. O. Di Simplicio, *Peccato, penitenza, perdono: Siena 1575–1800: la formazione della coscienza nell'Italia moderna* (Milano: FrancoAngeli, 1994); I. Fosi, *La giustizia del papa: sudditi e tribunali nello stato pontificio in età moderna* (Rome: GLF editori Laterza, 2007); P. Blastenbrei, "Violence, Arms and Criminal Justice in Papal Rome, 1560–1600," *Renaissance Studies* 20, no. 1 (February 2006): 68–87.

[36] C. Geertz, "Deep Play: Notes on the Balinese Cockfight," *Daedalus* 101, no. 1 (1972): 1–37; E. Muir, *Civic Ritual in Renaissance Venice* (Princeton, NJ: Princeton University Press, 1981); Weissman, *Ritual Brotherhood in Renaissance Florence*.

[37] M. Jurdjecic and R. Strom-Olsen, eds., *Rituals of Politics and Culture in Early Modern Europe: Essays in Honour of Edward Muir* (Toronto: Centre for Reformation and Renaissance Studies, 2016).

made the highly structured ritual lives of male sodalities a fruitful subject for readers of ritual history.[38] Historians of gender also used the ritual framework to analyze the construction and performance of gendered behaviours; masculinity, in particular, has been recognized as a performative, ritual set of relationships and behaviours.[39] So too with the concept of violence, which gives the historian examining ritual behaviour much to unpack: as Anton Blok argues, there is no such thing as senseless violence, and all violence carries meaning.[40] Ritual interpretation as a school of thought is wide and flexible enough that it has since branched into multiple interpretations.

Natalie Zemon Davis was the first to explore how the seemingly destructive violence of crowds could in fact be structured by ritual.[41] Her early work, collected in 1975 as *Society and Culture in Early Modern France: Eight Essays*, relied heavily on the interpretation of ritual behaviours to make meaning of the chaotic French sixteenth century. In Lyon, she found cohesive ritual languages spoken in common by artisans, labourers and lawyers that moved at levels much deeper than the divides of religion and state, or even the arrival of the printed word, could reflect.[42] Seeking to recover the voices of people who did not usually appear in chronicle narratives, Davis examined petitions for pardon, which were issued by the *ancien régime* French state in their thousands.[43] She argued that the process of crime, punishment and pardon – the

---

[38] J. F. Rondeau, "Homosociality and Civic (Dis)order in Late Medieval Italian Confraternities," in N. Terpstra, ed., *The Politics of Ritual Kinship*, Cambridge Studies in Italian History and Culture (Cambridge University Press, 1999); C. F. Black, "The Development of Confraternity Studies over the Past Thirty Years," in ibid.; Giovanna Casagrande, "Confraternities and Lay Female Religiosity in Late Medieval and Renaissance Umbria," in ibid.; D. Bornstein, "The Bounds of Community: Commune, Parish, Confraternity, and Charity at the Dawn of a New Era in Cortona," in ibid., 5; L. Nussdorfer, "The Vacant See: Ritual and Protest in Early Modern Rome," *The Sixteenth Century Journal* 18, no. 2 (July 1, 1987): 173–89.

[39] R. M. Karras, *From Boys to Men: Formations of Masculinity in Late Medieval Europe* (Philadelphia: University of Pennsylvania Press, 2003); T. W. Gallant, "Honor, Masculinity, and Ritual Knife Fighting in Nineteenth-Century Greece," *The American Historical Review* 105, no. 2 (April 1, 2000): 359–82; J. M. Hunt, "Carriages, Violence, and Masculinity in Early Modern Rome," *I Tatti Studies in the Italian Renaissance* 17, no. 1 (2014): 175–96; Kenneth Gouwens, "Meanings of Masculinity in Paolo Giovio's 'Ischian' Dialogues," *I Tatti Studies in the Italian Renaissance* 17, no. 1 (2014): 79–101.

[40] A. Blok, *Honour and Violence* (Malden, MA: Polity Press, 2001), chap. 6, "The Meaning of Senseless Violence."

[41] N. Z. Davis, "The Reasons of Misrule" and "The Rites of Violence," in N. Z. Davis, *Society and Culture in Early Modern France: Eight Essays* (Stanford, CA: Stanford University Press, 1975), 97–123, 152–188.

[42] "Printing and the People," in ibid., 189–99.

[43] N. Z. Davis, *Fiction in the Archives: Pardon Tales and Their Tellers in Sixteenth-Century France* (Stanford, CA: Stanford University Press, 1987).

judicial process – was itself a ritual process in which defendants understood the roles they had to play to save their necks, and judges allowed them to play these roles.

Davis and Muir share an interest in the close, anthropological reading of the documentary evidence of relationships, behaviour and social organization. Muir's work on the rituals of Venetian political and civic life led him to study the *Terra Ferma* and the Venetian dominions in Friuli, where during the sixteenth century a feudal code still loomed large in the law, and the state was absent but for itinerant soldiers guarding Venetian lands from Imperial raids.[44] A frightful massacre of one family and its partisans by another in Udine in 1511 provided the case study from which Muir expanded to discover a land where ritualized feudal power was made real by violence and control of natural resources. To Muir, the "Cruel Carnival" of 1511 was a violent outburst by a dying form of nobility that would later abandon violence in favour of "civilized" manners.[45] Unpacking the details of testimony about the massacre at Udine revealed a world of highly metaphorical violence, in which degradation of one's enemy both lifted one closer to the heavens and made dogs and dogmeat of one's foes. The deep entwining of violence, kinship and animal degradation focused Muir's attention on the ritualized elements of even the most explosive incidents of violence.

Where Muir focused on the exceptional rituals of violence that accompanied the final stages of an ancient vendetta, Robert Davis was more interested in the rituals of the mundane. Again, early modern Italy provided a wealth of materials that seemed to show violence permeating the daily lives of Italian cities. Any historian with a passing familiarity with Italian judicial archives will be familiar with the ubiquity of thrown rocks in the records of daily life. To Davis, the thrown rocks of Perugian boys were not merely the disruptive behaviour of unsupervised brats: they spoke a language, often conservative, that gave voice to artisan and peasant Italian politics.[46] Thrown rocks could indicate the dissatisfaction of a community with a ruler's bread policies, or with a town council's most recent decisions; they could also be brought to bear as instruments of civic defence, when marauding *condottieri* might threaten the city. Robert Davis showed how complicated the ritual significance of youthful

---

[44] E. Muir, *Mad Blood Stirring: Vendetta and Factions in Friuli during the Renaissance* (Baltimore, MD: Johns Hopkins University Press, 1993).
[45] Ibid., introduction.
[46] R. Davis, "Say It with Stones: The Language of Rock-Throwing in Early Modern Italy," *Ludica* 10 (2004): 113–28.

violence could be by examining the multiplicity of meanings attached to the common rock and its projection by force.

Davis's more recent work on rock throwing was informed by his earlier analysis of the more obvious and elaborate violence of Venetian bridge-fighting.[47] In this seminal work on the popular culture of violence in Italy, Davis decoded the chaotic bridge fights that regularly occurred in Venice. These were not animal expressions of brute competition by the city's lower classes. Rather, the violent competitions between neighbourhood groups for control of the city's liminal spaces were exercises in the formation of neighbourhood and civic identities, of masculine hierarchies and heroics, and of modern organized sport. The increasing state regulation of the bridge fighters robbed them of some of their fatal violence but none of their masculine bravado, as new forms of competition and new definitions of "champions" emerged to replace the armed and armoured fighters of the fourteenth century. Although the violence was real, the antagonisms were in many ways affected: rivalries between two loosely knit factions, rooted in early Venetian communal politics, were exploited, developed and made theatrical by a state apparatus that recognized the ritual power of organized, spectacular violence.

State use of ritual violence is itself an important element of early modern society. For Foucault, the *ancien régime* was distinguished from the modern penal state by a violent and punitive obsession with the bodies of subjects; mutilation, execution and desecration were the means by which the state demonstrated the total power it held over criminals.[48] Spierenburg's interpretation of capital and corporal punishment, much like his work on homicide, relies heavily on the civilizing process to explain the transformation of European penal practices from theatrical execution to policies of exile, incarceration and fiscal punishments.[49] Spierenburg argued the violence and theatricality of early modern judicial punishment was not just a means for the state to inflict terror. Rather, agrarian Europeans accustomed to the sights, smells and sounds of blood and death found the imposition of justice to be both just and enormously entertaining. Over time, as courtly values disseminated throughout society and new manners and sensitivities were inculcated, people turned away from the violent theatre of death in disgust.

---

[47] R. C. Davis, *The War of the Fists: Popular Culture and Public Violence in Late Renaissance Venice* (Oxford: Oxford University Press, 1994).

[48] M. Foucault, *Discipline and Punish: The Birth of the Prison* (New York: Vintage Books, 1995).

[49] Spierenburg, *The Spectacle of Suffering*; Spierenburg, *Violence and Punishment*.

Social historians of execution have looked at how communities participated in public executions, and how the forms of judicial killing spoke a language of justice and retribution that reenacted the very misdeeds of the condemned. An execution's purpose was to reintegrate the soul of the condemned into the community of Christians and, eventually, heaven. Terpstra and others are fascinated by the groups of laymen who formed confraternities dedicated to comforting the condemned on the eve of their execution and escorting them calmly to the gallows, where the condemned were encouraged to accept responsibility for their crime, repent of their sins, and welcome the good death that would allow them to join Christ in heaven.[50] This interpretation centres on the highly managed pageantry of death, in which the condemned was carted through the city's streets to visit the scene of the crime (where he or she could be mutilated); the homes of the most offended victims; the seat of judicial authority; and, finally, the hanging grounds, where the grim theatre had its final act. Religious ritual and spiritual process were the means to pacify the condemned, helping to further the goal of social peace in fraught circumstances. The ritual view of violence and execution allows historians to unpack the deeper languages of behaviour that are more contingent on time and place than the behaviour itself: at different times, violence means different things, and the ritual characteristics of a society and its violence help to elucidate that meaning.

The Civilizing Process

Beginning in the 1970s with the work of English medievalists James Given and Barbara Hanawalt, a growing body of historical research about North Western European crime and violence reveals an undeniable decrease in the number of everyday homicides committed by men against other men.[51] This evidence was collated by Manuel Eisner in his 2003

---

[50] N. Terpstra, "Theory into Practice."

[51] The bibliography of English crime is now too large to manage in a book on Italy, but it remains a rich locus of historical innovation concerning the place of women, the poor, immigrants and other marginalized groups in crime and its prosecution. Barbara Hanawalt, *Crime and Conflict in English Communities, 1300–1348* (Cambridge, MA: Harvard University Press, 1979); Garthine Walker and J. Kermode, eds., *Women, Crime and the Courts in Early Modern England* (Chapel Hill: University of North Carolina Press, 1994); Peter King, *Crime and Law in England, 1750–1840: Remaking Justice from the Margins* (Cambridge: Cambridge University Press, 2006); K. J. Kesselring, "Bodies of Evidence: Sex and Murder (or Gender and Homicide) in Early Modern England, c. 1500–1680," *Gender & History* 27, no. 2 (August 2015): 245–62; Sara M. Butler, "A Case of Indifference?: Child Murder in Later Medieval England," *Journal of Women's History* 19, no. 4 (2007): 59–82; Susan Dwyer Amussen, "Punishment, Discipline, and Power: The Social Meanings of Violence in Early

database, which reveals similar patterns across England, Scandinavia and the Netherlands.[52] To explain these long-term declines in interpersonal violence, European historians in the 1980s and 1990s embraced the claims of Norbert Elias. Elias's work argued that the French aristocracy was civilized by the absolutist state and by the court at Versailles.[53] From his work on France, Elias claimed that European society had been subject to a civilizing process in which violent instincts were progressively tamed and overcome. The main empirical support for this thesis comes from Pieter Spierenburg, whose work has been significant in bringing the discussion of violence to the foreground. Though it has attracted its critics, his work continues to dominate the discussion.[54]

Spierenburg and others identified male honour as the cultural trait that most conditioned the practice of interpersonal violence in the European past. Elite men of the medieval period were violent, they argue, because

Modern England," *Journal of British Studies* 34, no. 1 (January 1, 1995): 1–34; Malcolm Gaskill, "Reporting Murder: Fiction in the Archives in Early Modern England," *Social History* 23, no. 1 (January 1, 1998): 1–30; Malcolm Gaskill, *Crime and Mentalities in Early Modern England* (New York: Cambridge University Press, 2000); Barbara Hanawalt, *The Ties That Bound: Peasant Families in Medieval England* (New York: Oxford University Press, 1986); J. B. Given, *Society and Homicide in Thirteenth-Century England* (Stanford, CA: Stanford University Press, 1977); B. Hanawalt, "Violent Death in Fourteenth- and Early Fifteenth-Century England," *Comparative Studies in Society and History* 18, no. 3 (July 1, 1976): 297–320; B. Hanawalt, *Crime and Conflict in English Communities, 1300–1348* (Cambridge, MA: Harvard University Press, 1979); Rousseaux and Dwyer, "Crime, Justice and Society in Medieval and Early Modern Times: Thirty Years of Crime and Criminal Justice History: A Tribute to Herman Diederiks," *Crime, Histoire & Sociétés/Crime, History & Societies* 1, no. 1 (January 1, 1997): 87–118; J. M. Beattie, "The Pattern of Crime in England 1660–1800," *Past & Present*, no. 62 (February 1, 1974): 47–95; J. M. Beattie, *Crime and the Courts in England, 1660–1800* (Princeton, NJ: Princeton University Press, 1986); J. S. Cockburn, ed., *Crime in England, 1550–1800* (Princeton, NJ: Princeton University Press, 1977); J. A. Sharpe, "Quantification and the History of Crime in Early Modern England: Problems and Results," *Historical Social Research/Historische Sozialforschung* 15, no. 4 (56) (January 1, 1990): 17–32; T. Gurr, "Historical Trends in Violent Crime: A Critical Review of the Evidence," *Crime and Justice* 3 (January 1, 1981): 295–353.
[52] M. Eisner, "Long-Term Historical Trends in Violent Crime," *Crime and Justice* 30 (January 1, 2003): 83–142.
[53] Elias, *The Civilizing Process*.
[54] P. Spierenburg, *The Spectacle of Suffering: Executions and the Evolution of Repression: From a Preindustrial Metropolis to the European Experience* (New York: Cambridge University Press, 1984); Spierenburg, "Faces of Violence"; P Spierenburg, "Violence and the Civilizing Process: Does It Work?," *Crime, Histoire & Sociétés = Crime, History & Societies/International Association for the History of Crime and Criminal Justice* 5, no. 2 (2001): 87–105; Pieter Spierenburg, "Democracy Came Too Early: A Tentative Explanation for the Problem of American Homicide," *The American Historical Review* 111, no. 1 (February 1, 2006): 104–14; P. Spierenburg, ed., *Violence in Europe: Historical and Contemporary Perspectives* (New York: Springer, 2008); Spierenburg, *A History of Murder*; Petrus Cornelis Spierenburg, *Violence and Punishment: Civilizing the Body through Time* (Malden, MA: Polity, 2013).

men practiced an honour code that made volatile response to insults and slights the necessary standard of manhood.[55] Changes to male honour codes first rendered public violence ritualistic and performative and then distasteful and criminalized.[56] Honour as an analytical framework was especially significant for French and Italian historians, and important works have documented how civility, politeness and friendship shaped notions of honour and the boundaries of violence.[57] In Bologna, for example, Angelozzi argued that these changes to honour were wrought in the seventeenth century through a process of "disciplining" by means of a new chivalric code, the *Scienza Cavalleresca*, which prized above all a refined knowledge and grace as the litmus of male nobility.[58] The civilizing process and changes in masculine honour knit together neatly, and the interaction of honour and the long-term decline in interpersonal violence bears the weight of much analysis. Practices of masculine honour mattered, as did the relationship between male honour and judicial structures.

Social Strategists

In the late 1990s and 2000s, a group of historians and criminologists argued against the civilizing process, seeing violence as a more dynamic category that could not be reduced to an analysis of honour-based conflicts. A loosely knit counter-school critiques the idea that violence is largely regulated by biological drives that require taming and suppressing. Historians writing in this mould are no less concerned with the long-term dynamics of violence, but are more interested in the points where the decline was interrupted, and the political, social and economic

---

[55] Here these scholars echo some standard twentieth-century views on medieval nobility, which were well out of vogue by the time the civilizing process was taken up, but which remain classics of medieval historiography. Cf. Johan Huizinga, *The Autumn of the Middle Ages* (Chicago: University of Chicago Press, 1996); Stephen D. White, ed., *Feuding and Peace-Making in Eleventh-Century France* (Burlington, VT: Ashgate/Variorum, 2005); Tuten and Bilbao, eds., *Feud, Violence and Practice: Essays in Medieval Studies in Honor of Stephen D. White* (Burlington, VT: Ashgate, 2010); Stephen D. White, *Re-thinking Kinship and Feudalism in Early Medieval Europe* (Aldershot: Ashgate Variorum, 2005).

[56] Spierenburg, ed., *Men and Violence: Gender, Honor, and Rituals in Modern Europe and America* ([Columbus]: Ohio State University Press, 1998).

[57] Robert Muchembled, *Le temps des supplices: de l'obéissance sous les rois absolus, xv*ᵉ*–xviii*ᵉ *siècle* (Paris: A. Colin, 1992); Di Simplicio, *Peccato, penitenza, perdono*.

[58] Angelozzi and Casanova, *La nobiltà disciplinata*; Muir's work on the Friuli also employs the civilizing process to analyze masculine honour in Muir, *Mad Blood Stirring*. Recently, Stuart Carroll has pushed back against the idea of "disciplining," arguing that the *scienza cavalleresca* left plenty of room for, and perhaps promoted, the violent masculinity characteristic of Emilian elites. Carroll, "Revenge and Reconciliation in Early Modern Italy."

contexts of those interruptions. Randolph Roth, for instance, has engaged directly with the civilizing process theory to argue that its empirical underpinnings are faulty.[59]

Roth and others instead turn to "social trust," an analytical concept with roots in American sociology.[60] The concept of social trust implies that when individuals and communities recognize, accept and mutually adhere to their societies' rules and norms, fatal violence will be limited in its frequency.[61] Violence will increase when trust in one's neighbours or in the state breaks down. Social trust as an analytical concept helps us to understand homicide rates in early modern Italy since we have a strong documentary record of individual, community and political relationships, preserved in judicial records, correspondence and legislation.

Because violence is closely related to social trust, scholars have shown that it is a strategy of social interaction, employed when necessary to demonstrate social dominance or to defend a right.[62] In this view, violence is a rational goal or social strategy, a reasonable way to achieve one's goals, when one has the resources and skills to accomplish it. Carroll used the example of French nobility of the seventeenth century to show that, far from being curbed by the absolutist state, nobles continued to use violence to assert and project their social dominance. When the nature of political power moved from control of agrarian resources to the more complex forms of politics necessary to run a bureaucratic state, French nobles did not surrender their right to vindicatory, punitive and predatory violence. Similarly, Claudio Povolo and Mario Sbriccoli have referred to a practice of "negotiated justice"

---

[59] Cf. the debate in *Crime, History and Societies*: Pieter Spierenburg, "American Homicide: What Does the Evidence Mean for Theories of Violence and Society?," *Crime, Histoire & Sociétés/Crime, History & Societies* 15, no. 2 (January 1, 2011): 123–29; Randolph Roth, "Yes We Can: Working Together toward a History of Homicide That Is Empirically, Mathematically, and Theoretically Sound," *Crime, Histoire & Sociétés/Crime, History & Societies* 15, no. 2 (January 1, 2011): 131–45; Pieter Spierenburg, "Questions That Remain: Pieter Spierenburg's Reply to Randolph Roth," *Crime, Histoire & Sociétés/ Crime, History & Societies* 15, no. 2 (December 1, 2011): 147–50; Randolph Roth, "Biology and the Deep History of Homicide," *British Journal of Criminology* 51, no. 3 (May 1, 2011): 535–55.

[60] R. D. Putnam, *Bowling Alone: The Collapse and Revival of American Community* (New York: Simon & Schuster, 2000); Muir, *Mad Blood Stirring*; Edward Muir, "The Sources of Civil Society in Italy," *The Journal of Interdisciplinary History* 29, no. 3 (January 1, 1999): 379–406; Edward Muir, "The 2001 Josephine Waters Bennett Lecture: The Idea of Community in Renaissance Italy," *Renaissance Quarterly* 55, no. 1 (April 1, 2002): 1–18; Roth, *American Homicide*, 1–24.

[61] Roth lays out four conditions under which homicide rates will stabilize or fall; these conditions are developed for Bologna here. *American Homicide*, 18.

[62] S. Carroll, *Blood and Violence in Early Modern France* (New York: Oxford University Press, 2006), 49–59.

whereby Venetian elites used violence or the threat of violence to push their cases with both enemies and officials. The goal of this justice was not the punishment of malfeasance but the return to a previous state of equilibrium among conflicting parties.[63] We shall see that the Bolognese nobility exhibited a similar strategy, and how they reasserted their right to violence in the atmosphere of diminished social trust prevailing after the crises of the early century.[64] Violence, as a strategy chosen by belligerents, was one option in these negotiations.

If violence was a social strategy, its use was dependent on resources and it took place within defined social expectations. Daniel Lord Smail refers to violence in the context of legal pluralism. Disputants in social conflict were "consumers" of justice who could turn to self-help or the courts, whose strategies created an interlocking web of conflict prosecution and resolution, mediation and arbitration.[65] Violence was one of many options available to medieval Marseillaise, and men, women and children of various stripes and social orders employed it creatively in the judicial marketplace. Like Roth, Smail's functional and resource-based approach to violence has led him to embrace a scientific approach to history, what he terms the "Science of the Human Past."[66] Smail's wide-ranging interest in violence as a deep human behaviour also encompasses economics, and specifically debt, to account for the types of judicial and quasi-judicial violence prevalent in late medieval Italy.[67] Smail's functionalist approach to violence includes it as part of humanity's natural skill set, an approach not many historians are yet willing to make, despite the recent calls by non-historians to do so.[68] Some historians have

---

[63] Mario Sbriccoli, "Giustizia negoziata, giustizia egemonica: riflessioni su una nuova fase degli studi di storia della giustizia criminale," in G. Schwerhoff, M. Bellabarba and A. Zorzi, eds., *Criminalita e giustizia in Germania e in Italia: pratiche giudiziarie e linguaggi giuridici tra tardo medioevo ed eta moderna* (Bologna: Il Mulino, 2001), 345–64.

[64] Claudio Povolo, *L'intrigo dell'onore: poteri e istituzioni nella Repubblica Di Venezia tra cinque e seicento* (Verona: Cierre, 1997); Claudio Povolo et al., *Il processo a Paolo Orgiano (1605–1607)*, series Fonti per la storia della terraferma veneta 19 (Roma: Viella, 2003).

[65] D. Lord Smail, *The Consumption of Justice: Emotions, Publicity, and Legal Culture in Marseille, 1264–1423* (Ithaca, NY: Cornell University Press, 2003).

[66] D. Lord Smail, *On Deep History and the Brain* (Berkeley: University of California Press, 2008); D. Lord Smail, "Neuroscience and the Dialectics of History," *Análise Social* 47, no. 205 (2012): 894–909; D. Lord Smail, "In the Grip of Sacred History," *The American Historical Review* 110, no. 5 (2005): 1337–61; D. Lord Smail, "Neurohistory in Action: Hoarding and the Human Past," *Isis* 105, no. 1 (2014): 110–22.

[67] D. Lord Smail, "Violence and Predation in Late Medieval Mediterranean Europe," *Comparative Studies in Society and History* 54, no. 1 (January 1, 2012): 7–34.

[68] Pinker, *The Better Angels of Our Nature*; Ian Armit, "Violence and Society in the Deep Human Past," *British Journal of Criminology* 51, no. 3 (May 1, 2011): 499–517; Manuel Eisner, "Human Evolution, History and Violence: An Introduction," *British Journal of*

embraced the neuro-biological approach to violence.[69] Drawn by the similarities of violence across time and place, they seek to identify the deeper impulses of humanity that underlie masculinity and violence in different times and places.[70] It remains to be seen whether these studies will have a significant impact on the scholarship of early modern European violence.

Cultures of Violence and Peacemaking

There has been a recent wave of historians, cognizant of violence's ubiquity in early modern Europe, who ask how societies aimed to reduce levels and manage forms of violence through non-judicial means. Inspired by twentieth-century anthropology, historians readily applied the notion of "the peace in the feud" to explain both medieval and early

Criminology 51, no. 3 (May 1, 2011): 473–78; Roth, "Biology and the Deep History of Homicide." Pinker's melding of evolutionary psychology and the civilizing process has recently been strongly criticized by a group of historians. Richard Bessel, "Assessing Violence in the Modern World," *Historical Reflections/Réflexions Historiques* 44, no. 1 (March 1, 2018): 66–77; Joanna Bourke, "The Rise and Rise of Sexual Violence," *Historical Reflections/Réflexions Historiques* 44, no. 1 (March 1, 2018): 104–16; Sara M. Butler, "Getting Medieval on Steven Pinker: Violence and Medieval England," *Historical Reflections/Réflexions Historiques* 44, no. 1 (March 1, 2018): 29–40; Philip Dwyer, "Whitewashing History: Pinker's (Mis)representation of the Enlightenment and Violence," *Historical Reflections/Réflexions Historiques* 44, no. 1 (March 1, 2018): 54–65; Caroline Elkins, "The 'Moral Effect' of Legalized Lawlessness: Violence in Britain's Twentieth-Century Empire," *Historical Reflections/Réflexions Historiques* 44, no. 1 (March 1, 2018): 78–90; Linda Fibiger, "The Past as a Foreign Country: Bioarchaeological Perspectives on Pinker's 'Prehistoric Anarchy,'" *Historical Reflections/Réflexions Historiques* 44, no. 1 (March 1, 2018): 6–16; Mark S. Micale and Philip Dwyer, "Introduction: History, Violence, and Stephen Pinker," *Historical Reflections/Réflexions Historiques* 44, no. 1 (March 1, 2018): 1–5; Randolph Roth, "Does Better Angels of Our Nature Hold Up as History?," *Historical Reflections/Réflexions Historiques* 44, no. 1 (March 1, 2018): 91–103; Daniel Lord Smail, "The Inner Demons of the Better Angels of Our Nature," *Historical Reflections/Réflexions Historiques* 44, no. 1 (March 1, 2018): 117–27; Matthew Trundle, "Were There Better Angels of a Classical Greek Nature?: Violence in Classical Athens," *Historical Reflections/Réflexions Historiques* 44, no. 1 (March 1, 2018): 17–28.

[69] J. C. Wood, "A Change of Perspective: Integrating Evolutionary Psychology into the Historiography of Violence," *British Journal of Criminology* 51, no. 3 (May 1, 2011): 479–98; M. Eisner, "Human Evolution, History and Violence: An Introduction," *British Journal of Criminology* 51, no. 3 (May 1, 2011): 473–78; Roth, "Biology and the Deep History of Homicide"; Amy E. Nivette, "Violence in Non-State Societies: A Review," *British Journal of Criminology* 51, no. 3 (May 1, 2011): 578–98; E. A. Johnson, "Criminal Justice, Coercion and Consent in 'Totalitarian' Society: The Case of National Socialist Germany," *British Journal of Criminology* 51, no. 3 (May 1, 2011): 599–615; I. Armit, "Violence and Society in the Deep Human Past," *British Journal of Criminology* 51, no. 3 (May 1, 2011): 499–517.

[70] G. Hanlon, "The Decline of Violence in the West: From Cultural to Post-Cultural History," *The English Historical Review* 128, no. 531 (April 1, 2013): 367–400.

modern violence.[71] Premodern societies generally accepted a given level of violence conducted within legitimate boundaries. This legitimacy and acceptance meant that violence needed a corollary, found in the form of semi-organized processes of peacemaking. These peacemaking forums operated alongside the legal system, constituting a sophisticated system of arbitration across Europe.[72] An important innovation of the sixteenth century was religious missions, such as Jesuit companies that tried to make peace among feuding parties in seventeenth-century South Italy.[73] The "cultures of peacemaking" that produced these efforts acted as a foil to the early modern period's endemic violence, used by historians to demonstrate how unstable societies organized productive co-habitation in both town and country. Importantly, efforts at peacemaking were mostly adjacent to state action, or divorced from state policy entirely.

Italy stands out in the histories of violence and peace because of the richness of its archival sources. In the proceedings of a conference held by Georgetown University in 2010, authors argue that early modern Italians' obsession with male honour led them inexorably to the hot-blooded, quick-to-violence culture of masculinity that apparently characterized early modern Italian men.[74] A more nuanced set of ideas is found in Stuart Carroll's collection that focuses on the post-medieval West in general.[75] In his introduction, Carroll argues that historians of

[71] M. Gluckman, "The Peace in the Feud," *Past & Present*, no. 8 (November 1, 1955): 1–14; S. Carroll, "The Peace in the Feud in Sixteenth- and Seventeenth-Century France," *Past & Present*, no. 178 (February 1, 2003): 74–115; W. I. Miller, *Bloodtaking and Peacemaking: Feud, Law, and Society in Saga Iceland* (Chicago: University of Chicago Press, 1990).

[72] Nicole Castan was among the earliest to place arbitration alongside the judicial regime. John Bossy's influential, anthropologically informed history was important in pushing scholars to look at how violence and peace interwove. N. Castan, *Les criminels de Languedoc: les exigences d'ordre et les voies du ressentiment dans une société pré-révolutionnaire, 1750–1790* (Toulouse: Association des publications de l'Université de Toulouse-Le Mirail, 1980); N. Castan, *Justice et répression en Languedoc à l'époque des lumières* (Montréal: Flammarion, 1980); N. Castan, *Vivre ensemble: ordre et désordre en Languedoc au XVIIIᵉ siècle* ([Paris]: Gallimard/Julliard, 1981); N. Castan, "The Arbitration of Disputes under the Ancien Regime," in *Disputes and Settlements*, 219–60; H. Zmora, *The Feud in Early Modern Germany* (New York: Cambridge University Press, 2011).

[73] S. Cummins, "Forgiving Crimes in Early Modern Naples," in S. Cummins and L. Kounine, eds., *Cultures of Conflict Resolution in Early Modern Europe* (London: Ashgate, 2015), 255–80. Cf. also the introduction to *Cultures of Conflict Resolution* for a succinct overview of the literature on peacemaking and violence.

[74] S. Cohn, ed., *The Culture of Violence in Renaissance Italy: Proceedings of the International Conference: Georgetown University at Villa Le Balze, 3–4 May, 2010* (Firenze: Le lettere, 2012).

[75] S. Carroll, ed., *Cultures of Violence: Interpersonal Violence in Historical Perspective* (Houndmills: Palgrave Macmillan, 2007).

violence should resist ascribing too much agency or putting too much emphasis on fluid, unstable and often fluctuating notions such as honour. They should, he argues, look alongside moral and behavioural codes to determine the functional roles of much interpersonal violence within the constraints and boundaries of particular societies.[76] Rather than a focus on honour, the essays in *Cultures of Violence* deal with the gendered and religious overtones of interpersonal and state violence, with the transformation of vengeance and vindicatory violence within the context of developing courtly societies, with the role of class in violence in the nineteenth and twentieth centuries and with the legitimization of various types of maritime and aerial violence in the modern world. Although in this volume only Steven Hughes addresses Italy, the collected essays serve to remind Italianists that the Italian honour code is less exceptional than it first appears.[77] Functionalist readings of the violence apparently produced by rigid adherence to honour can offer more nuanced interpretations of past actors' behaviour and the goals of violence as social strategy.

A more recent historiographical school looks to modern science and philosophy of the emotions to explore and analyze the emotional contexts and processes of early modern violence. Like the cultural analysis of violence, an emotional analysis rests heavily on linguistic interpretation: emotional histories of violence focus on witness and, if possible, suspect testimony, or victim statements. A recent volume edited by Susan Broomhall and Sarah Finn collects a number of these analyses of early modern Europe.[78] The scholars therein take familiar issues of early modern crime and violence – judicial punishment, religious violence, interpersonal killing, medical treatment and "violent language" – and subject them to an emotional analysis that teases out the roles of anger, dishonour and love in cases of interpersonal, religious and political violence.

The lens of culture is now the dominant historical mode through which much behaviour, ideology, communication and societal structures are interpreted; so too with violence.[79] By eschewing the large-scale and

---

[76] S. Carroll, "Introduction," in ibid., 1–43.

[77] Steven Hughes, "Swords and Daggers: Class Conceptions of Interpersonal Violence in Liberal Italy," in ibid., 212–35.

[78] S. Finn and S. Broomhall, eds., *Violence and Emotions in Early Modern Europe* (Abingdon: Routledge, 2016).

[79] See, for instance, recent collections edited by Jonathan Davies and Pieter Spierenburg: P. Spierenburg, ed., *Violence in Europe: Historical and Contemporary Perspectives* (New York: Springer, 2008); J. Davies, ed., *Aspects of Violence in Renaissance Europe* (Farnham: Ashgate, 2013). In the Davies volume, Amanda Madden's contribution notes how the growing Este state was unable to restrain a culture of violence pervasive among

the comparative, cultural studies of violence focus on the intricacies and details of a society's prescriptions for and practice of violence. Incorporating a range of literary and historical sources, they seek to locate the meaning of violence and peacemaking within societies, without significant analysis of the incidence and characteristics of violence itself.

Men, Women and Children

Violence and particularly homicide are deeply gendered, though both foundational and recent work suggest that women frequently engaged in small-scale neighbourhood and domestic violence, some of which made it to the courts but much of which did not.[80] But women were rarely killers. Approximately 99% of accused killers in this book's sample of 658 intentional adult homicides were men. This statistic aligns with the findings of many studies of homicide across time and place.[81] As victims, women accounted for slightly more reported cases of homicide, but men remain the recorded victims of homicide in numbers over 90%. Unreported homicides of female victims by partners, husbands and male relatives are perhaps the most likely "dark figure" of homicide statistics that are unreachable through judicial and medical sources, though they remain well represented in literature and art.

The violent tenor of male childhood and adolescence has fascinated and troubled historians. Some have focused on the activities of official associations such as boys' theatre troupes in early modern France, and have generally seen any disorder as an unpleasant side note of these mini-societies.[82] When early modernists have addressed seriously the problem of youth violence, they have located its function and

Modenese elites. A. Madden, "'*Una causa civile*': Vendetta Violence and Governing Elites in Early-Modern Modena," in ibid., 205–24.

[80] J. Kermode and G. Walker, eds., *Women, Crime and the Courts in Early Modern England*; E. S. Cohen, "Open City: An Introduction to Gender in Early Modern Rome," *I Tatti Studies in the Italian Renaissance* 17, no. 1 (2014): 35–54; A.-M. Kilday, "'That Women Are but Men's Shadows': Examining Gender, Violence and Criminality in Early Modern Britain," in M. Muravyeva and R. Toivo, eds., *Gender in Late Medieval and Early Modern Europe* (New York: Routledge, 2013), 53–70; Kesselring, "Bodies of Evidence"; Giancarlo Angelozzi and Cesarina Casanova, *Donne criminali: il genere nella storia della giustizia* (Bologna: Pàtron, 2014).

[81] The multitude of studies completed in the late twentieth century is reviewed in M. Daly and M. Wilson, *Homicide* (New York: A. de Gruyter, 1988); Eisner, "Long-Term Historical Trends in Violent Crime"; Spierenburg, *A History of Murder*; Roth, *American Homicide*.

[82] S. Beam, *Laughing Matters: Farce and the Making of Absolutism in France* (Ithaca, NY: Cornell University Press, 2007); G. Parsons, *Siena, Civil Religion, and the Sienese* (Burlington, VT: Ashgate, 2004).

meaning in four distinct but related approaches. First, the "steam valve" explanation sees youth violence as a controlled expression of adolescent tension, and locates its origins in the familial and social structures of the early modern city.[83] The second approach gives youth violence a communal function; it helped perpetuate community norms and relayed social frustrations to elites.[84] In some readings, the group violence of young men allowed them to amass respect and loyalty among an in-group by targeting designated outsiders such as women and foreigners.[85] Finally, the semi-organized violence of youth is anthropological, part of a series of rites of passage that marked the transition of males from the isolated and protected world of childhood to the competitive environments of adult men.[86] Collectively, historians of youth violence locate its meaning in broader social structures and expectations.

Boys grow into men, and the socialization into violence that boys of all social classes received was reproduced in adult codes of honour, social status and patriarchy. Recent work on Italian masculinity has shown how adaptable its violence was to changing fashions and technologies.[87] Roman nobility took up travelling by carriage with enthusiasm, and traditional status conflicts over whose party had the right of way walking next to a wall turned into conflicts over whose carriage had the right of way at an intersection. Duelling, too, supposedly took the place of semi-covert revenge plots, and rigid adherence to a gentleman's honour became the measure of victory in limited arenas of bloodshed.[88] However, the formalized violence of the duel was itself criminalized because duellers were not restrained by its rules and expectations. In all its forms,

[83] O. Niccoli, "Rituals of Youth: Love, Play and Violence in Tridentine Bologna," in K. Eisenbichler, ed., *The Premodern Teenager* (Toronto: Centre for Reformation and Renaissance Studies, 2002), 75–94; D. Herlihy, "Some Psychological and Social Roots of Violence in the Tuscan Cities," in L. Martines, ed., *Violence and Disorder in Italian Cities, 1200–1500* (Berkeley: University of California Press, 1992), 129–54; G. Ruggiero, *The Boundaries of Eros* (New York: Oxford University Press, 1985), 3–15.

[84] N. Z. Davis, "The Reasons of Misrule," *Past & Present* 50 (1971): 41–75; R. C. Davis, "The Language of Rock Throwing in Early-Modern Italy," *Ludica* 10 (2004): 113–28; Muir, *Mad Blood Stirring*, 38–49.

[85] D. Boschi, "Homicide and Knife-Fighting in Rome, 1845–1914," in P. Spierenburg, ed., *Men and Violence*, 128–58; P. Spierenburg, "Knife Fighting and Popular Codes of Honor in Early Modern Amsterdam," in ibid., 103–27.

[86] M. Rocke, *Forbidden Friendships: Homosexuality and Male Culture in Renaissance Florence* (New York: Oxford University Press, 1996), 101–5; N. Z. Davis, "The Rites of Violence: Religious Riot in Sixteenth Century France," *Past & Present* 59 (1973): 51–91; N. Schindler, "Guardians of Disorder: Rituals of Youthful Culture at the Dawn of the Modern Age," in *A History of Young People*, 240–82; G. Duby, *The Chivalrous Society*, trans. C. Postan (Berkeley: University of California Press, 1977), 112–22.

[87] Hunt, "Carriages, Violence, and Masculinity in Early Modern Rome."

[88] M. Cavina, *Il sangue dell'onore: storia del duello* (Bari: GLF editori Laterza, 2005).

the performance and elaboration of masculinity retained the element of violence as a threat, act or symbol.

Microhistories of gender relations demonstrate the colourful ways in which early modern Italian men built their masculine *virtù* through violence. The streets of Rome were a veritable theatre of manhood where complex obligations and social networks involved members of Rome's many communities.[89] Thomas and Elizabeth Cohen have shown how deeply social mores, such as honour (whether male or female), penetrated social hierarchies and appeared in all socioeconomic groups.[90] Time and again, the Cohens' male subjects explained their disorder and violence as part of a process by which they were demonstrating to the world around them their masculinity and their right to certain privileges because of their *virtù*. Indeed, male solidarity expressed by violence became essential to contemporary understandings of community.[91] In Venice, by the seventeenth and eighteenth centuries, a libertine form of masculinity had emerged that involved gender-bending, sexual experimentation and a continued fascination with violence and the carnivalesque.[92] Interrogating the words and deeds of the men of the lower classes has shown how the performance and elaboration of masculinity's many forms was common to men of all classes and accounted for a great deal of their violence – which itself formed an integral part of masculine identities.

Historians of gender have paid increasing attention to the ways in which women participated in crime and violence as perpetrators, aiders and abettors, intervening bystanders, and provokers of conflict. Studies of women's homicide in early modern Europe have largely focused on women as victims of domestic violence or as perpetrators of infanticide.[93]

---

[89] T. V. Cohen, "The Case of the Mysterious Coil of Rope: Street Life and Jewish Persona in Rome in the Middle of the Sixteenth Century," *The Sixteenth Century Journal* 19, no. 2 (July 1, 1988): 209–21; T. V. Cohen, "The Lay Liturgy of Affront in Sixteenth-Century Italy," *Journal of Social History* 25, no. 4 (July 1, 1992): 857–77; cf. the trials transcribed and edited by the Cohens in T. V. Cohen and E. S. Cohen, *Words and Deeds in Renaissance Rome: Trials before the Papal Magistrates* (Toronto: University of Toronto Press, 1993).

[90] E. S. Cohen, "Honor and Gender in the Streets of Early Modern Rome," *The Journal of Interdisciplinary History* 22, no. 4 (April 1, 1992): 597–625.

[91] Muir, "The 2001 Josephine Waters Bennett Lecture."

[92] E. Muir, *The Culture Wars of the Late Renaissance: Skeptics, Libertines, and Opera* (Cambridge, MA: Harvard University Press, 2009), 13–60.

[93] Marco Cavina, *Nozze di sangue: storia della violenza coniugale* (Rome: Laterza, 2011); Kesselring, "Bodies of Evidence"; Laura Hynes, "Routine Infanticide by Married Couples? An Assessment of Baptismal Records from Seventeenth Century Parma," *Journal of Early Modern History* 15, no. 6 (January 1, 2011): 507–30; Gregory Hanlon, "L'infanticidio di coppie sposate in Toscana nella prima eta moderna," *Quaderni Storici* 38 (2003): 453–98; Joanne M. Ferraro, *Marriage Wars in Late Renaissance Venice* (New

Kesselring and Butler both argue that most prosecutions of accused female killers in England were for infanticide by young, single women.[94] For Italy there is no comparable measure of the prosecution and treatment of infanticide, though it has not escaped the attention of historians. Individual trials for infanticide and abortion opened new and fruitful avenues to study the formation of community ties and loyalty in peripheral villages governed by distant monarchies, or to expose the complex early modern mindset surrounding life, the soul and the law.[95]

Infanticide trials in seventeenth-century Italy are rare. Both Laura Hynes and Gregory Hanlon have pointed to a tendency to prosecute young, single mothers, as others have noted in the English case.[96] By extrapolating sex ratios at birth from parochial baptismal records, Hynes and Hanlon both argue that fluctuating ratios of male and female infants indicate the widespread practice of sex-selective family planning by infanticide among married couples in Emilia and Tuscany. Others suspect that abortion and other forms of birth control were a common form of family planning.[97] I do not here document sex ratios at baptism, but I address the prosecution and treatment of infanticide by both court and communities in papal Bologna.

Thirty years of gender history has done much for the study of violence, both focusing historians' attention on the critical notion of masculinity and its formation and demonstrating the wide range of women's agency and participation in crime and violence, as well as the gender violence of the early modern period. Marital violence and domestic politics were an early field in which gender historians provided necessary innovation: recognizing that much early modern domestic violence was accepted culturally, and that a husband's right to correct his family mostly went unchallenged in courts, they sought other ways to illuminate how women and families negotiated men's violence and created networks of mutual

---

York: Oxford University Press, 2001); Joanne M. Ferraro, *Nefarious Crimes, Contested Justice: Illicit Sex and Infanticide in the Republic of Venice, 1557–1789* (Baltimore, MD: Johns Hopkins University Press, 2008); Joanne M. Ferraro, "The Power to Decide: Battered Wives in Early Modern Venice," *Renaissance Quarterly* 48, no. 3 (October 1, 1995): 492–512.

[94] Kesselring, "Bodies of Evidence"; Butler, "A Case of Indifference?"

[95] Tommaso Astarita, *Village Justice: Community, Family, and Popular Culture in Early Modern Italy* (Baltimore, MD: Johns Hopkins University Press, 1999); Adriano Prosperi, *Dare l'anima: storia di un infanticidio* (Turin: G. Einaudi, 2005).

[96] Hanlon, "L'infanticidio di coppie sposate in Toscana nella prima eta moderna"; Hynes, "Routine Infanticide by Married Couples?"

[97] John Christopoulos, "Abortion and the Confessional in Counter-Reformation Italy," *Renaissance Quarterly* 65, no. 2 (June 1, 2012): 443–84.

support that might allow them to escape violent marriages.[98] Gender historians have also argued that codes of women's honour, requiring submission to male authority, excused much violence against them and made them more vulnerable to domestic and intimate violence.[99] Historians focusing on gender relations or childhood asked how the violent masculinity of the pre-modern West was taught to generations of peasant, artisan, merchant and noble men. When it became clear that women committed a wide variety of crimes in early modern Europe, historians shifted their attention to the gendered nature of prosecution, and to how women, communities and courts negotiated roles of gender and hierarchy.[100] Gender history is critical to the study of homicide precisely because it is such an overwhelmingly male phenomenon. Why this is so must be unpacked, as must the historical impact of masculine violence on women's lives.

In this book, then, I study the characteristics and frequency of homicidal violence in Bologna. The empirical research presented here enables us to test the patterns and characteristics of violence that are predicted by the civilizing process. The evidence points conclusively to a breakdown in social and institutional trust. The world was turned upside down in the wake of the crises of the 1620s and the 1630 plague, leading to a sharp increase of homicide. Both the state and communities attempted to deal with this violence with new peacemaking initiatives. The social networks and strategies operating during a mid-century breakdown in civic peace reveal how violence became a social strategy among both elite and ordinary communities. Women were prosecuted for homicide in this ambience, though assumptions made about Italian court practices are not borne out in the state of Bologna. Medieval tropes about the character of women's violence, analyzed by Trevor Dean, did not hold for early modern society.[101] By taking account of the evidence of seventeenth-century Bologna, we see how the legitimacy and character of institutions,

---

[98] Ferraro, "The Power to Decide"; Julie Hardwick, "Early Modern Perspectives on the Long History of Domestic Violence: The Case of Seventeenth-Century France," *The Journal of Modern History* 78, no. 1 (2006): 1–36.

[99] For instance, the recent chapters by Henri Bresc and Thomas V. Cohen in Dean and Lowe, eds., *Murder in Renaissance Italy*, 41–61, 62–83.

[100] P. Renée Baernstein and J. Christopoulos, "Interpreting the Body in Early Modern Italy: Pregnancy, Abortion and Adulthood," *Past & Present* 223, no. 1 (May 1, 2014): 41–75; Christopoulos, "Abortion and the Confessional in Counter-Reformation Italy"; J. Christopoulos, "Nonelite Male Perspectives on Procured Abortion, Rome circa 1600," *I Tatti Studies in the Italian Renaissance* 17, no. 1 (2014): 155–74.

[101] Trevor Dean, *Crime and Justice in Late Medieval Italy* (Cambridge: Cambridge University Press, 2007), chap. 6.

rather than their mere presence, are the significant factors influencing homicide rates in early modern Italy.

Defining and Prosecuting Homicide

This book does not answer the question of why people kill each other; it instead explores the ways they killed each other, the relationships of killers and victims, the locations and spaces where homicides stained the ground, and the ambience of a time and place that fostered extreme levels of bloodshed. It engages the ideas of Norbert Elias, and tests its evidence against the database of violence established by Manuel Eisner, which has grown in collaborative research since its first publication in 2003.[102] The definitions and understandings of homicide employed herein are hybridized from the best historical scholarship available, augmented with readings in the psychology, sociology and anthropology of violence.

What constitutes homicide is an easier question than what constitutes violence, which is understood differently across time and space. This fact complicates the study of historical violence because modern scholars reading historical documents often bring their modern perspective on Violence (with a capital "V"). Most modern readers would agree that burning a sack full of cats constitutes Violence, that it is abhorrent or at least immoral. Yet cultural historians have shown us that animal cruelty featured strongly in the ritual lives of early modern Europeans and performed certain community functions.[103] The study of violence is fraught with this definitional problem, and attempts to determine just "how violent" a society was become mired in relativism and comparison.[104]

Homicide is easier to define since its basic meaning is that someone has been found dead. This sine qua non makes homicide an attractive

---

[102] On the database as it stood in 2003, cf. Manuel Eisner, "Long-Term Historical Trends in Violent Crime," *Crime and Justice* 30 (January 1, 2003): 83–142. An online database is now maintained by Randolph Roth of Ohio State University. R. Roth et al., "Historical Violence Database: A Collaborative Research Project on the history of Violent Crime, Violent Death, and Collective Violence." http://cjrc.osu.edu/research/interdisciplinary/hvd, accessed September 24, 2015.

[103] R. Darnton, *The Great Cat Massacre and Other Episodes in French Cultural History* (New York: Vintage Books, 1985), 75–106.

[104] Cf. Neal Garnham, "How Violent Was Eighteenth-Century Ireland?," *Irish Historical Studies* 30, no. 119 (May 1, 1997): 377–92. Garnham concludes that eighteenth-century Ireland was more violent than England, but about as violent as rural parts of France at the same time. He is clear that this violence was "excessive" and blamed "a state that lacked both the means and the will to intervene" (p. 392).

object of study for historians concerned with unknown figures of unreported crimes in sometimes fragmentary documents: a body is difficult to hide forever, and someone's death usually aggrieved somebody else, who then sought some kind of justice.[105] From a stripped-down judicial standpoint, a homicide occurs when someone dies of unnatural causes, warranting an investigation into that death.[106] Scholars define it starting from this point, subsequently narrowing their analytical criteria. Spierenburg, for example, includes infanticide and the fatal violence of children and adolescents but excludes state and police homicides.[107] Roth, in his work on homicide in American history, includes judicial killings, but excludes non-adult homicides and disaggregates his homicide rates into discrete categories, each with their own sub-definitions.[108] The disagreements in analytical definitions between these two scholars, who represent the foremost arguments in the debate on historical homicide, are the result of methodological, evidentiary and institutional differences discussed below. Because of these same considerations, I here employ my own modified analytical definition.

Some 658 investigations or trials into homicide, 675 including infanticides, and 701 including accidents, inform this analytical scheme. Of these, 22 trials dealt with incidents that involved more than one victim. There were 19 double homicides, a figure that includes situations in which both the intended victim and their assailant were killed; two triple homicides; and one brawl that resulted in five deaths. Most homicidal acts, then, resulted in only one body, although they often involved more actors as both aggressors and victims. The number of killers is almost double the number of victims, although that number is itself misleading. In certain years, individual violence was the norm, particularly toward the end of the century under consideration. During the middle decades,

---

[105] In 1660, a skeleton was discovered in the bank of the Reno canal in Bologna, which coroners determined was that of a young girl who had gone missing in 1643. A man was subsequently accused and hanged for the killing. ASBo, *Torrone*, 6799, *in fine*.

[106] This is the most basic understanding at work among *Torrone* notaries, who, in about forty cases in this sample, initiated investigations of *homicidium* that were revealed to be accidental deaths or otherwise non-culpable.

[107] Spierenburg, *A History of Murder*, 114–64; Pieter Spierenburg, "Faces of Violence: Homicide Trends and Cultural Meanings: Amsterdam, 1431–1816," *Journal of Social History* 27, no. 4 (July 1, 1994): 701–16. On adolescent violence in Italy, cf. Niccoli, *Il seme della violenza*; Eisenbichler, *The Premodern Teenager*.

[108] R. Roth, *American Homicide* (Cambridge, MA: Belknap Press of Harvard University Press, 2009); R. Roth, "Yes We Can: Working Together toward a History of Homicide That Is Empirically, Mathematically, and Theoretically Sound," *Crime, Histoire & Sociétés/Crime, History & Societies* 15, no. 2 (January 1, 2011): 137–39. Cf. the debate between Roth and Spierenburg in *Crime, History and Societies* 15, no. 2 (January 1, 2011): 123–50.

group violence became prevalent, particularly from 1632 to 1660; in each of these years, the number of killers was close to, or more than, double the number of victims. The mid-century violence that plagued Bologna was deeply factional, and its roots lay in changing social structures that affected groups and classes of individuals collectively. In these years, the high levels of in-group violence practiced by nobility and increasing levels of violence between social classes demonstrate how violence can function as a barometer of social stability and economic aspirations.

At its most basic level, "homicide" referred to a death that required explanation – that is, was not apparently natural – and may have been caused by the act or failure to act of another individual or group. The presence of a body that alarmed somebody was enough to initiate a judicial process in the *Torrone*. Analogues exist to our modern typologies of homicide, ranging from accidental death or death by negligence to first-degree murder. In Bologna, the primary categories of homicide prosecuted by the *Tribunale del Torrone* were the following:

- *Homicidio casuale*: This term usually refers to a homicide whose cause is suspected to be or has been shown to be accidental; these include certain traffic incidents, falls, worksite accidents and some drownings. An additional important category of accidental death is accidental shootings, often by young boys of their siblings or friends. These cases were prosecuted as homicides and usually dismissed with the registering of a peace accord from within the family group. While some of these *homicidii casuali* are self-evidently accidental and can thus be excluded from an analysis of externally inflicted death, others register a degree of ambiguity felt even by the notaries and judges investigating the incident; in many cases some liability is determined. There are some twenty-five of these ambiguous cases in this book's sample.

- *Infanticidio*: Infanticide is a crime that was prosecuted with varying degrees of assiduousness at different times and in different places, and which is extremely difficult to track with any means of statistical validity. Infanticide is generally defined as the killing of infants under one year of age by one or more parents. Problems of reporting and discovery make the potential "black figure" for infanticide extremely large, a problem that Gregory Hanlon has proposed to solve by the induction of infanticide patterns through comparison of sex ratios at baptism to expected sex ratios at birth.[109] This method still lacks a means to provide precise measures of infanticide in either numbers or

---

[109] Hanlon, "L'infanticidio di coppie sposate in Toscana nella prima età moderna"; Hynes, "Routine Infanticide by Married Couples?"

gender proportions; as such, it can only hint at historical possibilities without providing concrete evidence.

- Tentatively accepting the assumption that substantially more infanticides occurred than were prosecuted, but unable to track these infanticides in any documentary fashion, the sample of cases here accounts for seventeen cases of infanticide prosecuted by the *Torrone* over the course of the century; infanticide investigations occurred in 1600, 1610, 1640, 1660, 1690, and 1700. The other five years (1620, 1632, 1652, 1670, and 1680) do not contain any records of infanticide trials. The presence or absence of investigations for infanticide should not be taken as evidence of the act's prevalence; rather, they reflect the court's current preoccupations. Tridentine reform called for the reporting of all births outside of wedlock, a requirement that theoretically reduced instances of infanticide by removing from a single mother the opportunity to birth a child in secret and dispose of it without anyone noticing. All cases tried by the *Torrone* were for the killing of newborn infants, often discovered shortly after the birth. These cases are ambiguous at best and often break down into a "she said/the neighbour said" situation, in which no satisfactory evidence could prove the circumstances of the child's death (or life) beyond a doubt. These cases generally ended in the mother's conviction, and in some cases, the father's as well; punishments ranged from banishment to execution.

- *Homicidio*: This is the largest typology of homicide identified by the *Torrone* and is a catch-all for violence that occurred spontaneously, over the course of an argument, or following some previous altercation. Homicides in this category tended to be crimes of opportunity or at least lacked clear signs of forethought and planning. Again, this is an ambiguous category whose borders may overlap with both *homicidio casuale* and other infractions. It refers primarily to the circumstances immediately preceding the attack and does not reflect the nature of the relationship between the killer and the victim, a variable that is critical in determining the killer's motivation and in classifying the homicide in more detail. These cases account for the large majority of prosecuted homicides and may correspond to modern notions of manslaughter and second-degree murder.

- *Homicidio appensate*: This is the analogue to modern (and pre-modern British) concepts of homicide with malice aforethought, or first-degree murder. This category appears most often in cases where the *Torrone* believed the murder to have been part of an ongoing relationship of enmity, often expressed as vendetta or revenge killings. Of course, revenge killings were often not labelled *appensate*. The geographies of violence can indicate a great deal about whether a killing was planned or not; for instance, those that take place in churchyards before or after mass speak to a deliberate decision to engage in violence in a culturally significant area. *Homicidio appensate* is a term *Torrone* judges used primarily to indicate their awareness of a recent conflict between the parties, but it does not definitively isolate these cases from other homicides that also contain obvious elements of planning and preparation.

- *Homicidio cum qualità assassinamento*: *Assassino* is a false cognate for English speakers. It refers not to killing for payment or by hire but rather to the forced taking of goods from someone's person; this is distinct from pick-pocketing and other minor forms of theft in that it was primarily a monetary crime, rather than object-driven, and distinct from armed robbery of houses or businesses in that it usually took place on a roadway or other route of transit.[110] It is related closely to banditry. *Homicidio cum qualità assassinamento* occurred when these violent waylays resulted in the victim's death. They were generally discovered when a search of the victim's cadaver revealed an empty purse, a message bag that had been emptied on the ground, or a jacket whose lining had been shredded in search of hidden pockets. Conversely, these crimes could be identified as "assassinations" when witnesses noted that the murder was motivated by the chance for material gain.

These five categories represent the *Torrone*'s view of homicide. Its most severe punishments were administered to those who committed infanticide and *assassinamento*, crimes that were considered more serious due to the helplessness of the victim or the craven motivation for material surplus. As signifiers of the *Torrone*'s priorities, they indicate that the court viewed most homicides as typical manifestations of enmity and anger in the city and countryside over which it held jurisdiction.

This study creates an additional set of typologies that more clearly reflect the subtleties and intricacies of homicides, and which refer to the relationships between killer and slayer, the degree of forethought, the group or individual nature of the act, and the level of predation that separates a homicide that occurred during a street fight from one that happened late at night, after a victim had been stalked home. These categories are artificially imposed to group homicide cases by similarity,

---

[110] Gregory Hanlon best labels *assassinamento* as "mugging." Gregory Hanlon, "Justice in the Age of Lordship: A Feudal Court in Tuscany during the Medici Era (1619–66)," *The Sixteenth Century Journal* 35, no. 4 (December 1, 2004): 1016.

identifying those that present more similarity than is at first visible if the categories of the *Torrone* are left unmodified. They comprise two main groupings that identify an act as either spontaneous or planned – each of these groupings divides into several sub-categories that reflect similarities in multiple variables.

Spontaneous homicides are rarely as spontaneous as they seem, and when analyzing cases in which violence erupted in the spur of the moment, it is important to remember that even the most sudden conflicts tend to have a history of their own; the issue in these cases is whether the parties entered into the situation intending violence. These motivations can usually be ascertained only by a close reading of the cases and the perspectives of victims and witnesses, although the geography and timing of homicides also matter here. For instance, cases in which an assailant waylays a traveller on the road can be either spontaneous or planned; whether the assailant lay in wait, and for how long, and what time the attack occurred may help indicate whether the attack was a crime of opportunity or a pre-planned attack of a habitual enemy. The database that informs this book divides the 701 homicide cases, both spontaneous and planned, into the following sub-categories:

- Male-on-male equal-status social confrontation: These homicides are among the most common of all cases, and include a wide variety of incidents, motivations, number of parties, locations and social classes. These are conflicts that well up in the course of everyday life, for instance, during a game of lawn-bowling in which one player accused another of unfair play.[111] The parties are not differentiated significantly by their social status in any of these cases. Their homicides are the regular barometer of the stability of community and social trust.[112]
- Male-on-male differential-status social confrontation: Less common than cases of spontaneous violence within social classes, these cases refer either to violence committed "upward," by relatively low-status individuals against elites – as when, on New Year's Eve 1631, a blacksmith rejected a nobleman's demands for obeisance, and then killed him in the ensuing firefight[113] – or to violence committed "downward," as when a member of the powerful Malvasia clan killed his employee Andrea during an argument over the spoils of the

---

[111] Archivio di Stato di Bologna (hereafter ASB), *Tribunale del Torrone, Atti e Processi*, 6780.

[112] Blok, *Honour and Violence*, chap. 7, "The Narcissism of Minor Differences," 115–31; R. Jacobi, *Bloodlust: On the Roots of Violence from Cain and Abel to the Present* (New York: Free Press, 2011), 143.

[113] ASB, *Tribunale del Torrone, Atti e Processi*, 5922.

1610 grape harvest.[114] A large number of these homicides indicates the dissolution of trust in social hierarchies and institutional structures.

- Male-on-male familial conflict: Fratricide was by no means unknown to early modern Bolognese, nor was violence between family members who were not related by blood. The archetypal familial homicide is fratricide, of which there were several over the century, in all social classes ranging from itinerant groups of "gypsies"[115] to the highest nobility.[116] Within all classes, fratricides occurred in the course of drunken arguments and during arguments over the division of patrimonies.[117] Given the ubiquity of kinship and its metaphors in Italian social life, familial violence, too, is a measure of local stability and the strength of neighbourhood bonds.[118]

- Male-on-female familial conflict: Uxoricide accounts for a small number (seven, approximately 1%) of cases across the century, and it occurred primarily within peasant and artisan families. The relative absence of uxoricide should not be taken as an indication of low levels of domestic violence by any means. Currently, there is no statistical analysis of the prevalence or absence of marital violence in Bologna that would allow for a proportional analysis of fatal violence.[119]

- Male-on-female social conflict: The largest proportion (ten) of these cases concerns jilted lovers or the jealous clients of prostitutes. The relationship between killer and victim matters here: was he her lover, jealous of her and enraged by the overtures of other men? Or was he a spurned potential partner, denied sexual access by a woman he considered to be a libertine, knowing that she regularly had relationships with other men, and furious that she should reject him? Both relationships appear in the record of violence, and they provide a window into the dangerous complexities of broken social and amorous relationships.

---

[114] ASB, *Tribunale del Torrone, Atti e Processi*, 4261, f. 231.
[115] ASB, *Tribunale del Torrone, Atti e Processi*, 6946, *in fine*, 1670.
[116] ASB, *Tribunale del Torrone, Atti e Processi*, 5857, f. 299, 1632.
[117] ASB, *Tribunale del Torrone, Atti e Processi*, 6635, *in fine*, 1652.
[118] On the interdependence of family and community identities, cf. K. A. Lynch, *Individuals, Families and Communities in Europe, 1200–1800: The Urban Foundations of Western Society* (Cambridge: Cambridge University Press, 2003). On the extension of kinship structures into bodies promoting social stability, cf. Terpstra, ed., *The Politics of Ritual Kinship*; Rondeau, "Homosociality and Civic (Dis)order in Late Medieval Italian Confraternities."
[119] While not providing a statistical analysis, Marco Cavina writes on the phenomenon of domestic abuse and violence in Bologna. Cf. M. Cavina, *Nozze di sangue: storia della violenza coniugale* (Rome: Laterza, 2011).

- Female-on-male familial violence: There is one case of husband-killing in the records, from 1690, in which a wife was convicted of poisoning her husband. This is an extremely rare phenomenon in the judicial records of early modern Bologna.
- Female-on-infant familial violence: Most accused female killers who acted alone (seven out of ten) were prosecuted for infanticide. Without a doubt, more infants were killed by desperate parents, faced with the brutal algebra of necessity in a rural society of endemic poverty, than led to trials in the *Torrone*; lacking a verifiable number for these cases leaves researchers imputing a level of violent behaviour to mothers and fathers that cannot be shown without sensitive reading of the appropriate sources.[120]
- Female-on-female/female-on-male social conflict: Women were not frequent killers, and those who killed outside their family were often aiding and abetting their male relatives in the prosecution of their conflicts (nine out of eleven). Female killers were an extremely small minority, particularly if one ignores imputed infanticides and female participation in primarily male conflicts. The two definitive cases of female-on-female homicide both stem directly from a woman's attempt to guard fragile resources during vulnerable times of the year.

This schema is more useful for the organization of a database than for deployment in a book, in part because the sample size for many of the categories is so small, while male-on-male violence overwhelmingly dominates the record of homicide. But it helps to define the terms of this argument: that the social structures influencing peace in Bologna trembled through the seventeenth century and that homicidal violence accompanied their trembling. Homicide, for early modern Bolognese and for this book, was the wrongful killing of another person that required compensation to either the victim's kin or to the state. As advised by Roth, this included police or law enforcement murders; from Spierenburg, it included adolescents, who still needed to make peace even for accidental killings. When the *Torrone* ruled a death an accident and all indicators point in that direction, I exclude that death from homicides; but when an accident was protested as a homicide or satisfaction was made to the victim's kin, that death is included as a homicide. This is admittedly an expansive analytical definition. But it encapsulates the ubiquity of fatal violence in this early modern society, even at its most peaceful. With aggregate homicide rates never reaching lower than about 13 per 100,000, early modern *bolognesi* saw many killings. Their grief

---

[120] Hynes, "Routine Infanticide by Married Couples?," 520–30.

over wrongful deaths pushed them to seek redress, which brought them to the notaries of the *Torrone*.

The Shape of Homicide in Early Modern Bologna

The homicides in this book were all investigated or prosecuted by the *Tribunale del Torrone*, which became a particularly vivid symbol of papal rule by consolidating its control over criminal law in Bolognese territory. The *Torrone* refined its process and practices throughout the seventeenth century. It employed its judicial apparatus not to dominate and punish the bodies of a population, but to attract ordinary *bolognesi* to its services rather than taking their litigation to a noble *padrone*. It possessed specific legislative powers and experimented with firearms regulation across the century, with policies ranging from a complete ban on firearms to the mustering of an armed rural militia. Aware that its police force was "one step removed from the very criminals they were hired to catch," the court attempted to regulate and professionalize the *sbirri* who carried out its arrests.[121] In punishment, the *Torrone* demonstrated a considered and restrained approach to violence. Contumacy and consequent exile were the most likely and common results of homicide trials. By mid-century, exile was more often under the threat of galley service than of death. Executions in Bologna became rare events, averaging less than two per year in the 1690s. Executions were more often for robbery or counterfeiting than for homicide, and the elaborate theatre with which Foucault characterized *ancien régime* executions had long disappeared.[122] Few killers were executed due to the *Torrone*'s role as both an adjudicator of conflict and a potential party to it. The court preferred to leave killers alive and to foster the conditions under which peace might be made and the killer returned to his community and pardoned (Chapter 2).

However, the presence of a centralized and bureaucratic criminal court failed to achieve the reduction of homicide rates seen under similar circumstances in England and the Netherlands. Rather, as Chapter 3 demonstrates, *bolognesi* continued to kill each other at high rates in the pursuit of revenge and romance, to defend their families and properties or to take someone else's. In large part this is due to the decline of trust in political and social institutions over the course of a series of economic, natural and political disasters in the early decades of the century.

---

[121] S. Hughes, "Fear and Loathing in Bologna and Rome the Papal Police in Perspective," *Journal of Social History* 21, no. 1 (October 1, 1987): 98.

[122] Foucault, *Discipline and Punish*, chap. 1.

Domestic and family homicides prevailed in both town and country. Almost one-seventh of sampled homicide prosecutions accused the victim's relatives by blood or marriage. Uxoricide loomed large in the records of domestic violence and appears in generally consistent numbers across the century, while the city's prostitutes were themselves a vulnerable population. The court responded more harshly to uxoricide and other domestic homicides than to banal male–male interpersonal violence or the killing of marginalized women. Women killers were seen as an aberration and treated as such by the court, through their numbers remained small. Most feared by authorities were the figures of the female poisoner and the young, unmarried mother who killed her child. These fears were deeply shaped by cultural ideals of gender and honour, which played themselves out in the experiences Bolognese women had as wives and mothers. Records of violence show that one's kin were a source of both comfort and conflict (Chapter 4).

Violence in the rural world was conditioned by environmental and economic instability. The *Torrone* made haphazard efforts to provide security, justice and conflict resolution to rural communities, eventually drawing rural *bolognesi* into the judicial fold. Still, food instability and the epidemic of 1630 severely impacted demographic structures, property portfolios and labour markets. The thirty years following the plague saw drastic changes in rural homicides, particularly in conflicts over property, food and money. Prosecutions for some forms of homicide, like infanticide, are unique to the *contado* and present particular analytical challenges. Homicide in the *contado* was much less susceptible to police and judicial action than it was within the city, where the apparatus of the state was stronger and more visible. Achieving general regional stability by the end of the century aided rural communities in returning homicide rates to where they were in 1600 (Chapter 5).

Urban homicides were more governed by tensions reemerging from cracks in Bologna's political regime. Radical elements of Bologna's nobility rejected the civility on offer by papal magistrates. After a period of quiescence, leading noble clans such as the Barbazza and Malvezzi returned to, and amplified, the private warfare and practices of vendetta-as-politics that characterized the medieval regime.[123] Other noble families, such as the Paleotti and the Pepoli, advanced their interests through

---

[123] The concept of vendetta-as-politics is not unique to Bologna. A fine example from Italy includes Osvaldo Raggio, *Faide e parentele: lo stato genovese visto dalla Fontanabuona* (Turin: G. Einaudi, 1990); Daniel Lord Smail, "Factions and Vengeance in Renaissance Italy: A Review Article," *Comparative Studies in Society and History* 38, no. 4 (1996): 781–89.

papal bureaucracy and governance, and so responded with violence to renewed oligarchic agitation. These resurging nobles formed and presented their masculine and political identities through skilful violence, using swords when guns were easily available. In mid-century, anti-papal sentiment peaked with a series of murders of judicial and governmental officers by aggrieved nobles and their henchmen. Although rooted in the politics of rural power, this process was primarily an urban one (Chapter 6).

The disruption of social peace that occurred in Bologna complicates our understanding of the sharp decline of interpersonal violence in much of Europe during the same period. The resurgence of noble factionalism following a period of quiescence shows that the civilizing process was – or, better, civilizing processes were – contingent on the participation of multiple orders of society. When a powerful sector, such as noble families whose rural privileges were sharply curtailed by successive papal legates, rejected the terms of central authority, gains made in creating a more ordered elite class were lost and violence resurged. However, the acts of Bolognese nobility also counter a strictly functionalist argument in which violence is part of a considered political strategy: by the seventeenth century, papal rule over Bologna was a reality and the most successful Bolognese nobles recognized this fact and accommodated themselves to its new institutions. For these elites, violence was not a means to succeed.

Moreover, it was artisan and labouring communities that drove the *Torrone*'s ascension as the supreme court of the land. In the turbulent judicial marketplace of late medieval and early modern Bologna, during multiple transitions between oligarchic, podestarial, feudal and papal justice, Bolognese communities over time voted with their feet. The increasing volume of testimony dedicated to the mundane struggles of everyday life buttressed and helped to finance the court's displacement of the patchwork of seigneurial tribunals that operated in the shadows of rural fiefs. In Bologna, where the nobility retained their capacity for violence in the face of a centralized judicial regime, any civilizing process that occurred was the result of blacksmiths, butchers and farmers settling their conflicts on paper, beneath the shadowy bulk of the *Torrone*, rather than with knives in the hot summer fields of Medicina, on narrow mountain roads near Camugnano or behind taverns in Castel Bolognese.

2   The Tower of Justice

Introduction

When Julius II conquered the city of Bologna in 1506 and expelled the Bentivoglio oligarchs, he was faced with the difficult task of restraining the city's nobility and curbing their independence. After the failed Bentivoglio rebellion in 1509, Julius vowed to strip the noble families of their traditional rights and privileges. This meant removing the nobles' right to exercise justice both within the city, by influencing the operations of the podestarial court, and in their feudal territories in the city's hinterland, through the direct operation of criminal and civil courts of first instance.[1] The city's papal sovereign needed to curb the noble class's hereditary privileges of justice, while its inhabitants wanted the efficient and reliable vehicle for conflict resolution they had never received under medieval courts. One solution was the creation of a centralized criminal court, known as the *Torrone*, after the imposing medieval tower its offices occupied.

Bologna's courts remained in a state of flux during the first decades of papal rule. Gradually, the papal legates – Cardinals installed as city governors – increased the power and reach of the *Torrone* and inserted papal representation firmly into the system of criminal justice. The inefficiencies of podestarial justice drove plaintiffs, lawyers and jurists toward a centralized legatine court. The judges and notaries of the *Tribunale del Torrone* cemented inquisitorial and summary procedures and claimed a monopoly over criminal justice in Bologna and its environs. But the process was a slow one: the *Torrone* finally secured its judicial monopoly at the end of the seventeenth century. Paradoxically, it did so because of, not despite, the nobility's continued resistance to the court's jurisdiction, which created a wave of violence in the mid-seventeenth century. Rural

---

[1] Giancarlo Angelozzi and Cesarina Casanova, *La giustizia criminale in una città di antico regime: il tribunale del Torrone di Bologna, secc. XVI–XVII* (Bologna: CLUEB, 2008), p. 21.

bolognesi increasingly brought their conflicts to the *Torrone* for resolution, rather than to a court operated by local feudal powers.

The *Torrone*'s basic structure and function was established by the mid-sixteenth century, while similar courts were developed elsewhere in Italy; it persisted in much the same shape until the eighteenth century. In response to a powerful and rebellious nobility, the court established a more professional structure than the courts operating in contemporary states. In Florence, for example, Cosimo I had effectively redirected Florentine nobility away from oligarchical competition and toward bureaucratic service as the route to political power. Brackett saw the centralized criminal court as an important aspect of sixteenth-century Florentine governance and surveillance. It extended the reach of the Medici dukes into the *quartieri* of the city and the many *ville* of the Tuscan state, much as Cosimo I used patronage and clientage to staff major charitable institutions and hospitals.[2] Despite the continued existence of multiple criminal courts in Rome throughout the sixteenth century, the increasing centralization of Roman political power around the College of Cardinals brought these courts into closer operation and influenced the use of inquisitorial procedure by all. Nevertheless, Roman criminal tribunals remained, as Irene Fosi argues, inefficient, ineffective and incapable of delivering justice.[3]

The first half of the sixteenth century witnessed the development of such courts in the many duchies of the Lombard plain and throughout central Italy, such as Parma, which became the hereditary duchy of the Farnese in 1548 and cemented its criminal jurisdiction with the public

---

[2] J. K. Brackett, *Criminal Justice and Crime in Late Renaissance Florence, 1537–1609* (Cambridge: Cambridge University Press, 1992); N. Terpstra, "Competing Visions of the State and Social Welfare: The Medici Dukes, the Bigallo Magistrates, and Local Hospitals in Sixteenth-Century Tuscany," *Renaissance Quarterly* 54 (2001): 1319–55; J.-C. Waquet, *Corruption: Ethics and Power in Florence, 1600–1770* (University Park: Pennsylvania State University Press, 1992). Waquet in particular notes how the Medici dukes allowed nobility a certain leeway in graft and other opportunities for private profit off the public purse, in exchange for absolute loyalty to the Medici regime in what he terms an exercise of "machine politics." Terpstra notes that Cosimo's patterns of cronyism and patronage in charitable staffing and funding played a similar role, drawing formerly restive noble families into a domesticated Medici household, where the duke played the benevolent father to all.

[3] G. Signorotto and M. A. Visceglia, eds., *Court and Politics in Papal Rome, 1492–1700* (Cambridge: Cambridge University Press, 2002); P. Blastenbrei, "Violence, Arms and Criminal Justice in Papal Rome, 1560–1600," *Renaissance Studies* 20 (2006): 68–87; I. Fosi, *La giustizia del Papa: sudditi e tribunali nello stato pontificio in età moderna* (Rome: Laterza, 2007). Blastenbrei argues that the ineffective justice of Rome was a result of "the lasting refusal of the great majority of the Roman population to cooperate with the organs of the papal criminal justice, and the predilection of the average Romans for arms," but does not provide reasons why these two situations should have obtained.

execution of a large group of nobles in 1612.[4] In Siena, the Medici courts pacified a politically restive urban nobility and adjudicated the minor quarrels of everyday life in rural hamlets such as Montefollonico.[5] Venice operated central urban courts but was unable to establish a reliable jurisdiction in its vendetta-ridden *terra ferma* empire.[6] In the South, in the Kingdom of Naples, representatives from the Royal Court served as a court of second appeal for rural plaintiffs whose feudal overlords retained a robust local privilege of justice.[7] These structural differences between North and South were perhaps not so significant, as Hanlon and Torre have argued that Lombard nobles enjoyed extensive jurisdictional privileges well into the eighteenth century – much longer than the legislation might imply.[8] No matter the structure of local and feudal justice, all of the states that instituted centralized, inquisitorial courts did so at the expense, in both reduced potency and reduced income, of the hereditary nobility who enjoyed extensive power under the medieval systems, podestarial, feudal or legatine.

The consolidation of the *Torrone* in Bologna was a process that lasted almost a century and a half, from at least 1525, the court's earliest mention in documentary evidence, to the late seventeenth century, or perhaps longer. Indeed, the court truly eliminated the last vestiges of feudal jurisdiction only in the eighteenth century, following significant reforms instituted by Benedetto XIV.[9] An explanation for the long and

---

[4] G. Hanlon, *The Hero of Italy: Odoardo Farnese, Duke of Parma, His Soldiers, and His Subjects in the Thirty Years' War* (Oxford: Oxford University Press, 2014), 1–10; C. Rose, "'To Be Remedied of Any Vendetta': Petitions and the Avoidance of Violence in Early Modern Parma," *Crime, Histoire & Sociétés/Crime, History & Societies* 16 (2012): 5–27.

[5] O. Di Simplicio, *Peccato, penitenza, perdono: Siena 1575–1800: la formazione della coscienza nell'Italia moderna* (Milan: FrancoAngeli, 1994); G. Hanlon, *Human Nature in Rural Tuscany: An Early Modern History* (New York: Palgrave Macmillan, 2007).

[6] G. Ruggiero, *Violence in Early Renaissance Venice* (New Brunswick, NJ: Rutgers University Press, 1980), 18–40; E. Muir, *Mad Blood Stirring: Vendetta and Factions in Friuli during the Renaissance* (Baltimore, MD: Johns Hopkins University Press, 1993), 13–50.

[7] T. Astarita, *Village Justice: Community, Family, and Popular Culture in Early Modern Italy* (Baltimore, MD: Johns Hopkins University Press, 1999).

[8] G. Hanlon, "In Praise of Refeudalization: Princes and Feudataries in North-Central Italy from the Sixteenth to the Eighteenth Century," in N. Eckstein and N. Terpstra, eds., *Sociability and Its Discontents: Civil Society, Social Capital, and Their Alternatives in Late Medieval and Early Modern Europe* (Turnhout: Brepols, 2009), 213–25; A. Torre, "Feuding, Factions, and Parties: The Redefinition of Politics in the Imperial Fiefs of Langhe in the Seventeenth and Eighteenth Centuries," in E. Muir and G. Ruggiero, eds., *History from Crime: Selections from* Quaderni Storici (Baltimore, MD: Johns Hopkins University Press, 1994), 135–70.

[9] Angelozzi and Casanova, *La giustizia criminale in una città di antico regime*; Angelozzi and Casanova, *La nobiltà disciplinata: violenza nobiliare, procedure di giustizia e scienza cavalleresca a Bologna nel XVII secolo* (Bologna: CLUEB, 2003); Angelozzi and

arduous nature of this process may be found in the functional use of criminal justice in early modern Italy. The theoretical purpose of the court, according to its *Constitutione* of 1556, was to prosecute and punish malefactors.[10] However, a thorough reading of its *processi* and the records of punishment indicate that, as under the earlier courts, its functional purpose was different: officials, plaintiffs and defendants viewed the court as a forum for conflict resolution.

Accusatorial procedure traditionally placed the judge as an arbitrator between two private parties. The *Torrone* served a similar role, although it made dispute resolution a public matter between the court, the imputed criminal and his or her kin, the victim and his or her kin, and the communities around them. Initiated by a local bailiff or by a private citizen through a *denuncia* to the court, *ex officio* process drew entire communities into an elaborate process in which men, women and children explained to the notaries and themselves the circumstances of a murder, arson, or a simple fight between two drunks in a bar. Through this process they confronted and discharged strong emotions, such as the impulse to revenge, and were guided by notaries' skilful questioning toward reconciliation and, perhaps following a period of enforced separation of the parties, finally toward forgiveness. The purpose of the *Torrone* was therefore not to execute every murderer in the papal state, but to prevent cycles of revenge violence from breaking out in both urban and rural contexts, and among all levels of Bolognese society. Indeed, analysis of the court's execution patterns reveals that the state carried out very few of its death sentences. Inquisitorial procedure in Bologna thus allowed the state to expand its role in conflict resolution into the daily life of the most remote villages. While subject to occasional reform, the court retained its basic structure throughout the sixteenth and seventeenth centuries and grew in power as *bolognesi* resolved quarrels through its channels rather than the violent sponsorship of feudal nobility.[11]

Casanova, *La giustizia criminale a Bologna nel XVIII secolo e le riforme di Benedetto XIV* (Bologna: CLUEB, 2010); T. Di Zio, "Il tribunale del Torrone," *Atti e Memorie della Regia Deputazione di storia patria per le provincie di Romagna* 43 (1992): 333–48; Di Zio, "Il tribunale criminale di Bologna nel se. XVI," *Archivi per la storia. Rivista dell' Associazione nazionale archivistica italiana* 1–2 (1991): 125–35.

[10] ASBo, *Assunteria del Torrone, Bandi e Stampe, Constitutiones Turroni Bononie*, 1566, f. 1r–4v.

[11] On the origins and structure of the court, cf. C. Rose, "Violence and the Centralization of Justice in Early Modern Bologna," in Sarah Rubin Blanshei, ed., *Violence and Justice in Bologna: 1250–1700* (Lanham, MD: Lexington Books, 2018), 101–22. The entire collection is an excellent resource on the political nature of both violence and justice in the medieval and early modern city.

Procedure

Inquisitorial procedure was at the heart of the *Torrone*'s approach to crime and conflict resolution. *Inquisitio*'s usefulness in finding the "truth" of a crime made it more effective than accusation procedure in arbitrating conflicts, rather than punishing them. A series of reforms in the 1590s boosted the court's credibility by forcing its notaries and officials to be more transparent in their dealings with the public, by condemning the practice of taking bribes by notaries and *sbirri*, and by publicly advertising the strictly regulated fees that they charged for various services. These reforms were designed to bring ordinary *bolognesi* further into the *Torrone*'s fold. Finally, the court's use of violence – torture during interrogation, and corporal and capital punishment – demonstrates how the *Torrone* strayed from *inquisitio*'s lofty goals of ensuring that all crime was punished, and indicates that the court was far more interested in containing and suppressing cycles of revenge violence than it was in punishing individual acts; its contrary treatment of thieves indicates that its treatment of theft, too, was meant to dampen the victim's impulse to revenge by providing satisfaction through the court's channels. These procedures made the *Torrone* a useful option for *bolognesi* seeking resolutions to conflicts that otherwise might have been arbitrated by the local feudal noble, thus allowing the court's control of everyday life to expand throughout the seventeenth century.

Fundamentally, the *Torrone*'s work relied on ordinary peoples' participation in an elaborate network of information. Simply put, for inquisition to function, the court had to be made aware of crimes. Local bailiffs played a crucial role in the first phase of criminal process, the denunciation. Because homicide engendered emotions among whole communities, trials for this heinous act provide the clearest, fullest view of criminal trials in action. But how was the court in Bologna made aware of a man from Castiglione who was robbed and killed on his way to sell some livestock in the city market?[12] Or of a landlord's murder at the hands of his delinquent tenant, who had refused to pay rent?[13] The *massari* and *mestrali*, as local bailiff figures, provided the first response to major crimes such as this. Upon the commission of a crime, the victim or any witnesses were obliged to inform the local official, as in the case of the robbery-homicide noted above. Here, the victim's wife first went to the local *massaro* to report the crime. The *massaro* served both as the *Torrone*'s contact in the area and as the source of public participation in

---

[12] ASBo, *Tribunale del Torrone, Atti e Processi*, 5840, f. 384.   [13] Ibid., 6782, *in fine*.

justice: upon hearing of a crime, he was obliged to first ring the tocsin and gather all the local men in the square. With all the men gathered, the *massaro* led a search party to apprehend the delinquent, which in the vast majority of cases was a fruitless attempt (the time it would have taken to ring the bell and gather the men provided a useful window of escape to killers, who were generally local and against whom the community bore no particular animosity). The search party would typically search the accused's home and the homes of his parents and brothers, if they were in the same town. With the criminal having fled, typically into a self-imposed exile in Modena before the trial process even began, the bailiff's second obligation was to inform the court of the crime with or without the consent of the victim or his relatives.[14] Travelling to the court's central office in Bologna's *palazzo comunale*, the local official presented his *denuncia* to one of the *Torrone*'s eight notaries, who were arranged about the palace's courtyard and who shared equal competence over crimes of all sorts.

While most often submitted in an official capacity, denunciations were also given by a variety of other actors. Chief among these semi-official sources for information on crimes were the physicians and barbers of the city's major hospitals and the villages. Peter Blastenbrei has claimed that the *relazioni dei barbieri* (barbers' reports) of Rome were a unique source in that city, but they are present from an early period in Bologna, collated among the other stages of *Torrone* investigations (a boon to historians, these are grouped together in dedicated fascicles rather than separated among dispersed archival casebooks).[15] In Bologna, physicians and surgeons were required to make denunciations sometime before 1588, as evidenced by a 1588 decree against "the doctors and barbers who do not denounce."[16] Physicians at the *Ospedale di Santa Maria della Morte*

---

[14] This was not a popular job. Locals angry at seeing a friend or relative reported to the court harassed and sometimes assaulted these rural bailiffs as they travelled to Bologna. See the edict exhorting people to let their *massari* execute their duties in peace, ASBo, Bandi e Notificazione, Series I, No. 5, no folio, *bando* of August 21, 1585, "Bando che non si possi gridar dietro alli Contadini che conducono Delinquenti in mano della Corte." The *Torrone* also expected these *massari* to act as first-line surveillance, particularly with regard to bandit activity, ASBo, Bandi e Notificazione, Series I, No. 5, no folio, *bando* of September 5, 1584, "Bando che li Massari debbano quando passano li Banditi per li loro Communi venire Subito a denonciarli."

[15] Blastenbrei, "Violence, Arms and Criminal Justice in Papal Rome, 1560–1600," 69. Blastenbrei makes a persuasive case that these *relazioni* can give a rough idea of levels of violence, and they play a significant role in his larger study of crime in Rome.

[16] ASBo, Bandi e Notificazione, Series I, No. 5, no folio, *bando* of December 31, 1588, "Bando sopra quelli che non perseguitano li delinquenti e li medici e barbieri che non denontiano." Importantly, this also reiterates the long-standing requirement that all citizens had a responsibility to report crimes to their local official.

(known as the *Ospedale della Morte*) and that of *Santa Maria della Vita* were required to, and generally did, submit reports of all suspicious wounds that they treated, noting their nature, judging the wound's seriousness, and suggesting what type of weapon caused it. They submitted these descriptions for simple assaults as well as wounds that became fatal. If the notary deemed it appropriate, the surgeon's report initiated a full *Torrone* process; at the very least, the notary was usually dispatched to interview the victim in the hospital before he was released or died. Like the *massari*, the city physicians and rural barbers permitted the *Torrone* to penetrate the dense community networks that might otherwise occlude crimes. Between the *massari*, the *medici* and an amorphous group of informants known as *amici*, the *Torrone*'s intelligence and surveillance network gave papal officials the information necessary to effectively control the complex apparatus of the Bolognese state.

With a *denuncia* having been made, the notary decided whether the case warranted a summary procedure or a full inquisition. For simple assaults, minor property damage, and other small quarrels, the notary recorded the *denuncia* into his casebook (of which a notary might produce twenty a year, between 300 and 600 folios each), assigned a simple fine according to the infraction, and sent the *massaro* back with the decision. For more serious cases such as robbery, serious assault, rape, arson, theft or communal disorders, the notary was dispatched to investigate the crime in situ and gather enough information for the judge to make a decision. In urban cases, a judge or *sotto-Auditore* often went directly to the investigation as well. For rural crimes, the notary and a group of *sbirri* embarked on an outriding (*cavalcate*) to the village. A late attempt to keep track of the details of all of these *cavalcati* records 170 of these investigations between July and December 1689, which gives a sense of how busy these notaries were.[17] The dispatch of a notary and *sbirri* constituted the beginning of a full inquisition, which proceeded by beginning with an investigation of the immediate facts of the crime.

In cases of serious assault or homicide, this meant an inspection of the wounds or the body. If the victim was in the hospital, this was usually performed by the doctor who reported the wounds and two witnesses, the notary and a medical assistant. If the victim was in the streets, in his house or otherwise outside the city, this inspection was performed by the notary and two locals who knew the victim. Generally in threes, although sometimes with a fourth, these men described the victim's appearance,

---

[17] ASBo, *Assunteria del Torrone, Registro Cavalcati* 1689–91.

clothes and possessions; the nature, location and cause of all visible wounds; and the victim's name, age and origin. In cases of poisoning and other ambiguous deaths, a physician might perform an autopsy.[18] If the victim was not a local, the notaries might order that the body be left exposed in a public area until someone could identify it.[19] They noted where the body was found, where locals had moved it to, and where the crime was alleged to have taken place. These body inspections are extremely important as they allowed the *Torrone* to establish who the victims of violent crime actually were. Equally, the inspections drew members of communities into the judicial process by holding villages accountable for identifying victims of crimes. This process brought the victim's close friends and relatives into direct contact with the apparatus of justice that was to resolve their claim against the people who had injured their kin. The body inspection phase of a trial doubled as both information-collecting and an opportunity for the notary to assess the local community's attitude toward the victim, the imputed and the crime itself. This attitude could then inform the notary's approach to the third phase of the inquisitorial trial.

The interrogation of witnesses was a varied affair, dependent on the nature of the crime, the witnesses being interviewed, the victim and his or her status, and the notary's personal preferences. Some crimes warranted the interrogation of three witnesses, others of hundreds. If the victim was of a high enough status to afford a lawyer, this phase might be doubled by the provision of witnesses for the accused after the initial phase of notarial interrogation. But despite the multitude of ways in which interrogating witnesses might proceed, a few general patterns stand out. First, interrogation was never piecemeal: the notaries always had a plan and a list of both witnesses and questions they were after. The initial list of witnesses was formulated on the basis of both the *denuncia* and the initial investigation, and it usually included the immediate kin (particularly mothers and sisters) of the victim and imputed criminal, to establish a firm sense of *publica fama* and each person's role in his or her community. Citations were issued to both witnesses and suspects to appear before the notary on a given day, with increasingly severe fines for those who did not appear at the appointed times. Several prepared lists of questions survive as miscellanea in the casebooks, such as that prepared for the interrogation of Domenica Bertazzori, a former servant of Giulia Zaccaria, in 1600.[20] Like many others, Domenica's interrogation proceeded from simple to complex questions: Did she know why she had been called by the

---

[18] ASBo, *Torrone*, 5876, f. 432v–35v.   [19] Ibid., 5869, f. 395–400.
[20] Ibid., 3232, loose folio.

notaries? Had she spoken to any other witnesses who were called by the *Torrone*? How did she know the victim? Why did she leave her service? How long did she work for her mistress before leaving? Did she know if there had ever been any arguments between her mistress Giulia and her killer Giulio? Did she know if he had repeatedly offered her 4 *ducatoni* for a broken *cetera* (a musical instrument)? Again, what was the nature of her service to Giulia, where did she stay after leaving her, and why did she leave? Was she aware that if she was lying, she would be sent to prison, and did she admit that Giulio had fired her from Giulia's service? Had Giulia told her many times to go to Giulio's and get either the *cetera* or the money? These were the questions the notaries decided beforehand, before writing, "and other questions at the discretion of the interrogator according to the answers given." The interrogation of witnesses, a technique used by the notaries to investigate the social network of entire communities rather than isolated crimes, was both highly orchestrated and extremely flexible, making it very useful for compelling the loyalties of *bolognesi*. It is perhaps noteworthy that this list from 1600 was prepared in Italian, rather than Latin, indicating that the interrogation room was a more vernacular space than we might imagine. It seems that most ordinary interrogations took place in the local Italian, though sometimes students and other scholars were questioned in Latin, at least as far as their knowledge allowed.

Of course, recalcitrant witnesses could be threatened with worse than prison if they refused to cooperate. As part of the interrogation phase, both witnesses and accused criminals could be tortured by the court, which maintained records of torture sessions. The *Torrone* only tortured using the rope hoist, and, although a comprehensive statistical analysis is precluded by the sheer size of the *Torrone*'s archival holdings, it appears that the use of torture declined across the seventeenth century along with the use of capital punishment. As a legal proof, torture remained within the *Torrone*'s competency, but functionally, it became less important and less prevalent because it was ineffective at attaining reliable information, and more often overwhelmed or broke a prisoner than caused them to confess deep secrets.[21] In cases when torture might have been effective, witnesses were often sufficiently cognizant of the legal strictures surrounding torture that they could avoid it – for example, a witness could have a physician certify to the court that their back was already too injured by labour and age to withstand a torture session.[22] The legal restraints on torture were followed when it did occur, and authorities

[21] Cf. ASBo, *Torrone*, 4216, f. 83r–5v; 3202, f. 286.   [22] Ibid., 3270, f. 153r.

were careful not to maim or permanently disfigure suspects or witnesses, such as Anna Trevisana, whose torture was abruptly ended when a physician declared that her arms could not sustain another drop of the rope.[23] While the selection here precludes the comprehensive review of torture that would give a full picture of its use and prevalence, torture was used at least into the 1630s as a means of proof in interrogation. If in custody, witness and suspect alike could be tortured.

With an initial round of witness interrogations completed, further citations were issued by court officers. Typically, someone accused of a violent crime that carried a heavy fine or corporal punishment fled the locale in the aftermath and took up residency either elsewhere within Bologna's borders or in one of its neighbouring states. *Sbirri* posted citations in major villages and border towns calling the imputed to appear for interrogation and sentencing. Three citations were issued before a criminal was declared absent, at which point he could be killed with impunity by citizen and bandit alike.[24] With the citations dispensed and the criminal either in exile or recovering from interrogation, the notary collated the evidence and gave it to the judge, who then reviewed it and presented his view of the crime and his sentencing. If present, advocates for the accused were then given the opportunity to review the evidence and present counter-arguments and technicalities. Most cases, however, were resolved without lawyers' input. The judge determined every step of the process, evaluated the evidence, and pronounced sentence.[25]

In sentencing, the judge was not bound by a strict schema. The death sentence could be applied in cases of theft, assault to officials, homicide, sodomy, counterfeiting, heresy, rebellion, banditry and spying. However, the actual application of capital punishment declined significantly over the seventeenth century, following a spike in the 1580s during the campaign to cleanse bandits from the *contado*.[26] Throughout the early years of papal rule and until the 1540s, the legates used the power of the *Podesta*'s court to summarily execute significant members of the anti-

---

[23] Ibid., 5904, f. 437v–40v.

[24] ASBo, *Bandi e Notificazione*, Series I, No. 5, no folio, *bando* of October 31, 1584.

[25] For more on the history of judicial process in Bologna, cf. M. Vallerani, "Criminal Court Procedure in Late Medieval Bologna: Cultural and Social Contexts," in Blanshei, *Violence and Justice in Bologna*, 27–54; S. Blanshei, "Bolognese Criminal Justice: From Medieval Commune to Renaissance Signoria," in ibid., 55–82; T. Dean, "Invesigating Homicide: Bologna in the 1450s," in ibid., 83–100.

[26] N. Terpstra, "Theory into Practice: Executions, Comforting, and Comforters in Renaissance Italy," in N. Terpstra, ed., *The Art of Executing Well: Rituals of Execution in Renaissance Italy* (Kirksville, MO: Truman State University Press, 2008), 118–58, especially p. 123.

papal opposition. But with the legate established and the *Torrone* integrated into the judicial system by the late sixteenth century, capital punishment lost its usefulness and became another emblem of inefficient and ineffective medieval justice. While the period 1540–1600 saw Bologna execute 917 men and women, this number was only 556 from 1600 to 1700, an average of 5.5 per year compared to the average 15.25 from 1540 to 1600.[27] In the final three years of the seventeenth century, one person was executed annually, and none executed in 1696. A large spike in executions in the 1640s reflects the increased presence of disbanded armies and deserters in North Italy following the Thirty Years' War; a similar spike in 1630 reflects the increased hold of the *Torrone* over the city during the plague crisis, and most of the eleven men executed in 1653 were involved in the brazen public murder of the *Torrone sotto-Auditore* Giacinto Pungelli. The pattern is clear: the *Torrone* executed criminals who represented a threat to the security of the state and the court's hold over that state. As the court grew more powerful with each of the crises noted above, execution was less useful as a demonstration of the *Torrone*'s power, which by the late seventeenth century was better represented as mercy.

With capital punishment waning, the *Torrone* instead used convicted criminals to man the oars of the papal galleys in the Mediterranean. Sentences could range from one year of service to perpetual galley service, which was a functional death sentence that fell on someone else to carry out.[28] Punitive incarceration was possible but rarely employed, since it was both expensive and considered extremely cruel. Corporal punishment could be employed for minor quarrels and disputes, while mutilation and maiming were reserved for heresy and other deviant categories. However, most people who committed simple infractions received a simple fine, the amount of which was left to the judge. Pecuniary punishment made it possible to avoid overly harsh punishment of poor *bolognesi* while making some small exchange – even a few *quattrini* – the basis for the court's accepting the criminal back into society's fold. This was the true purpose of punishment for minor crimes: not to hurt or mutilate, but to balance crime and punishment – to order compensation for the offence committed so that normal societal relations could resume.

This drive to balance offences – through punishment or vengeance – perhaps explains a great deal of the prevalence and importance of outlaws

---

[27] Ibid., 121; ASBo, *Cronaci delle Giustizie seguite in Bologna del 1030 al 1750.*
[28] Cf. Damasio Zavagli's sentencing to ten years of galley service at the age of twenty-two. ASBo, *Tribunale del Torrone, Atti e processi*, 6592, *in fine.*

and contumacious bandits in North Italy later in the sixteenth century and throughout the seventeenth. Under the *Torrone*'s inquisitorial system, contumacious banditry became the de facto punishment for a wide swath of crimes. Some criminals in custody were explicitly punished with banishment, such as the gang of young men following a murder in 1700. Others were banned because they were contumacious, and were exiled with the provision that they would be executed if they were found, such as a certain Sabbatino, who had fled into the *contado* after robbing and murdering the priest who employed him as a servant.[29] Lombard and Central Italian bandits had a deserved reputation for theft, murder, rape and robbery, and the *Torrone* first took action against them in the 1580s and 1590s, resulting in the late-century spike in executions noted above. The 1580s and 1590s saw a great deal of legislation exhorting *bolognesi* to assist in reporting and capturing bandits whenever possible; employing a carrot and stick approach, these *bandi* promised significant rewards to those who turned in bandits, and threatened heavy punishments against individuals and communities who failed to do so.[30] The campaign to purge the Bolognese hinterland of violent bandits was part of a broader project in the papal states, and some of this legislation thus appears in the pope's name.[31] Because bandits could remain highly involved in their local communities, the campaign against bandits provided the *Torrone* with an opportunity to penetrate those communities through carrot-and-stick participation in the judicial system such as catching bandits for reward.

If the numbers of captured and killed bandits is any indication, the success of the late sixteenth-century campaign against bandit criminals was considerable but was nevertheless transitory and depended to a large extent on the continued participation of the *bolognesi* least under the *Torrone*'s thumb. This group, the rural peasantry, eked out their livings on farms near the borders of Modena and Ferrara, the closest significant states to Bologna and the most popular destinations for exiled and banished *bolognesi*. The need to maintain the vigilance of these *contadini* and their capacity to repel bandit incursions led the *Torrone* to decree, on June 17, 1614, that all residents in these borderlands were required keep in their house at all times at least one, and preferably two, loaded wheellock arquebuses, and had to carry one with them at all times when out in

---

[29] ASBo, *Torrone*, 7535.2, *fasc.* 8.; 7536, *fasc.* 31.
[30] Cf. the latest of the sixteenth century, which promises *contadini* 200 *scudi* for killing a *capobandito* and 400 for turning him in alive. ASBo, *Bandi e Notificazione*, Series I, No. 5, no folio, *bando* of July 6, 1590.
[31] Ibid., *bando* of July 23, 1585.

their fields and around their villages.[32] This obligation made the *contadini* the first line of defence against invading bandits, but also resulted in a flood of firearms to the *contado* that continued to plague the *Torrone* through the rest of the century. Within two and a half years the decree was reversed, due to the many disorders and homicides that accompanied the sharp rise of firearms ownership.[33] The *Torrone*'s experiment with militia control of bandit incursions only served to create conditions under which bandits flourished and everybody was armed. The problems caused by banditry continued to plague the *Torrone* throughout the seventeenth century.

Most important is the fact that banditry was often a temporary stage in a criminal process that could stretch for years, and even decades. Following a homicide, the killer most often fled the district and was banned as a contumacious killer, to be executed if captured, but as noted above, this sentence was rarely carried out. However, while under ban, the killer himself could be killed with impunity unless he was able to make peace with his victim's family, and thus receive pardon from the legate. The final stage of the *Torrone*'s process, the crucial acts of peacemaking and pardon, mediated the ban and allowed the offended party and his or her kin a period of separation in which the violent emotions engendered by social conflict could be tempered, and hatred turned first into forgiveness and then friendship. Here the *Torrone*'s goals to prevent the outbreak of cycles of violence and to ensure that peace was obtained are most obvious. While not explicit in the documentation, many trials imply that notaries and officials of the *Torrone* applied significant pressure on victims and their kin to accept their enemies' overtures for peace. Forged with the sponsorship of the court, the peace accord brought the temporary state of outlawry to a close and reintegrated the offender into Bolognese society.

A peace accord – the formal instrument by which enmity was made into friendship – could be difficult to obtain while the contumacious offender was formally subject to judicial murder upon sight, and thus bandits had to seek ways to influence the course of events from beyond the borders. The most common means for this to occur was through the sponsorship of a noble family. In 1600, the Ronchetta and Tozzi clans of the district of Aiano, in the mountains south of the city, engaged in a

---

[32] ASBo, *Legato, Bandi*, 1600–1700, *bando* of June 7, 1614.
[33] Ibid., *bando* of December 20, 1616.

vendetta exchange that left at least three dead and many others wounded.[34] By November, the violence had moved from Aiano and into the city as the two families brought their networks of kin and friendship into the conflict. The quarrel attracted the attention of the *Torrone*, whose notaries arranged for a peace conference between the leading members of the family in the palace of Signore Galeazzo Paleotti, a member of one of Bologna's leading noble families.[35] This conference was ultimately unsuccessful because one of the Ronchetta family's young scions, Battista, the nephew of the patriarch, refused to make peace along with his other male relatives; nevertheless, a peace accord was signed between the two families and young Battista was confined to house arrest in Bologna until he capitulated to the peace. In fact, he and his cousin Nicola fled into contumacy rather than face that punishment.[36]

In many cases, the process was much less fraught, and peace became a regular aspect of the process of criminal justice. Of the 701 homicide trials collected in this sample, at least 212 were settled with a notarized peace accord granted by the victim's kin to his killer, which brought the process to a conclusion and commuted the killer's sentence of banishment, galley service or death to pardon, and a return home to his community. Often these pardons stipulated a further period of separation between the parties, such as a three-year period in which the killer could not return to the village where he committed the homicide, but was otherwise free to move about the *legato*. The formulation of peace became such an important part of Bologna's criminal process that by the 1650s, an entire government council, the *Assunteria de Liti e Paci*, was formed to facilitate peacemaking between high-ranking noble families. Although it does not seem to have been a very active council, the *Assunteria* was involved in forging a peace in at least one major conflict, which involved members of the Ghisilieri, Bentivoglii, Ercolani, Malvezzi and Calderani families. It was mediated by high-ranking members of the Fibia and Pepoli families.[37] It is difficult to overstate the importance of peacemaking for the criminal court of Bologna in the seventeenth century. These formal structures for making peace and ending conflict allowed the *Torrone* a full measure of social control, which augmented their use of inquisition procedures in increasing the court's effective hold over *bolognesi* from all areas of the *legato*.

---

[34] ASBo, *Tribunale del Torrone, Atti e Processi*, 3173, f. 147; 3184, f. 298–418; 3185, f. 162–326r; 3246, f. 176.

[35] Ibid., 3246, f. 176–185v.   [36] Ibid., 218.

[37] ASBo, *Assunteria de liti e paci, Atti dell'Assunteria e di Paci, 1658–72*, f. 1v–53r.

The Public Trust: Reforming the *Torrone*

The *Torrone* was not, at first, the sole forum for judicial resolution in and around Bologna. The medieval and Renaissance judicial regime was podestarial and had limited control over the *contado*, while its role in the city was more responsive than proactive in the control of violence. The *Torrone* first rose from the ashes of the medieval courts as a means for the Pope to eliminate the nobility's practice of operating private courts on feudal lands in the countryside. It emerged, then, as part of a judicial marketplace in which control of the population was bid on by the Papacy, by republican families who wished to see power flow from the Senate, and by oligarchic factions such as the Malvezzi who wished the Papacy banished and the Bentivoglio reinstated. What the *Torrone* offered, according to its own documentation, was a regular and predictable justice available to all subjects, free of the web of allegiances and kinship that plagued seigneurial justice in feudal courts.

If its offer was an impartial justice available to all *bolognesi*, the *Torrone* needed to make the case that its functionaries, and particularly its notaries, were accountable and that their work appeared to be and was transparent. Gaining effective jurisdiction over the farthest reaches of the jurisdiction required establishing a measure of social trust in its institutional capacities. In essence, this meant that the *Torrone*'s judges and notaries were challenged to prove to rurals that they offered better forms of conflict resolution than did the arbitration of feudal landlords, who might be swayed in their judgment by factors outside the conflict at hand.[38]

What did early modern people want from their courts? They were not dupes of a sinister and omniscient Foucauldian panopticon: if the residents of Aiano, the small hamlet that hosted a violent feud at the turn of the century, wished to hide their troubles from the authorities in Bologna, they could. The city was 42 kilometres away in a straight line, and the winding paths through mountain vales made it farther still. Hanlon notes that "justice" carried specific meanings for early moderns, that were at once simpler and more complex than its modern ideal.[39] Justice fell somewhere between vengeance and restitution for rural seventeenth-century Italians, and lordship meant finding the proper balance between these factors in order to promote the continuance of

---

[38] On the reform of Italian magistrates, cf. D. Chambers and T. Dean, *Clean Hands and Rough Justice: An Investigating Magistrate in Renaissance Italy* (Ann Arbor: University of Michigan Press, 1997).

[39] Hanlon, "Justice in the Age of Lordship."

social peace and the abeyance of local conflicts.[40] Hanlon's Tuscan peasants, however, were living in an area that was expressly feudal, under the legal jurisdiction of an established marchese. In Bologna, central and peripheral authorities often found themselves in conflict, a situation complicated by the fact that the central authority of Bologna's court was a peripheral arm of Roman power. In a judicial marketplace such as early modern Bologna, where users of the court employed litigation and prosecution among many strategies of conflict, the *Torrone* was challenged to represent its justice as the most reliable justice.

To that end, the papal legates and the *Torrone* itself initiated a series of reforms to criminal procedure in the late sixteenth and early seventeenth centuries, designed to give justice at least the appearance of fairness and transparency. Already by 1576, under the signature of Gregory XIII, the *Torrone* had a publicly posted rubric of fees and emoluments payable to notaries for their services.[41] Cardinal Legate Antonio Maria Salviati, in 1586, promulgated a *bando* that publicized his rules for the timely delivery and execution of court citations, in response to complaints about the "frauds and evils of the executors of the city and *contado* of Bologna," which stipulated that all citations from the court were to be delivered within four days of being written.[42] This *bando* was the carrot in improving the lot of city officials dealing with the messy business of delivering court citations and transporting witnesses and suspects to the city. The stick had come a year before – in 1585, Salviati had published a decree stipulating that anyone who harassed or assaulted *Massari* or others acting in the court's name would be subject to three drops of the rope in public and a stiff fine of 50 *scudi* (minors were merely given fifty lashes).[43] Salviati's successor, Enrico Gaetani, soon after assuming the legation, publicly castigated shopkeepers who did nothing to stop crimes in commission, but also offered rewards for those who did – his *bando* described both prize and penalty for those who intervened to prevent crime or neglected to do so.[44] These late sixteenth century *bandi* envisioned rural communities that regularly accessed the resources of the court, because it presented itself as a reliable (and reliably priced), neutral alternative to local justice.

The sixteenth-century campaign against banditry was also an opportunity for the city to access rural communities by involving them directly.

---

[40] Ibid., 1008.

[41] ASBo, *Bandi e Notificazione*, Series I, No. 4, *bando* of October 20, 1576. This particular document is a Latin text distributed to officials, which calls for vulgar translations to be posted around the city.

[42] ASBo, *Bandi e Notificazione*, Series I, No. 5, *bando* of February 10, 1586.

[43] Ibid., *bando* of August 21, 1585.   [44] Ibid., *bando* of February 19, 1587.

Throughout the 1580s, *bandi* regularly exhorted communities to report and apprehend bandits whenever possible, as Legate Salviati did on June 12, 1585, specifying that communities should if possible apprehend the leader of a bandit gang in order to weaken the whole.[45] In 1589, the Vice-Legate Camillo Borghese offered *denominazione*, the lifting of a ban from oneself or a relative, to anyone who killed or captured a bandit, while reminding subjects of the penalties for not doing so.[46] This strategy of drawing the peasantry into the *Torrone*'s orbit through their participation in capturing bandits paid off. On March 4, three days after Borghese had promulgated his *denominazione*, the Auditor of the *Torrone* signed off on Francesco di Sante Minozzi's pardon for acts of banditry and peace-breaking, because Francesco had killed the notorious bandit Domenico Malagei.[47] By requiring the participation of *contadini* in the control of rural violence, Borghese was attempting to break apart the webs of allegiance and codes of *omertà* that operated outside city walls. Criminals themselves were offered respite if they turned in bigger fish, as when Borghese offered immunity to any accomplice who would name his co-conspirators in an attack on Count Ridolfo Campeggi, or when he extended the rewards offered for the capture of bandits even to gang leaders who turned other gang leaders in to the court.[48] By the dawn of the seventeenth century, the court sought opportunities to insinuate its agents and its judicial protocol into the farthest reaches of the Bolognese state.

The reform of *Torrone* procedures continued and a new public rubric, published in Italian in 1595, laid out the judicial process and the roles of notaries and judges, including especially the head notary's responsibility for the conservation and security of the goods and pledges of witnesses. In 1599, Vice-Legate Orazio Spinola published a reform of *Torrone* record-keeping that would have significant effects on the documentary record of the judicial process – a boon to future historians, though likely just more paperwork for the staff of the *Torrone*. In this decree, Spinola dictated that two copies of every sentence were to be maintained, one in the ongoing books of acts kept by the *Torrone* and one immediately deposited into the archive.[49] More than this, the decree also empowered notaries to assign sentences in the absence of a judge, who would later confirm them. This change in process enabled notaries to adjudicate many of the summary cases of conflict encountered in the countryside,

---

[45] Ibid., *bando* of June 12, 1585.   [46] Ibid., *bando* of March 1, 1589.
[47] Ibid., *bando* of March 4, 1589.
[48] Ibid., *bando* of August 25, 1589, *bando* of July 6, 1590.
[49] ASBo, *Bandi e Notificazione*, Series I, No. 6, *bando* of November 1, 1599.

and it increased the pace of justice since witnesses and suspects no longer faced the long walk to Bologna to receive adjudication. At the same time, because the decree empowered notaries, it altered the form of their record-keeping in a way for which historians should be grateful. Criminal processes were now required to be kept integral, with all materials from denunciation to petition and pardon either conserved or copied into booklets organized by notary and by date. A single process was now located in a single book and conserved in a single archive. This allowed for the efficient and timely management of archives and for easy access to records of past processes, which court users could request for a fee. The reforms of the late sixteenth century were all intended to draw users to the court by advertising its neutrality and its efficiency, and by offering tangible benefits to those who participated in its judicial program.

While the *Torrone* sought to improve its public relations through community involvement in controlling crime, it was also reforming its internal conduct in the early seventeenth century. In 1607, Cardinal Legate Iustiniano published the "Orders to Be Observed by the Notaries of the *Torrone*, regarding both Matters and Fees," a document that lists in painstaking detail the duties and responsibilities of the eight *Torrone* notaries.[50] The rules are clear and numerous. Notaries were required to, among other things:

- Fully render the process without leaving gaps in the text to fill in by memory later, and note this assiduousness with the phrase "*non se adstringens*" at the end.
- Write directly in the books of *processi*, never on sheets of paper.
- Only take the names of complainants if they were freely given.
- Never investigate the background of complainants during a process.
- Report to the head notary, every fifteen days or whenever a book was filled, the names of all those processed at their bench during that time. Notaries were also required to submit those books promptly to the archive, and maintain an index of all loose paper, acts and other documents separate from the books, which was also to be submitted to the *caponotaio*.

These requirements were all intended to ensure the integrity of *Torrone processi* and to reassure users of the court that its powers would not be turned upon them. The right of anonymous complaint and the ban on background checks by notaries protected complainants from judicial

---

[50] ASBo, *Assunteria del Torrone*, 3c, *Constitutioni e bolle del Torrone*, 1488–1623, "Ordini da Osservarsi dalli Notari del Torrone, cosi intorne alle Cause more alle Mercedi loro," 1607.

prejudice and from the possibility that their adversary might hear of their complaint. These measures were enacted to protect the integrity of the process and prevent notaries from taking advantage of their positions at the expense of court users. Two further measures were meant to ensure a timely process: first, quarrels and complaints were to be immediately shown to the head notary who would judge whether to pursue an investigation. The second gave urgency to rural justice by stipulating that when a notary was called to the *contado*, he had to go immediately; if he could not be found at the office or at home, the messenger was to immediately report this and a substitute notary would be sent. These rules of order for notaries were meant to counter a reputation for greed and self-interest, and to bring users to the *Torrone* as a reliable forum for justice.

Access to neutral justice was a pillar of the *Torrone*'s bid to win users in the *contado* away from illegitimate judicial forums. Justice, however, had its costs, most of which were borne by complainants or the court. The *Torrone* reformed this by shifting some costs onto the accused and absorbing others, while implementing measures to ensure access to justice by the poorest of *bolognesi*. When the accused appeared, they were charged five gold *scudi* for a full defence, and three if they admitted guilt to receive absolution. If they were judged truly innocent, the court ate the expense.[51] Witnesses under interrogation were required to pay the notary for his services, but these costs were eased (by 50%) for minor crimes without bloodshed or when multiple family members were questioned (the family paid as one). If they could not afford the fees, the very poor had their costs reduced by up to 75%. In a city where the judiciary had a long reputation for capriciousness and political manipulation, the *Torrone* advertised itself as separate from the internecine conflicts that dominated Bolognese society's echelons. The final stipulation of the 1602 *Ordini* was that the head notary face reappointment every ten years, with the criteria being that he had performed adequately and had not cultivated power and interest groups around the city.

The fiscal integrity of notaries was particularly important in this stage of the *Torrone*'s development.[52] In this sense, Bologna was almost a century ahead of its ruling city, Rome, in effecting meaningful reform

---

[51] Ibid., "Ordini di NS Papa Clemente Ottavo Sopra l'osservanza delle Constitutioni del Torrone, e Altro," 1580, reproduced 1602.

[52] Laurie Nussdorfer details the development of the notarial profession in Rome, noting how by the seventeenth century it was highly regulated and restricted to a smaller number of notaries than in the Medieval. She argues that reform of notarial practice in Rome was motivated by papal financial needs, and that popes viewed the notaries of Rome as sources of venal income. Laurie Nussdorfer, *Brokers of Public Trust: Notaries in Early Modern Rome* (Baltimore, MD: Johns Hopkins University Press, 2009), 140–50.

of notarial procedures in court (a second set of reforms, under Pope Benedict XIV, took place in the eighteenth century).[53] These reforms make it clear the *Torrone* was responding to a general mistrust of its notarial staff; it is equally clear that to do so was not an easy task, as the reform measures were repeated in *Torrone* legislation throughout the century. Beyond the processual stipulations already noted above, which guaranteed the integrity of investigations, several regulations touched directly on the comportment and behaviour of notaries themselves. The limits on what notaries could charge were particularly emphasized, indicating a general concern with notarial greed. The 1607 reforms included a wide ban on notaries accepting any emoluments or bribes beyond those laid out in the salarial tables that were published publicly.[54] Since much of their work with the public involved copying various acts such as petitions and peace accords that emerged from cancelled *processi*, notaries were explicitly limited in what they could charge for copying services: half a giulio for petitions; for copies of pardons or peace accords, no more than one lira. The notaries were also responsible for receiving the sureties given by parties where the court had imposed a peace accord. For homicides, the notary took half a scudo; for non-mortal bloodshed, three giulii from each individual party to the peace; for simple assaults without bloodshed, three giulii in total sufficed.

The 1602 document the *Ordini di NS Papa Clemente Ottavo*, first published in 1580, is more explicit about the emoluments and the limits on notarial salaries.[55] Fees for notarial services were generally low, and moreover, they were pegged to the severity of the crime under investigation. Thus, in most corporal or pecuniary cases, the fee for a notary to compile the paperwork was 2 scudi; but if the possible fine for the delict was 2.5 lire or less it was reduced to 3 soldi, whereas if it was 200 lire or more, the scudi were augmented by 7 soldi. These fees were halved in cases of minor conflict without bloodshed. In the name of efficiency, the *Torrone* allowed notaries and subjects to combine multiple crimes into a single process, which could then be paid for with a single fee. This document went so far as to prescribe a complex schema of fees for individual paper acts, and it ran three manuscript folios on each side.

[53] Nussdorfer, *Brokers of Public Trust*; Angelozzi and Casanova, *La giustizia criminale a Bologna nel XVIII secolo e le riforme di Benedetto XIV*. Nussdorfer notes how meaningful reform of the Roman notarial class occurred only in the eighteenth century.

[54] ASBo, *Assunteria del Torrone*, 3c, *Constitutioni e bolle del Torrone*, 1488–1623, "Ordini da Osservarsi dalli Notari del Torrone, cosi intorne alle Cause more alle Mercedi loro," 1607.

[55] "Ordini di NS Papa Clemente Ottavo Sopra l'osservanza delle Constitutioni del Torrone, e Altro," 1580, reproduced 1602.

Every document conceivably produced by a notary of the *Torrone* was given a price, with possible modifications and reductions noted alongside the circumstances that warranted them. The collection and management of these fees was then regulated under a series of provisions that make clear the *Torrone*'s goal of improving the trustworthiness of its notaries. The regulations were as follows:

1. Messengers and notaries may not accept any money except that laid out in the fees.
2. All citations, messages and notices must be delivered as soon as possible and without delay to assure "the swift passage of justice."
3. Only the Head Notary may receive or disburse payments.
4. Copyists may not write on the original books, on pain of being fired (or worse, at the Governor's discretion).
5. Any ex-notaries who attempt to access the records of justice will be banned from the state.
6. There should be no more than 8 substitute notaries, and they must remain nearby the offices of the *Torrone*, and they will change posts every 8 days; notaries should be prepared to pass on records to substitutes in case they are unable to work.
7. Trials may not be taken out of the office or copied, unless given signed permission by the Head Notary and his reviewer; all copies made must be equal to and of equal quality as originals.

The measures implemented to reform notaries' behaviour are illustrative of the widespread distrust to which the *Torrone* was responding. Ordinary *bolognesi* could be forgiven for viewing the court as an intrusive force. Witnesses were reticent to give information to notaries for fear that it might be used against them in the future and could be maddeningly uncooperative.[56] As the *Torrone* remained a representative of papal, and therefore non-native, power, *bolognesi* continued to treat many criminal acts as civil conflicts, bringing them instead to the vestiges of podestarial justice, such as the *Tribunale della Rota*.[57] Aware of these difficulties and the general distrust of professional notaries among the population at large, the judges of the *Torrone* and their masters in the Senate sought to improve the public image of the court's visible faces – the notaries who for the most part handled the daily operations of justice.

---

[56] Cf. ASBo, *Torrone*, 3258, 1600, f. 78r–81v, in which a witness seems to be deliberately wasting the notary's time by expounding on the many reasons he could not know the answer sought.

[57] Angelozzi and Casanova, *La giustizia criminale in una città di antico regime*, 43.

This late sixteenth-century series of reforms differed significantly from the early attempts by papal governors to ensure a regularly operating court. In the 1530s, ease of access had been critical, and legislation had dictated that one member of the *Rota* per week be assigned the duty of handing down summary justice to all face-to-face complainants with minor quarrels.[58] A 1535 statute laid out the rubric of punishments for fatal violence, in an attempt to regularize the investigation and punishment of homicides.[59] The punishments were surprisingly harsh: anyone who committed a homicide was immediately banned from the state, on pain of death; no pardons were to be granted to homicides, even if the killer was able to make peace with his or her victim's families, and even if the banned killer in turn killed one or several other bandits; multiple homicides were ineligible for the lifting of the ban. These were unexpectedly harsh measures for a court that, in both its medieval antecedents and in its mature form, much preferred the composition of banishment to debt, and tended to use justice as the means to force conflicting parties to make peace – a pattern it shared with other Mediterranean courts that developed over this period.[60] The mid-sixteenth century turn to repression is probably best explained by the Papacy's need to assert authority and dominate the newly subdued people of Bologna. The aim of these homicide punishments was almost certainly the expulsion of significant numbers of factional supporters from the province, easing the legates' ability to maintain order and peace.

By 1600, then, the *Torrone* had enjoyed some sixty years of authority over Bologna.[61] In that time it had made significant headway in eliminating the noble prerogative of justice, but many of the noble clans continued to operate feudal courts in the *contado*. It had, however, become the only legitimate criminal court of Bologna, and had piggybacked on medieval offices like the local bailiff, which allowed it to achieve a certain continuity of tradition as well as to gain a trusted insider in rural villages. The homicides that occurred at the turn of the century reflect this trend: Bologna was beginning to recover from the traumas of the papal conquest, and interpersonal violence was generally prosaic: revenge, romance and robbery dominate the records of 1600, uncomplicated by high politics, rebellion or disaster. Indicted homicide rates were comparable to other Italian cities such as Rome at the same time.[62]

---

[58] ASBo, *Bandi e Notificazioni*, Series I, No. 3, f. 13, *bando* of February 9, 1536.
[59] Ibid., f. 6–8, *bando* of August 3, 1535
[60] Smail, "Violence and Predation in Late Medieval Mediterranean Europe," 32–34.
[61] The earliest mention I find of the *Torrone* in statutes is 1541. ASBo, *Bandi e Notificazioni*, Series I, No. 3, f. 95.
[62] Eisner, "Long-Term Historical Trends in Violent Crime," 97.

The *Torrone* took an active interest in discerning, investigating and ultimately adjudicating homicides, but its approach was not necessarily punitive. Rather, it sought to establish a forum under which peace could be made – or forced – between the killers and their victims. Establishing itself as the sole font of criminal justice was not the first step in a Foucauldian transformation of sovereign power, but rather the new court's appropriation of the larger Mediterranean pattern by which communities transmuted debts of violence into financial and social liabilities.[63] Sentencing and execution rates for homicides were negligible, and the city focused its violence on those who robbed pilgrims or those who forged keys. The homicides that occurred in 1600, 1610 and 1620 and the treatment they received from the court demonstrate a city relatively "civilized" by the standards of the age.[64]

The seventeenth century dawned on a *Torrone* affirmed in its status as the sole criminal forum in Bologna, and on a population who continued to use violence as a regular strategy of social conflict. However, the homicides that occurred in these years indicate a period of stability in this society, where violence was primarily mundane and did not challenge the presiding hierarchies and structures of social and political authority. Factional violence is practically absent from the record of homicides in 1600, and most homicides occurred during arguments between people who knew each other and whose conflicts had a limited social scope. Public noble violence was not an issue in these years. Broad swaths of the population brought their minor and mortal quarrels to the *Torrone* for adjudication, such that sometime in the 1620s the *Torrone* reformed its record-keeping to account for the mounting volume of both the number of cases and the effusive statements taken in their investigation. A fragile peace reigned over Bologna, and the *Torrone* took much of the credit for it, developing a reputation for autocracy and haughtiness.[65]

The early century's relatively low rates of indicted homicides are legible in this light. Early modern Bologna was a society in which the primary purpose of criminal justice was not to eliminate the criminal, but rather to ensure the conditions of peace and order were restored within the communal body. Those communities, in turn, had good reasons to turn to the *Torrone* to resolve minor quarrels before they turned to homicidal violence, knowing that the minor fine they might pay was less

---

[63] Smail, "Violence and Predation in Late Medieval Mediterranean Europe."

[64] Eisner, "Long-Term Historical Trends in Violent Crime," 94–100; Spierenburg, *A History of Murder*, 62–65.

[65] Angelozzi and Casanova, *La giustizia criminale in una città di antico regime*, 43.

onerous than the hardships of exile, the expense of securing a notarized pardon, or the possibility, however slight, that the *Torrone* might hang a killer if he was caught. The indicators of a relatively thick atmosphere of social trust were present in Bologna at the time: significant political upheaval lay in the past and the future; a criminal court was effectively combining exemplary punishment for theft with mediation of social conflicts; and the local nobility had recently come together with the Papacy to clear the roadways and mountain passes of dangerous bandits. Run-of-the-mill violence remained commonplace throughout these years, and the records of homicides are far outnumbered by the records of fistfights, slaps, thrown rocks and even missed gunshots. Early modern *bolognesi* were accustomed to conflict and tolerated a great deal of violence in their communities, and at the turn of the seventeenth century, they were able to restrain it such that fatal violence remained comparatively low. The remaining years of the seventeenth century destroyed that equilibrium as warfare and environmental disaster reared their ugly heads.

If the *Torrone* was created to bring a measure of regularity and reliability to the complex judicial system that operated in medieval Bologna, the ambitions of legates, judges and notaries made it a much more powerful instrument of control and coercion than its founding members had envisioned. A document printed sometime after the death of Paul V in 1621 reveals the growing ambitions of its judges in a "proposal-response" format. This document, entitled "A Record of Certain Matters to Discuss from the Illustrious Lords of the Torrone with the Most Illustrious and Excellent Lord Judge of the Torrone, with His Responses Given Point by Point," establishes the *Torrone*'s responsibilities, as seen by its judge.[66] The judge's responses to the suggested limits on *Torrone* activity indicate his view of the court as the state's primary office of social control.

Each proposal addressed a contentious aspect of the *Torrone*'s authority and provided the *Torrone*'s justification for it. The first proposal put forward was that the *Torrone* should not involve itself in minor quarrels, as these were not important enough to garner its attention.[67] The judge responded that if these crimes might lead to enmity, greater quarrels and violence, then the *Torrone* should involve itself. On the second point, that the *Torrone* should not seek out additional witnesses but instead be

---

[66] ASBo, *Assunteria del Torrone*, 3a, *Constitutiones Turroni Bandi e Stampe*, "Ricordo di alcuni part.ri da trattarsi dall'Ill.mi SS.ri Conf.e et Assonti del Torrone col molto Ill. mo et Ecc.mo Sig. Auditore di esso Torrone, con le rispose da esso S.r Auditore date a capo per capo," n.d. (1627?), no folio.

[67] Ibid.

satisfied with information provided in initial testimony, the judge responded that if he felt it necessary, the *Torrone* would seek other witnesses. Both these points reflect the *Torrone*'s ambition to act without significant limits or oversight. Third, that *sbirri* should not injure or otherwise mistreat prisoners "as they presently do for no good reason." The judge fully agreed but despaired of how to achieve that goal, as prisoners were often uncooperative in their arrest. Fourth, the *Torrone* was not to ride into the countryside except for homicides, assassinations and other grave crimes, to which the judge simply responded that he could not think of a single instance in which a notary was dispatched for a crime other than those cited.[68] The fifth, sixth and seventh points addressed notarial abuses, and the judge agreed that notaries should cease their corrupt ways, although he had already tried everything he could think of and thought that the good done by catching criminals outweighed the bad of a bit of notarial graft.[69] The next three points all addressed the *Torrone*'s procedures for capturing and interrogating suspects, and the judge agreed that the *Torrone* should provide a quick and transparent process.

By the end of this document, the responding judge grew impatient with his reviewers. He brushed off the notion that notaries should submit all receipts for audit every three months, saying they already did so – to him. He similarly rejected the reforms instituted by Paul V in Rome, arguing that they were designed for Rome and would not function in Bologna. He did agree that notaries should make a better effort to faithfully record the exact words of witnesses, except that sometimes details might be excluded to protect witnesses. Taken as a whole, the fourteen points disputed in this document make clear that the *Torrone* viewed its role in Bologna as a unique vehicle for the resolution of conflicts and diffusion of peaceful order throughout both the city and hinterland. From his first response (that the *Torrone* had authority to insert itself directly into even the most minor quarrels of peasants) to his fourteenth (that the *Torrone* was a repository of sensitive information, over whose publication the court held responsible custody), this judge declared the court's sweeping competence and independence, downplayed its corruptions, and justified its domination of Bologna on the grounds that the city was unique and required the *Torrone*'s guiding hand.

Moments such as the plague of 1630, when increased jurisdiction over daily life allowed the *Torrone* to increase its power and justify those

---

[68] Ibid.   [69] Ibid.

increases, were tempered by a series of reforms to mitigate the court's independence and ensure a transparent fiscal and judicial structure. The first of these reforms occurred in 1563, with the subjugation of the *Torrone*'s finances and the office of the *caponotaio* to the officers of the *Monte di Pietà*.[70] Another series of reform attempts took place in the 1590s and 1600s, when the court's eager campaign to gather information about banditry in the *contado* gave rise to notarial corruption. In 1595, Vice-Legate Annibale Rucellai published his "Orders to Be Observed in the Criminal Court of the Torrone of Bologna," both as a broadsheet posted in public spaces around the city and *contado* and as a document provided to the *Torrone* as its guiding orders.[71] This document defined the scheme of payments and emoluments for notaries, and the procedures they had to follow in keeping records of cases. It was supported in 1596 with a bull by Pius V giving the *Monte* authority over all of the *Torrone*'s notaries in addition to the Head Notary, and confirming the court's jurisdiction over all areas of the *legato*.[72] Another bull, published in 1602, reproduced the same schedule of fees that dated back to 1580.[73] The first fifty years of the *Torrone*'s operations witnessed reforms designed to professionalize and standardize its notarial staff and eliminate the types of petty corruption for which they were known in many public offices.

Five years later, in 1607, the Legate Giustiniani pushed the reforms further, making the *Torrone*'s casebooks and its finances transparent and accountable. A new set of orders governed the documentation of cases and the preservation of evidence.[74] Notaries were ordered to transcribe testimony word for word, instead of in shorthand; to bring evidence to judges at an appropriate time in the investigation, not before or after; to interrogate witnesses individually, rather than in pairs or groups, and to record their testimony directly into the casebooks; and they were not to conduct interrogations for "serious crimes" without a judge's order or assistance, nor to accept any more payment than stipulated in the rubrics for defence examinations. Notaries were not to interrogate every person who came in to make a denunciation, but were to take that person's name and write the denunciation in full, with its date. These rules all managed

---

[70] Angelozzi and Casanova, *La giustizia criminale in una città di antico regime*, p. 36.
[71] ASBo, *Assunteria del Torrone*, 3c, *Constitutioni e bolle del Torrone*, 1488–1623, "Ordini da Osservarsi nel Foro Criminale del Torrone di Bologna," 1595, no folio.
[72] Ibid., "Per il Torrone," 1596, no folio.
[73] Ibid., "Ordini di NS Papa Clemente Ottavo Sopra l'osservanza delle Constitutioni del Torrone, e Altro," 1602, no folio.
[74] Ibid., "Ordini da Osservarsi dalli Notari del Torone, cosi intoro alle Cause, come anco alle Mercedi loro," 1607, broadsheet.

the relationships between notaries and witnesses or suspects, regulating the dynamic between the parties to ensure that notaries did not abuse their positions. The next series ensured that cases would be preserved adequately and would be accessible for future use: copyists were not to write on original documents in any way; as soon as the notary has finished a process ("in neat, legible writing") he was to record the case in the Head Notary's notebook. Similarly, denunciations and quarrels were to be sent immediately to the Head Notary, who reported daily to the legate; every two weeks, or when they completed a casebook, notaries were to report to the Head Notary the names of everybody processed at their bench and turn over all their books as soon as they were filled; finally, they were to retain a full inventory of their own papers and turn this inventory over to their successors. A third set of orders publicly regulated the scheme of payments notaries could receive for making copies of pardons and registering peace accords, and it stipulated situations when they were forbidden to charge for these services (such as when a process was cancelled, but a full pardon not granted). These fees were low, a matter of soldi and quattrini for the most part, and many, such as for receiving copies of pardons and *grazie*, were dependent on the person's ability to pay.

The sheer volume of the *Torrone*'s archive, and its long tenure as the central criminal court in Bologna, indicate that it achieved some success in its aims. This is in part because it served the purpose that people wanted: a forum for the public, not private, resolution of disputes that involved entire communities alongside the victims, criminals, and the central court. Much of this progress was illusory, and the judges of the *Torrone* had a vested interest in promoting the success and impartiality of its work. They wielded inquisitorial procedure as the supposedly neutral alternative to capricious feudal justice. As the city's governance stabilized through the sixteenth and seventeenth centuries, the *Tribunale del Torrone* modified inquisition procedures to ensure that it effectively upheld state power while simultaneously increasing the penetration of its power into all corners of the province and into the minutiae of Bolognese daily life. With absolute rule came central, inquisitorial criminal justice, both to empower the city's new sovereign and to reduce the hold of its vicious nobility over the conflicts and concerns of the *contadini*, blacksmiths and wool-sellers of the *legato*.

State Homicide: Executions, 1600–1700

The uneasy peace of the early seventeenth century was built on a late sixteenth century campaign of repression and execution in the

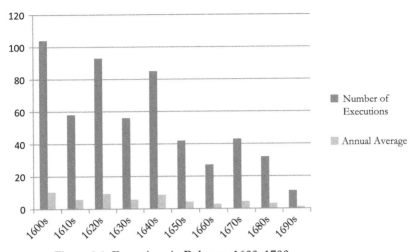

Figure 2.1 Executions in Bologna, 1600–1700.
Source: ASBo, Cronaci delle Giustizie seguite in Bologna del 1030 al 1750

countryside and a law-and-order push in the city. Beginning in the 1580s, an effort to secure the roads and mountain passes around Bologna took the lives of many bandits and made bandits of many men. In its seventeenth-century punitive approach to violence, however, the *Torrone* demonstrated that its primary concern was not the vengeful punishing of private conflict. When it executed people, it did so because their crimes damaged the court or other city institutions, or because they were thieves. The court was paranoid of threats to its authority and leery of intervening with a heavy hand in private homicides that it viewed as properly resolved through peacemaking channels. These early years of the century thus show little institutional stability: although the court was legitimate enough to adjudicate many homicides, it achieved this legitimacy through the violent repression of threats to its authority. The execution patterns of the century's first three decades bear this out, shown in Figure 2.1.

In the decade 1590–99, the *Torrone* executed some eighteen people annually, according to the journals kept by the city's confraternity of comforters, the company of *Santa Maria della Morte*.[75] A detailed look at those numbers reveals that spikes in the comforter's journal found in the *Archivio di Stato* in Bologna list 255 executions between 1600 and 1629, or 8.5 executions per annum, and 46% of the century total. A mere 28 of

---

[75] Terpstra, "Theory into Practice," in Terpstra, ed., *The Art of Executing Well*, 124.

those executions were for homicides, and in most of those cases the court did not execute the killer because of the homicide itself. Rather, executions of killers fit into the more general pattern of executions exposed here. Perpetrators of homicides were executed when their violence had threatened the institutions of society, such as the court, the family, or state relations. Thus, in 1600, the first nobleman of the century died at the hands of the *Torrone*: Signore Francesco Bezzelli of Verona, who in August had murdered his servant in Piazza San Martino while visiting Bologna.[76] He was not hanged for this offence, however. Bezzelli pinned the murder on a local street urchin named Pietro, and held his story long enough for the *Torrone* to sentence the street urchin to death for attacking a nobleman's retinue. When further questioning revealed Bezzelli's ruse, he was hanged for perjury and abuse of the *Torrone*, not for the murder of his servant. Bezzelli's high status made this execution atypical, and he was decapitated rather than hanged, though his head was posted on the gates facing Verona.[77] He was one of ten executed in 1600.

In other years between 1600 and 1629, the number of executions ranged from one (in 1615, 1616) to twenty-one (in 1625). The two men killed in 1615 and 1616 were hanged as thieves, which remained common.[78] In 1625, of the twenty-one people killed, ten were killed in groups of two and three for various robberies, thefts and murders committed during their careers as bandits.[79] The others included a serial robber, a thief who had falsely accused someone of murder, and a jail-breaker. Six of the twenty-one were killers: a mother sentenced for infanticide was beheaded on August 6; a priest who violated his orders by shooting Signore Cesare Ghisilieri was decapitated on May 10; and the man who stalked Alessio Bignardi dalla Palla and murdered him was hanged and quartered on May 31. On August 9, Tomaso Ambrosini was hanged after he killed his brother-in-law, and on September 23 Girolamo Alborano was hanged as a bandit for outlawry he incurred after killing the *sbirro* of Medicina. On December 6, one other killer was hanged for hunting his victim at night before killing him. The homicides the *Torrone* punished with death were unusual, not bred of the ordinary conflict within communities that accounted for most homicides. The victims were unusual: an infant and a relative by marriage. The killers – a young mother and a priest sworn against violence – were similarly unusual. The circumstances were sinister: high-ranking men stalked through the

[76] ASBo, *Torrone*, 3227, f. 358.   [77] ASBo, *Cronaci*, execution of September 27, 1600.
[78] Ibid., executions of June 27, 1615, and September 3, 1516.
[79] Ibid., executions of February 1 and August 20, 1625.

streets and eliminated at night, not during an open conflict. These killers were executed not because they killed, but because their killings broke the line of social conflict and threatened social trust. And then, still, homicides remained in the minority of executed crimes.

With twenty-one executions, 1625 was the most active year in the century for the *Torrone*'s hangman, due in large part to the four multiple executions that took place. Eighteen were executed in 1627, and seventeen each in 1607 and 1610. In 1627, sixteen of the executions were of thieves, and only one of a killer (who had killed his wife, and was also technically a thief; he killed her for her jewels).[80] One other man was hanged for counterfeiting Venetian ducats.[81] In 1607, two of seventeen executions were for homicide, both of priests in religious orders.[82] None of the seventeen in 1610 was for a homicide. Again in these years, the vast majority of executions were for theft, particularly when it involved breaking and entering, or took place on roadways with threats of force.

Why execute robbers and not killers? Why did the *Torrone* treat theft as though it were a greater threat to society than murder? Theft is a qualitatively different act than homicide: violence was a social act that could occur between relations and friends as a legitimate, albeit disruptive, aspect of community. Even a homicide did not preclude the killer's reintegration into that community if he could make peace with the aggrieved kin. Theft, on the other hand, is inherently anti-social. It occurs outside community relationships and is often committed by outsiders. The thief was more contemptible than the killer; the state, by taking action against thieves, sowed belief within communities that the court was a legitimate recourse for aggrieved parties. Communities wanted punishment of theft and mediation of violence, and the *Torrone* strengthened its hold on justice by giving them both. The laws of banditry and peace allowed the court to bind both communities and criminals to itself through petty financial obligations that served as guarantors of fealty. By executing thieves, the *Torrone* made itself the forum that mediated homicidal conflicts, paradoxically by neglecting to physically punish the killers.

The *Torrone* executed people mostly by hanging. From 1600 to 1629, 194 of 255 (76%) executions were performed by hanging. By the seventeenth century the court had for the most part dispensed with the elaborate theatre of execution that it had used in the sixteenth century to

---

[80] Ibid., execution of October 9, 1627.   [81] Ibid., execution of September 27, 1627.
[82] Ibid., executions of August 18 and October 13, 1627.

demonstrate its firm hold on power and the bodily consequences of rebellion.[83] Most of the condemned were not subject to the public humiliations of being carted around the city and tortured at the sites of their victims' houses or the locations of their crimes. Instead, they were conducted solemnly from the *Torrone*'s cells in what is now the Palazzo Comunale and hanged in the Piazza Maggiore or the Piazza del Mercato, now the Piazza VIII Agosto and still the site of a weekly market. Hanging was the most frequent means to execute criminals whose crimes, while warranting execution, were generally prosaic in nature.

More elaborate modes of execution were reserved for those who committed crimes against the state or particularly heinous crimes. On March 10, 1600, two men were taken from the prison in a cart to the Piazza Maggiore where they were each given two "large cuts." From there, bleeding, they were processed to the bank of Taddeo Ghelli, which they had robbed, and cut twice more; twice again they were sliced open at the house of the *Procuratore* Grati, and twice more at the gate "beneath the butchers." Finally, back in Piazza Maggiore and beneath the Ringhiera, the balcony from which members of the Senate and the legate watched, the right hands of both men were amputated. There, they were hanged and quartered.[84] These men were not simple thieves and their execution was calibrated to reflect that. First, they had robbed Ghelli's bank of 15,000 gold scudi in coin and then fled to Hungary. When Ghelli's agent, the *Procuratore* Grati, caught up with them in Vienna, they shot an arquebus at his notary. Somewhere in their adventures, they had also killed a butcher named Taddeo Abelli. They suffered for each of these crimes in stages along their execution, and their deaths were meant to give satisfaction in turn to each of the aggrieved parties, including the butchers' guild. These spectacular, moving theatres of death were rare, however, and rarer still as the years passed. The next occurred in 1601, when the young man from Cesena (a foreigner, importantly) who had killed Signore Alessandro de' Bianchi was processed through the streets, had his hand cut off in front of the Palazzo Bianchi, and was hanged and quartered in the piazza. A similar spectacle would not recur until 1606.

Spectacular executions in this period were reserved for severe crimes of morality and crimes against the state. Robbing pilgrims on their way to Rome would get you hanged, as would abducting a woman and holding her hostage to rob her.[85] Two prisoners who might have avoided the

---

[83] Cf. the description of a multistaged, heavily symbolic execution in Bologna in January 1540 in Terpstra, "Theory into Practice," 118–19.

[84] ASBo, *Cronaci delle Giustizie*, execution of March 10, 1600.

[85] Ibid., executions of October 30, 1610, and May 26, 1607.

ignominy were put in the cart after they murdered a guard, took his keys and money, and broke out of prison. Finding the gates out of the palace barred, they locked themselves in the chancery until the *Torrone*'s *sbirri* retrieved them. They were brought in a cart to each city gate before returning to Piazza Maggiore, where they were torn with hot pincers, tied to stakes, had their throats cut and were quartered.[86] These were not ordinary crimes: pilgrims were sacrosanct and under the Papacy's protection; the woman's abduction, with intimations of violation, compounded the already capital crime of robbery. The escaped prisoners challenged the authority of the court and the city and killed a court agent in the process: their grim fate was necessary, in the *Torrone*'s eyes, because their crime challenged institutional strength.

Accused heretics and homosexuals were also burned in this period, five of each between 1600 and 1629. These men were not investigated by the *Torrone*, but its officers imprisoned the victims and carried out the execution. Five men were burned between 1607 and 1614 for *sodomia* or "*il peccato nefarioso*."[87] The *Torrone* investigated cases of sodomy only when the complaint was of violation, usually of someone's son.[88] These men appear to have been processed as sodomites in the Archiepiscopal court, and the language used – *the nefarious sin* – demonstrates that for this society, homosexuality fell into the narrative of sin and purgation; fire became the means to cleanse the sin. The case was similar for the five alleged Lutherans burned: one of them died alone in 1618, and his comforters noted that "He conversed in the Conforteria, and left assured of himself with a moral security of his sin."[89] Four more died together in 1622, after committing some sort of "abuse done publicly in *San Petronio* the previous day."[90] The record of their execution is accompanied by a panic-stricken comforter's notes on the growing fears of Lutheranism in the city. With the exception of one counterfeiter (whose coins challenged both the power of the state and God, since they faked papal currency), only accused sodomites and Lutherans died by fire.[91]

The *Torrone*, then, continued to execute significant numbers of people in the early seventeenth century, exercising the physical punishment that constituted the heavy stick of the push to pacify Bologna and its countryside. But the target of its violent repression was not the violence of *bolognesi*. As recorded by the comforters of *Santa Maria della Morte*, the

---

[86] Ibid., execution of August 27, 1611.
[87] Ibid., executions of November 10, 1607, January 23 and August 7, 1610, February 20, 1613, and August 18, 1614.
[88] ASBo, *Torrone*, 4290, f. 212r.   [89] ASBo, *Cronaci*, execution of November 5, 1618.
[90] Ibid., four executions of November 28, 1622.
[91] Ibid., execution of October 16, 1610.

crimes that merited execution were those that challenged institutional structures, such as the system of property ownership which theft and robbery violated, the power of the court which the Veronese Francesco Bellezzi demeaned with his perjury, or the Catholic dogmas that made sodomy and Lutheranism actionable sins. The *Torrone* did not, generally, execute killers who killed during conflict within, or even between, communities. In large part, this is because most killers immediately fled to contumacy and incurred de facto capital sentences of banditry – but these were mediated with a fine and a peace accord, not with their lives.[92] As the example of the Ghelli bank bandits shows, plaintiffs would go to extraordinary lengths – even to Hungary – to apprehend criminals, and extradition treaties between Bologna and neighbouring states had existed since at least 1539.[93] The *Torrone*'s execution policy demonstrates that violent conflict between its subjects was not its primary concern and warranted state violence only when the violence was combined with more nefarious issues. Again, social and institutional trust worked on homicide: by giving communities room to make peace among their members in the semi-formalized channels of mercy, contumacy and pecuniary punishment, the *Torrone* encouraged users to bring these very complaints to the court for mediation. At the same time, the court assured its users that outsiders who robbed their homes or abducted their daughters would be punished with maximum severity, thereby further buttressing its power.

In many ways both the Foucauldian and Eliasian readings of the decline of execution in Europe are correct: as the court amassed power and control in Bologna, and as urban and peasant communities followed non-violent avenues of justice, the need for exemplary execution became less pressing – even for crimes that breached the contract between state and citizen. The influence of papal justice was wielded through soft measures, such as mediation, rather than through the rack and the rope. But contra Foucault, the state was not engaged in a sinister project to survey the thoughts of ordinary citizens or to imprison their movements: the *Torrone* took a measured approach to justice that considered the impact of its decrees in terms of whether they would breed or quell

---

[92] Cf. the work of Daniel Smail, who has developed the most convincing view of the mediating, and collecting, role of Mediterranean courts, and of the function of contumacy within their jurisdictions. D. Smail, "Violence and Predation in Late Medieval Mediterranean Europe"; Daniel Lord Smail, *The Consumption of Justice: Emotions, Publicity, and Legal Culture in Marseille, 1264–1423* (Ithaca, NY: Cornell University Press, 2003).

[93] ASBo, *Bandi e Notificazioni*, Series I, No. 3, f. 59, "Che li banditi del S. Duca di Firenze non siano sicuri nel Territorio di Bologna ecc," August 23, 1539.

distrust and conflict among the population, and against the judicial system. Nor, as an Eliasian reading would have it, did the *Torrone* actively disseminate a new set of non-violent values through its penalties. Its approach to justice presumes a broadly casual acceptance of the efficacy of some violence in social action, but it sought to channel the social fallout of that violence away from revenge and toward peace. Meeting interpersonal violence with state violence eroded the *Torrone*'s ability to slow revenge violence, and executions rapidly declined to negligible levels over the remainder of the seventeenth century.

While the state and people of Bologna suffered through the crises of the mid-*seicento* that bookend much of my argument, the *Torrone* executed 210 people from 1630 to 1659, of whom 205 were men and five were women. The early years of this period were dominated by executions for thefts and crimes specific to plague and quarantine. Executions of killers in the 1630s (14 out of a total 56) breached the understanding of violence's normalized place in society that informed much of the *Torrone*'s approach to justice. Murderers were hanged when they preyed on victims, especially if they did so as part of a conspiracy or for heinous material ends, such as killing their relatives to receive their inheritance before the plague arrived.[94] When homicides breached the acceptable social boundaries and a servant killed his master, the *Torrone* executed the servant; so too with a husband who was condemned for poisoning his wife.[95] Only four of the fourteen executions for homicide were carried out after 1635, indicating that the execution of killers in the early 1630s was largely related to the continuing instability wrought by plague and crisis.

The 1640s also saw the *Torrone* executing killers primarily when their crimes transgressed the reasonable defence of self, kin and community that judges usually treated mercifully. The threat of marauding soldiers, recently deserted from the Italian campaigns of the Thirty Years' War, resulted in a higher tally of executions overall in the 1640s (85 from 1640 to 1649) than in the previous decade.[96] Fully 29 of the 85 condemned criminals in this decade were soldiers condemned for various delicts, from desertion to homicide (compare to three soldiers among the

---

[94] ASBo, *Cronaci*, executions of Francesco Riccabene, January 2, 1630; Francesco di Giovanni, soldier, May 4, 1630; Mariano Imadesi, March 16, 1630; and Domenico Magnani, December 18, 1632.

[95] Ibid., execution of Giacinto Sabbatini, May 7, 1631, and Bartolomeo Frassetti, December 18, 1631.

[96] On the Italian campaigns, which saw armies transitting Bolognese territory, cf. Hanlon, *The Hero of Italy*; Gregory Hanlon, *Italy 1636: Cemetery of Armies* (Oxford University Press, 2015).

56 executed in the 1630s). Outside of the soldiery, slayers were condemned to death for the same reasons as in the previous decade: they killed in ways that damaged hierarchical structures of society and threatened the state's ability to administer non-violent conflict resolution. The husband and wife were hanged in 1640 for burying their daughter's murdered husband in a field opened the decade, and the hanging of a hired assassin of a Casalecchio man closed it in 1649.[97] The overall growth of executions in Bologna during the 1640s betrays the fault lines cracking in Bolognese society: soldiers caused disorders in the *contado*, and the basic hierarchies of social order and conflict resolution were under threat by the radically altered economic and demographic circumstances of the post-plague world.

The *Torrone* seemed less concerned with order and apparently had fewer soldiers troubling its territory during the 1650s, when the number of executions dropped by over 50% to 42. With 21 of these executions carried out as punishment for homicide, this decade had the largest proportion yet (50%) of executions for killing. The signs of Bologna's brewing civil war were visible in the court's efforts to pacify internecine and anti-papal revenge violence through demonstrative executions. Three of these executions were for the murder of a *Torrone* judge, an incident explored further in Chapter 6.[98] Two more were of the killers of two members of the powerful de' Grassi clan who had profited during the papal occupancy through participation in the newly reformed Senate.[99] The other fifteen were primarily urban: servants and minor players of noble houses who did their part for their clans by killing one another in Bologna; and the homicides associated with robbery and predation that accompanied the breakdown of social peace in mid-century Bologna. The executions of the 1650s show a court straining against that breakdown and attempting to firmly quell the resurgence of public violence and revenge-as-politics.

The court obviously changed its approach in the 1660s: there were only twenty-seven executions across the decade, the fewest so far in the century. Nine men were executed for homicide, showing that the court retained a heightened interest in violence. But, following the drastic measures taken to pacify the nobility in the 1650s, its focus returned to the interpersonal violence that transgressed acceptable social orders: the

[97] ASBo, *Cronaci*, executions of Diamante Mori and Domenico di Lumese Bonvoglii, January 17, 1640, and Alessandro Brighani, November 6, 1649.

[98] Ibid., executions of Filippo Stefanini, Mario Stefanini and Francesco Vitale, April 26, 1653.

[99] Ibid., executions of Alessandro Barbieri, February 14, 1652, and Giovanni Antonio Malisardi, May 5, 1657; Gardi, *Lo stato in provincia*.

nine executed killers were all condemned for uxoricide, peace-breaking or being paid assassins. In this period, when the factional disorders wracking the city brought homicide rates to an urban civil war of 104 per 100,000, the court did not execute noblemen. Again, the slippery concept of social trust helps to explain this: in the fragile political arena of Bologna, the court's overreach in condemning the nobility's traditional practices by executing its violent members would only rend the breach further. Better to attempt mediation or, as happened in Bologna, remove the problem through large-scale political exile.

The rapid decline in executions continued through the remainder of the century, with only 85 carried out in 1670–1700. A minor spike occurred in 1671 and 1672, a time of poor harvests and elevated grain prices; bread riots in Bologna in 1671 led to three executions, and homicides involving resources and violence against authorities were punished with execution as well.[100] Another *tumulto* in the city in 1677 saw four men hanged for sacking the *bottega* of Antonio Maria Uttini.[101] Thefts and counterfeiting coins – crimes that broke boundaries of property and ownership which were guaranteed by law, and crimes which threatened the sovereignty of the pope in Rome or his representatives in Bologna – remained the primary target of judicial violence during these decades.[102] The violence prompted by noble factionalism in mid-century had dissipated and the court returned its attention to the mundane regulation of social and economic life that occupied its primary interests: achieving primacy as Bologna's judicial forum for resolving social conflict.

Conclusion

The transition from the podestarial courts to the *Torrone* marked the establishment of a new, more centralized, administrative system of justice; but only gradually did it evolve into an instrument of control that offered a venue for resolving disputes, bringing litigants to court instead of to blows. It did so in part by returning to and amplifying the late thirteenth-century emphasis upon fact-finding and interrogating witnesses, and by use of peace accords and letters of pardon to broker

---

[100] Ibid., executions of Giovani Tura, April 2, 1671; Domenico Cesarini, May 2, 1671; Pietro Piazza, July 30, 1671; Carlo Galata, September 16, 1671; and Domenico Bondi, October 21, 1671.

[101] Ibid., executions of Antonio Donati, Angelo Maria Busacchi, Marc'Antonio Boriani and Vincenzo Crespellani, October 9, 1677.

[102] E.g., ibid., executions of Paolo Cantelli Lievre, January 14, 1673; Agostino Masetti, October 8, 1681; and Francesco Antonio Taruffi Zanotti, April 26, 1698.

reconciliation – again a continuity of a medieval practice.[103] In this sense, the maturation of the *Torrone* system was also a "bottom-up" process: litigants of all stripes turned to the courts, just as they had turned away in the fourteenth century with the decline of accusation procedure. Yet the *Torrone* also differed significantly from the podestarial courts, not only in its centralization and professionalism, but in its emphasis on making dispute resolution a public matter that involved entire communities. The long transition from private to public justice proceeded between the thirteenth and seventeenth centuries in an uneven manner. But by the end of the seventeenth century, the public dimension in criminal justice had reached a new level of efficacy and cohesion.

As the *Torrone* grew in power, the scope of its presence in Bolognese life made it more than a forum in which social actors resolved their differences. Judges of the *Torrone* could promulgate legislation concerning law and order: as early as 1583, *auditori* declared new public security measures and an official policy against bandits.[104] The court's judges were closely linked to the legatine government; in 1596 the *Auditore del Torrone* also served as the vice-regent of papal authority in the city.[105] Firearms regulation and the roles of rural bailiffs and militias also fell under the *Torrone*'s administrative purview. The *Torrone*'s self-advertising as a neutral and impartial forum for conflict resolution was misleading in this light: centralized criminal justice and the *Torrone*'s active efforts to control behaviour through legislation and decree were critical to the maturation of papal rule over Bologna.

---

[103] Angelozzi and Casanova, *La nobiltà disciplinata*, 289–300.
[104] ASBo, *Bandi e Notificazione*, Series I, No. 5, *bando* of September 5, 1584.
[105] Ibid., Series I, No. 6, *bando* of March 11, 1597.

3   Homicide in Bologna, 1600–1700

Introduction

On October 19, 1600, the patriarch Francesco "Righo" della Ronchetta was taken from his prison cell and brought to the palace of Signore Galeazzo Paleotti in Bologna. There, Paleotti, a member of a prominent senatorial family who was sponsoring a peace conference between the feuding clans of the Ronchetta and Tozzi from Aiano, was waiting with a notary. The notary demanded from Francesco della Ronchetta an account of all the men in his kin group and their last known whereabouts. Francesco obliged. He had seen his cousin Taddeo Tanetti just the evening before, when Taddeo had visited him in prison and was sent to find a good lawyer. The notary and Signore Paleotti fixated on Battista della Ronchetta, Francesco's nephew and the oldest member of the clan's younger generation. When Francesco had last seen his nephew three months before, their parting words had been ominous: Battista had said, "I have been shamed and I hold myself one who does not want peace."[1]

This was a problem, because just the day before, Giovanni Pellegrino Tozzi was shot dead within city walls, and Battista had spoken his parting words as he stormed out of the peace conference that brought together these feuding shepherds. Francesco supplied the tantalizing hints of a backstory: "The peace we were making was between the Tozzi and the Righi and we the Ronchetti, and the hatred is old between the Ronchetta and Tozzi and Righi houses, for which many men have died."[2] It was this feud that Paleotti was attempting to mediate, during which process he took Battista into his household as a servant. When Battista refused to make peace and fled the house, Paleotti expelled him from service. Battista was now presumed to have killed Giovanni Pellegrino Tozzi while pursuing his unsatisfied vendetta.[3]

---

[1] ASBo, *Torrone*, 3246, f. 178r.   [2] Ibid.
[3] These are not the wealthy noble factions of sixteenth-century Friuli, though the case looks similar in many ways. The Ronchetti and Tozzi were minor landowners, holders of local power in their mountain pass but with no wider influence or power. These were small

79

This rural feud between minor landowners and the efforts made by Bolognese authorities to quell its violence encapsulate both this chapter's argument and Bologna's sociopolitical situation at the opening of the seventeenth century. In 1600, the *Tribunale del Torrone* had effectively established its jurisdiction and a measure of peace over the urban core: within the city, homicide rates between 1600 and 1620 were comparatively low when measured against contemporary rural rates or later urban ones. Moreover, following the bitter conflicts between papal authorities and the local nobility that occupied much of the sixteenth century, certain families of the city's nobility, such as the Paleotti noted above, had accommodated papal dominance and become active members of the city's Senate, or had entered the papal ranks through the chapters of both the Cathedral and the Basilica.[4] Yet the authority of judges and notaries remained fragile, especially outside the safety of city walls, where a legally disciplined population was more of an ideal than a reality.[5] The campaign waged against banditry in the papal states in the late sixteenth century had indeed made the roads and waterways safer places, but borderlands remained fraught with local conflict. The state struggled to penetrate the communities of the many villages and hamlets that dotted both the plain and the mountain valleys to the south. More to the purpose of the Papacy, the cleansing of bandits had directed the energies of a restless nobility toward violence that served both themselves and the state. By securing the roadways that ran through their traditional landholdings, nobility performed their feudal duties that they maintained were their hereditary privilege even a century after the papal conquest. Here, hanging bandits stood in for dispensing justice, though many nobles also reestablished illegitimate feudal tribunals in their lands at this time.[6] At the beginning of the century, then, the *Torrone* had made headway on reining in interpersonal violence within the city and was reaching to the *contado* to extend its sphere of influence.

mountain folk with vital hatreds of their own. Cf. E. Muir, *Mad Blood Stirring: Vendetta and Factions in Friuli during the Renaissance* (Baltimore, MD: Johns Hopkins University Press, 1993), in particular chap. 4, 110–33.

[4] J. M. deSilva, "Ecclesiastical Dynasticism in Early Modern Bologna: The Canonical Chapters of San Pietro and San Petronio," in G. M Anselmi et al., eds., *Bologna: Cultural Crossroads from the Medieval to the Baroque: Recent Anglo-American Scholarship* (Bologna: Bononia University Press, 2013), 173–85.

[5] Cf. the *bando* of August 21, 1585, assigning punishments for those who harassed, assaulted or otherwise impeded *massari* as they carried out their duties, particularly transit of prisoners. The theme of this *bando* repeats throughout the seventeenth century. ASBo, *Bandi e Notificazione*, Series I, No. 5, Bando of August 21, 1585.

[6] G. Angelozzi and C. Casanova, *La nobiltà disciplinata: violenza nobiliare, procedure di giustizia e scienza cavalleresca a Bologna nel 17. secolo* (Bologna: CLUEB, 2003), chap. 3.

The homicidal violence that occurred in 1600, 1610 and 1620 reflects this uneasy stability. More homicides were investigated in 1600 than in either 1610 or 1620, a fact that demonstrates the court's continued concern with rural banditry and its attempts to assert more control over rural areas. The homicides that did occur took place primarily in the orbit of family and sociability, and are typical of a society with strong institutions and strong social bonds but which suffered endemic poverty in both urban and rural contexts, not to mention extreme economic inequality. Love and lust feature in many of the homicides that occurred in these samples, as does highway robbery and the pursuit of vendetta in person and by hired proxy. At the outset of the seventeenth century, the Bolognese *contado* remained a dangerous and violent land, while the city itself was comparatively peaceful. What separated the century's early years from the rest was the absence of any major noble feuding that characterized medieval and Baroque Bologna. Artisans, labourers and merchants killed each other, their families, their lovers and occasionally their employers. The success of the sixteenth century had been the relative pacification of the fractious local nobility, a peace that depended upon the Papacy's ability to co-opt noble violence into civil society. A civilizing process took place in Bologna during the sixteenth century, consciously wrought by Julius II and his successors, often with great bloodshed.[7] However, civilizing processes are fragile at best, and Bologna's artisan and labouring classes continued to practice a quotidian violence that reflected the instability of their lives in a profoundly stratified early modern city.

This chapter draws its analysis primarily from 701 investigations into unexplained deaths drawn from the *Torrone*'s archives in approximate ten-year gaps. In each year, every investigation and trial into a cadaver – including those that begin and end with a body inspection – were collected into a database, which was then winnowed to represent only deaths confirmed as homicides by the notaries of the *Torrone* and their medical witnesses. All pertinent variables were drawn from deep reading of the trials themselves. The run of investigation/trial evidence totals more than 1,000 books conserved in the *Archivio di Stato di Bologna*. All years except the sample from 1652 are complete. Some 25% of the books from 1652 are water-damaged beyond usability, necessitating an extrapolation of homicide rates from the 75% that permitted analysis (several years on either side of 1652 are in worse condition, hence this approach). These sources permit a broad reconstruction, gleaned

---

[7] N. Terpstra, "Theory into Practice: Executions, Comforting and Comforters," in N. Terpstra, ed., *The Art of Executing Well*.

from a large body of judicial materials, of the primary characteristics and patterns of homicidal violence in eleven decennial years spanning 1600–1700.

Characteristics of Homicide in 1600

This book works with "indicted homicide rates" of killings investigated, adjudicated and resolved by the *Torrone*.[8] Population figures for the city were calculated by Bellettini from a variety of parish censuses and other surveys that were undertaken at irregular intervals by Bolognese and church authorities.[9] Population figures for the countryside are more difficult to come by, but from the figures that were collected also appear to have been relatively stable throughout the seventeenth century; an early period of growth was followed by a drop after 1630 and a steady rise back to pre-plague levels. The average population throughout the century was about 65,000 city inhabitants and 165,000 rural inhabitants, for a total provincial population of approximately 230,000 individuals.[10]

In 1600, we have firm figures for town and country. Bellettini accounted for 62,844 city-dwellers and 144,951 *paesani*, for a provincial population of 207,795 individuals.[11] This puts 1600 toward the low end of population figures, though not so much as to appear extraneous. The *Torrone* accounted for 58 homicides from January to December 1600; removing accidents (6) and one infanticide trial leaves 51 definitive cases of killing. Using the *Torrone*'s accounting, indicted homicide rates for 1600 were 30.2 per 100,000 in the city, 27 per 100,000 rural, and 28 per 100,000 as an aggregate rate for the province. Having extracted infanticides and accidents, we arrive at definitive homicide rates of 25 urban, 24.1 rural, and 24.5 aggregated for the province. This places 1600 toward the high end of the spectrum of homicide rates for the years sampled here, with the fourth-highest aggregate rates after those of 1632, 1652 and 1660. A comparison to modern homicide rates also provides a meaningful benchmark for these aggregate figures. According to the *United Nations Office for Drugs and Crime Global Study on Homicide 2011*, the homicide rate of the province of Bologna, and much of North Italy, was somewhere below 1 per 100,000 in 2005, making it one of the safest

---

[8] These indictments are a reliable guide to the general levels of fatal violence extant in the region. Although it is impossible to say whether the *Torrone* was made aware of every killing, the "black figure" of unreported homicides is likely small, and would only serve to paint a bleaker picture of Bologna's experience in the seventeenth century.
[9] A. Bellettini, *La Popolazione di Bologna di Secolo XV all'Unificazione Italiana* (Bologna: Zanchelli Editore, 1961), 25–27.
[10] Ibid., 48.   [11] Ibid., 25–27, 48.

areas of Europe in terms of homicidal violence.[12] Thus, the seventeenth century in Bologna started with a relatively high incidence of violence, particularly when one factors in accidents and infanticides; the occurrence of violence was also approximately equal in town and country. This near parity of rates is typical of the end of the century, but is not a pattern that carried throughout the century. Indeed, the divergence between urban and rural rates is indicative of varying attempts to control violence in the city and to cleanse the countryside of disorder; it also indicates that social structures changed around major events of the century such as the plague of 1630. The characteristics of urban and rural violence could be quite different, however, a fact that again indicates the *Torrone*'s tenuous authority outside the city.

In 1600 there were 51 homicides, 16 of which were urban and 35 rural. Within this annual count, however, there are significant fluctuations by season and month. The annual rhythms of homicide are predictable, although they oscillated mildly year by year. In 1600, homicides occurred as shown in Figure 3.1.

Figure 3.1 demonstrates the annual rhythm of violence in Bologna in 1600. This pattern was typical and remained a near-constant characteristic of homicide across the century. The year began relatively peacefully, with three deaths occurring in January and two in February, before a rapid spike to six each for the months of March and April. The early months of spring were often considerably more violent than the first months of the year, and Blastenbrei (among others) is quick to attribute the spike to disorders and social inversion surrounding Carnival.[13] While this was true in Bologna in certain years, it does not appear to account for the sharp uptick in violence during March and April of 1600: none of the killings had the hallmark features of carnival violence – namely, spontaneous public aggression fuelled by alcohol intake during or following the festivities. In one case, which occurred on March 30, 1600, a group of young men, several of whom were banned and likely snuck into the city during Carnival, came to blows outside the Palazzo Bentivoglio, and one of them ended up dead.[14] The argument appears to have predated the encounter. Carnival violence is more visible in other years throughout the century, and it is easily identified by the presence of masked revellers

[12] UNODC, *Global Study on Homicide 2011: Trends, Context, Data*, ed. John Gibbins, www.unodc.org/documents/data-and-analysis/statistics/Homicide/Globa_study_on_ homicide_2011_web.pdf, accessed October 22, 2013, p. 76.

[13] P. Blastenbrei, "Violence, Arms and Criminal Justice in Papal Rome, 1560–1600," *Renaissance* Studies 20, no. 1 (2006): 71; E. Muir, *Ritual in Early Modern Europe* (Cambridge: Cambridge University Press, 1997), 87–89.

[14] ASBo, *Torrone*, 3202, f. 28.

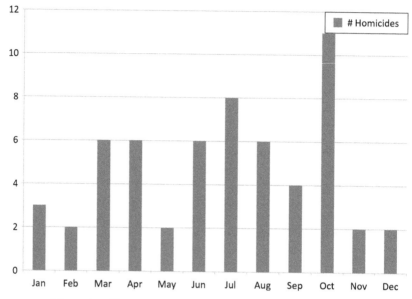

Figure 3.1 Homicides per month, 1600.
Source: ASBo, Torrone, 3171–264

and itinerant groups of singing drunks. If anything caused the higher number of homicides in March and April, it is likely related to the social and labour rhythms of the season, but it cannot be pinned specifically on Carnival from an analysis of the homicides themselves. The only homicide that specifically displays these traits was one of the two in February, indicating that Carnival was not only early in this year but also relatively peaceful in terms of fatal violence.[15]

The spike in homicides in spring was followed by a lull in May, with two homicides investigated, before summer inaugurated an annually typical season of high temperatures, high tensions and explosive tempers. June and July were, in many different environments and geographic areas, months in which the mad blood stirred.[16] In North Italy, this is partly explained by the agricultural calendar, according to which people harvested the winter and spring supply of grain and grapes in late summer and fall; by June, these supplies were often running low in

[15] ASBo, *Torrone*, 3192, f. 104.
[16] Shakespeare, *Romeo and Juliet*, III.I.4; Blastenbrei, "Violence, Arms and Criminal Justice," finds a totally distinct pattern for urban Rome in which violence declines during the summer months, as people fled the oppressive heat of the city for the countryside.

poorer sections of the population. June and July were thus difficult months to begin with. They also were the time to settle scores. Three of the six homicides that occurred then were vengeful, for previous insults perceived or real. Two more occurred during a heated argument between a group of soldiers and a mixed group of students and artisans who resided in Bologna. The fatal brawl occurred in a brothel during arguments over the soldiers' treatment of the women. In July, six of eight homicides were brought on by sour relationships between acquaintances, for shoddy business dealing (1), for inappropriate relations with someone's female relatives (2), for perceived failings of the clergy (1) or for other long-standing hatred and rivalry (2).

August continued this trend of high violence, but as the population prepared for the late summer and early fall harvest, land rights played a more significant role in the month's violence (2), and family reputation was at stake in two cases as well. In one of these cases, a son killed his father's second wife, whom he accused of being a prostitute prior to marrying his father;[17] the other occurred during the Ronchetti–Tozzi feud discussed at the opening of this chapter.[18] The first of the remaining two involved the murder of a servant by a Veronese nobleman who had attempted to blame a local Bolognese street urchin for the crime; the other was an unsolved mystery in which the eleven-year-old victim's mutilated corpse was found in the woods after he had been sent to trade a horse in the nearby town of Barbarolo.[19]

September witnessed another brief lull, with only four homicides, but October proved violent. This was typical of October, the end of the harvest season for both grain and grapes. This was a time when agricultural labour was drawing to a close, and exhausted Bolognese lashed out against relatives and enemies alike. Three cases were of men killing lovers or potential lovers.[20] One cousin murdered another in the pursuit of a vendetta between two factions; one man killed his acquaintance over unpaid debts; two masons killed a young man of the Alberti over his shameful treatment of a lady; and another young man killed his fellow dancer in an argument over a girl. Two of the remaining homicides went unsolved, and the last was part of the feud from Aiano.

By November, violence had returned to the low level seen at the beginning of the year, and stayed there through December. The four

---

[17] ASB, Tribunale del Torrone, Atti e Processi, 3252, f. 223.

[18] ASB, Tribunale del Torrone, Atti e Processi, 3224, f. 275.

[19] ASB, Tribunale del Torrone, Atti e Processi, 3228, f. 358; 3227, f. 279. This Veronese nobleman was the only person indicted for homicide who was executed in 1600. ASBo, *Cronaci delle Giustizie seguite a Bologna del 1030 a 1750*, execution of September 27, 1600.

[20] ASB, Tribunale del Torrone, Atti e Processi, 3257, f. 29.

cases over those two months all involved conflict within families. The male-on-male violence characteristic of the hot months (when land, women and social and material resources were all hotly contested) was not a feature of the end of the year. A father killed his daughter's persistent suitor; a man hired a bandit to murder his uncle on the road to his mother's house; a brother murdered his sister for unclear reasons; and a long-standing rivalry between two families from Luminasio was resolved with the murder of the twenty-five-year-old scion of the Frasanetti family. Thus concluded twelve months of violence in Bologna, ending as they began: with a whimper that rose to a scream in the summer months, before dying off as the weather turned cold and people's thoughts turned first and foremost to survival through the winter.

The *Torrone*'s failure to regularly record the ages of killers is an impediment to a full reconstruction of homicide. Criminologists, sociologists and historians agree that most homicidal violence is committed by males aged eighteen to thirty-five, which roughly corresponds to the vague period that early modern Bolognese referred to as "youth."[21] However, although they may not have been able to regularly or accurately record the ages of slayers, the notaries of the *Torrone* collected most of the ages of victims, via a protocol of the *Torrone*'s trial process. Cadaver inspections, which were common to early modern Italian judicial systems, assiduously noted the gender, age, appearance and clothing of homicide victims, and of assault victims on their way to becoming victims of homicide.[22] Thus, we have a reliable indicator of the ages of these victims, for approximately 500 of the 701 total deaths including infanticides and accidents. This cannot reveal in any concrete way the ages of killers, although age can indicate in a rough way the social networks in

---

[21] Daly and Wilson, *Homicide*, 284–88; Eisner, "Long-Term Historical Trends," 112–15; Spierenburg, *A History of Murder*, 90; on Italian youth, cf. O. Niccoli, *Il seme della violenza: Putti, fanciulli, e mammoli* (Rome: Laterza, 1995); Elizabeth Crouzet-Pavan, "A Flower of Evil: Young Men in Medieval Italy," in G. Levi and J. C. Schmidt, eds., *A History of Young People, Vol. 1: Ancient and Medieval Rites of Passage*, trans. Camille Naish (Cambridge, MA: Harvard University Press, 1997), 173–221; M. Rocke, *Forbidden Friendships: Homosexuality and Male Culture in Renaissance Florence* (New York: 1996); R. Karras, *From Boys to Men: Formations of Masculinity in late Medieval Europe* (Philadelphia: University of Pennsylvania Press, 2003).

[22] Cf. Blastenbrei, "Violence, Arms and Criminal Justice," 70, for more on the *relazioni dei barberi*. Here, as in many other ways, the *Torrone* proves itself ahead of the curve in judicial organization. Whereas in Rome these *relazioni* are in a separate archival *fondo* and were considered a supplementary tool of judicial activity, in Bologna the *relazioni* formed a crucial part of any criminal investigation into violence. When they do not begin a process, they are the first recourse after initial denunciation; they are conserved as a part of the entire criminal process, in the same file as witness testimonies, interrogations, sentences and appeals.

which the victim operated. In many cases where a victim seems unusually old, he was the elder party in a faction, attacked by the younger men of another faction.

In 1600, the average age of a homicide victim was thirty-three, with outliers on both sides. The three infanticides prosecuted in this year dragged the average down, while the accidental deaths of two seventy-year-old men and a fifty-five-year-old brought it up. Another forty-five-year-old died after falling to the ground while being chased around the rooftops by *sbirri*; his death remains in the homicide count. At the same time, twelve-year-old Francesca balances out the death of fifty-year-old Paolino Rossi. Removing all the outliers, the picture is essentially unchanged, and the average age of victims stays at thirty-three. There are some patterns within each age grouping. Older victims were more likely to die as a result of targeted attacks, such as when Ercole de Benedetto answered his door late at night only to be shot in the face by a group of his enemies.[23] Deaths that occurred in the heat of argument, or in other spontaneous outbursts of violence, were more likely to involve young men, as in the post-Mass argument that led to the death of twenty-five-year-old Francesco Frasanetti.[24] Women tended to die older than men, as a proportional measure among the smaller absolute numbers of female victims. In 1600, apart from twelve-year-old Francesca, who in fact died while defending her mother from a lover's enraged son,[25] no woman under the age of thirty appears to have been killed, although it should be noted that three of the eight women killed in 1600 were not identified by age during inspections of their bodies. In Bologna, at the beginning of the seventeenth century, the years from fifteen to thirty-five were particularly dangerous for active young men, although there was no guaranteed safety in age.

We have more reliable information for the sex of killers than for their ages, and equally reliable information for the sex of victims. Of the fifty-one definite homicides that occurred in 1600, forty-three (84%) involved male victims, and in every one of these cases except one where no killer was ever identified, the killers were also male. In the eight (16%) cases involving female victims, all the killers were also male. Thus, once putative infanticides are removed from the sample, the murdering class of 1600 was entirely male. The number of killers per victim is also worthy of analysis, as collective action can indicate not only forethought and violent intent but also the social regularity of violence as a means of

---

[23] ASB, Tribunale del Torrone, Atti e Processi, 3204, f 297.
[24] ASB, Tribunale del Torrone, Atti e Processi, 3253, f. 301.
[25] ASB, Tribunale del Torrone, Atti e Processi, 3195, f. 303.

fostering both competition and cooperation. The fifty-one homicides were committed by eighty-one killers; fourteen (27.5%) of the homicides were committed by groups of two or more men working in concert. Of these, there were three groups of four killers, four groups of three killers, and eight pairs of killers. These groups were composed of family members, co-workers, or faction members. The factions were based around a core of family members – in this year, the Ronchetti and Tozzi clans who actively feuded throughout 1600. Additionally, an unknown number of *sbirri* contributed to the death of Michele di Cheli during a botched arrest in Budrio in April.[26] Group violence was not abnormal in seventeenth-century Bologna, and its prevalence speaks to the powerful role in male sociability that violence continued to play at the outset of the seventeenth century. This role, emergent from the strong bonding power of cooperative violence and its communicative effectiveness, would not abate through the century, demonstrating that civilization and violence went hand in hand in Bologna.

Further, for any given year, it is important to analyze the means of homicide as an insight into the immediate situational emotions of homicidal acts. Killing is difficult and requires the killer to overcome significant psychological barriers to the taking of a life.[27] As a general rule, this difficulty lessens with the killer's physical distance from his victim, and with the psychological distance provided by advanced weaponry.[28] This means that it is easier to bash someone with a rock than it is to strangle him with bare hands; easier to stab someone with a pitchfork than with a dagger; and, importantly, much easier to shoot someone with a firearm from ten paces than to stab him up close. By the beginning of the seventeenth century, firearms ownership was common in the province of Bologna, a situation exacerbated by a piece of 1614 legislation mandating firearms ownership among rural *bolognesi* to combat bandit incursions.[29] In 1600, the fifty-eight total deaths, including the removed infanticides and accidents, were accomplished with the variety of weapons as shown in Figure 3.2.

In 1600 – and in all but two of the eleven years sampled across the century – the largest proportion of homicides were committed with rudimentary firearms known as the *archibugio a ruota* (wheel-lock

---

[26] ASB, Tribunale del Torrone, Atti e Processi, 3200, f. 151.

[27] D. Grossman, *On Killing: The Psychological Cost of Learning to Kill in War and Society* (New York: E-Rights, digital edition, 2009), section III, chapter 1.

[28] Ibid., section III, introduction.

[29] ASBo, *Bandi Intorno al Torrone, Bando che gl'Habitanti ne'Communi convicini alli confini di Prencipi esterni debbano tenere in casa gl'archibugi, portarli con essi, correre alla stremita*, June 7, 1614.

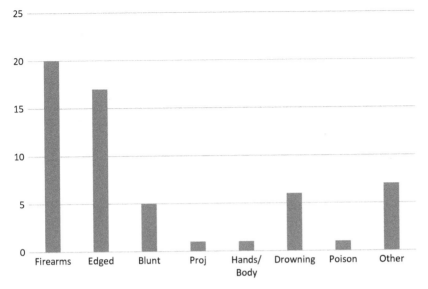

Figure 3.2 Homicides by weapon used, 1600.
Source: ASBo, Torrone, 3171–264

arquebus) or the *archibugio a fuoco* (match-lock), which were increasingly common across North Italy. Twenty (39%) of the fifty-one confirmed homicides were committed with a firearm, indicating that guns were the weapons of choice for killers by the beginning of the century. A flood of firearms into the *contado* in the late sixteenth and early seventeenth centuries made the *archibugio* a cheap and easily available weapon to a wide variety of social groups, despite aggressive legislation to require licenses for firearms and to ban their possession or use in populated areas.

The second most commonly used tools in homicide were a variety of edged weapons. From knives and daggers (though rarely the elite *stiletto*) to swords, and including agricultural and pastoral implements such as hoes, pitchforks and boar spears: these weapons accounted for seventeen (33%) of our confirmed killings. Firearms and edged weapons were the primary means used to kill in 1600, followed by an unusually large proportion (in this sample) of "unknown weapons" from seven cases (13%) that were definitively homicides, but whose circumstances of the death were unclear. The six drownings noted in Figure 3.2 were all deemed accidental, making the next category of homicide blunt weapons, such as purpose-designed clubs or whatever piece of wood was handy; these were used in five homicides (9%). Projectiles (rocks),

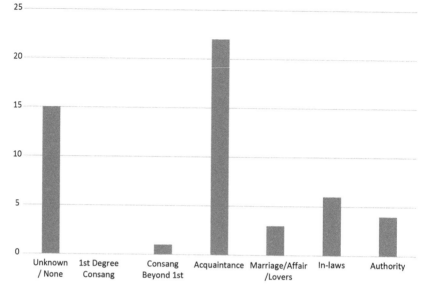

Figure 3.3 Homicides by relationship, 1600.
Source: ASBo, Torrone, 3171–264

poison and strangulation accounted for one homicide (2%) each. Although killers had a wide variety of weapons and weapon-like tools at their disposal, in 1600 they first chose the *archibugio* and then the blade to commit their violence, indicating a comfort with violence and a familiarity with weaponry that pervaded all levels of society. With only minor exceptions, this pattern held across the century, despite repeated attempts by legates to curtail gun violence and the efforts of urban *sbirri* to disarm the populace.

The question remains, who were the killers and victims to one another?[30] The relationships of the killers and victims are broken down by number of homicides in Figure 3.3. The *Torrone* established the relationships between killer and slain in most cases. In 1600, twenty-two (43%) of killers were known to their victims and were of the same social group or community, and of roughly equal social status. Ten killers slew family members, though none killed an immediately consanguineous relative. In-laws were the more likely family member to murder. Four killers did so, either exercising or protesting familial authority.

---

[30] On the relationship between violence and kin networks, cf. Raggio, *Faide E Parentele*; Smail, "Factions and Vengeance in Renaissance Italy. A Review Article."

We do not know the relationships between the killer and his victim in fifteen cases. Usually a relationship is unclear only in cases where a killer is never identified, thus making it impossible to determine how or if they knew their victim. Three of these cases, in which the killer was identified, were homicides committed by people whose relationship to their victims is unclear. They might have known each other: a priest was killed by a group of workers,[31] and two soldiers were killed by a group of Bolognese during a brothel argument turned brawl.[32] Those three homicides clearly fit into the category of spontaneous male-on-male conflict. Another, in which a group of people called out their victim's name and then gunned him down in his doorway, was clearly the denouement of some sour relationship.[33] Homicides that were committed by persons totally unknown to the victim and in which the killer was identified included the murder of a Roman by two Bolognese during the course of an argument[34] and a roadside robbery committed by bandits.[35] Thus, the larger part of homicides in 1600 were in fact committed by people who knew each other at least by name and acquaintance, rather than between strangers.

That situation bespeaks a relatively stable society in which violence occurred within daily conflict, an unfortunate reality that early modern Italians were accustomed to and, indeed, embraced to a large extent. But these homicides were censured not by the repressive action of state forces but by a court-mediated process of community censure. Killers were sentenced as guilty in twenty-eight of fifty-one indicted *processi*, and in fifteen cases, the record notes that they later received pardon after making peace with their respective victim's relatives. Of the twenty-eight sentenced to hang, only one did so. The *Torrone* did not police violence with the use of violence at this time, and in every case, the condemned men suffered exile for lengthy, often indeterminate, periods of time. Rooted in persistent Mediterranean structures, this customary approach to conflict resolution functioned when social trust was relatively thick and communities could withstand the occasional violent rupture.

This brings us back to our feuding shepherds from Aiano, and the chaos that their ongoing conflict inflicted on their local areas through 1600. In the several criminal *processi* that arose from the disorder, no one was punished. Nobody executed, nobody found to be primarily responsible for the disquiet, and only a few of the parties formally banished, though none in perpetuity. Yet the judge of the *Torrone* still clearly took

---

[31] ASBo, *Torrone*, 3224, *in fine*.   [32] ASBo, *Torrone*, 3223, *in fine*.
[33] ASBo, *Torrone*, 3204, *in fine*.   [34] ASBo, *Torrone*, 3200, f. 73.
[35] ASBo, *Torrone*, 3171, f. 301.

an active interest in the goings-on of small mountain towns, enough that he brought the feuding principals together under a banner of peace. The peace conference shows several things. The factionalism of Bolognese nobility was not binary antagonism against papal rule. Some of the nobility had advanced their family fortunes through accommodation of papal rule. These families supported the *Torrone* project and participated in its judicial program, acting as elite sponsors of peace accords between rural *bolognesi*. Here the Paleotti family filled this role, and Signore Galeazzo, acting as a good patron, sought to bind these families to the peace by bringing young Niccolo della Ronchetta into his service. By 1600, the *Torrone* had won the acquiescence of certain Bolognese nobility, who by this point were grouped loosely into papal (oligarchic) and anti-papal (republican) factions.[36]

Moreover, the *Torrone* and Paleotti had the ability to host such a peace conference, apparently without significant coercion: by their report, the patriarchs of each family had voluntarily confined themselves to the city and had pledged themselves to the peace conference. In the day-to-day life of the feud, their word was bond in their home territories, and violence was restrained to the peripheries of each faction; servants primarily suffered the violence. When both Francesco della Ronchetta and Antonio Tozzi removed themselves from their local hierarchies, tensions flared, and Niccolo, the son of Francesco, murdered his counterpart, Giovanni Pellegrino Tozzi. Ironically, by imposing the peacemaking process, the *Torrone* inadvertently amped up this feud's violence by removing it from its home territory, where local social hierarchies had hitherto limited its bloodshed. That the *Torrone* was established as a legitimate peacemaking body did not mean that it was effective in making that peace.

1610 and 1620: A Peaceful City, a Blood-Soaked Plain

The situation seemingly only improved in the next two decades. Immediately apparent in the homicide records of 1610 and 1620 are a significant drop in the number of urban homicides and a general reduction in levels of violence. Bellettini gives population figures for both city and *contado* in years close enough to 1610 and 1620 that they function as

---

[36] For the impact of these factions on public life, cf. N. Terpstra, "Republicanism, Public Welfare and Civil Society in Early Modern Bologna," in G. M. Anselmi et al., eds., *Bologna: Cultural Crossroads from the Medieval to the Baroque: Recent Anglo-American Scholarship* (Bologna: Bononia University Press, 2013), 205–16.

good estimates. In 1606, the city's population was 65,417 and the *contado*'s 161,083, for a provincial population of 226,500.[37] The *Torrone* trial records accounted for 34 total homicides in 1610, with the majority (29) concentrated in the *contado* and an extreme, and slightly dubious, low of five in the *città*. These absolute numbers translate to an overall homicide rate of 15 per 100,000, a rural rate of 18 per 100,000, and an urban rate of 7.6 per 100,000. Removing five accidents, three from the *contado* and two within the walls, as well as one infanticide, we are left with 28 definitive homicides, three in the city walls and the remaining 25 in the hinterland. These figures translate into consolidated homicides rates of 12.4 in aggregate, 15.5 in the countryside, and an urban rate of 4.6. The urban figures for this year and for 1620 appear remarkably low in comparison to the years on either side; it must be noted, however, that the decade 1610–1620 and the years on either end featured a strong push to reduce crime within the city walls and to restrain the violent groups of noble retainers who were thought responsible for the majority of urban violence.[38] Urban violence tumbled significantly in the first three decades of the seventeenth century before the cumulative weight of regional war and stagnation met the shock of the 1630 plague and inverted that pattern.

Bellettini provides population figures for the year 1617 of 67,871 for the city and 171,976 for the country, making a total population of 239,847.[39] Note here the rapid growth of the rural population since 1610, which gained 10,000 inhabitants in a decade, and approximately 27,000 from 1600 to 1620. Perhaps accompanying the rapid population growth, a slight increase in homicide numbers between 1610 and 1620 also increased the indicted homicide rate. Using the *Torrone*'s accounting of homicides, the year 1620 featured five urban homicides and 36 rural homicides for a total of 41 deaths. These figures translate into homicide rates of 7.4, 21 and 17, respectively. After removing from consideration another six fatal accidents, the final count of homicides for 1620 stands at three urban, 32 rural and 35 in total. The revised homicide rates for these counts are an urban rate of 4.4, a rural rate of 18.6 and a total rate of 14.6. Thus, despite the sharp drop in homicide rates between 1600 and 1610, particularly in the urban environment, violence rebounded with a slight increase in homicide rates in the ensuing decade, indicating that

---

[37] Bellettini, La popolazione di Bologna, 25–27.
[38] Angelozzi and Casanova, *La nobiltà disciplinata*, 370; G. Angelozzi and C. Casanova, *La giustizia criminale in una città di antico regime: Il tribunale del Torrone di Bologna* (secc. XVI–XVII) (Bologna: CLUEB, 2008).
[39] Bellettini, *La popolazione di Bologna*, 26–27.

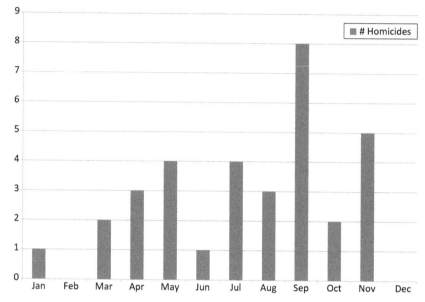

Figure 3.4 Homicides by month, 1610.
Source: ASBo, Torrone, 4203–323

whatever successes the police forces of Bologna may have had in curbing homicidal violence were fragile and temporary, subject to the pushback from a population that continued to view violence as an appropriate expression of social tension and a means to resolve it. The city was well under heel, if the *Torrone*'s records are reflective of actual homicides in the city

As in 1600, violence in these two years followed a regular annual rhythm, although there are some slight differences between the three years. The distribution of homicides by month for the year 1610 is shown in Figure 3.4.

As shown in Figure 3.4, 1610 began quietly before levels of violence grew toward their customary summer highs. The one death noted for January was the putative infanticide mentioned above, in which a male infant was found in a canal; no trial ensued because it was impossible to identify the child.[40] Carnival was also generally peaceful this year, with no homicides occurring in February. In March, the *Torrone* investigated an apparent suicide[41] and the vicious murder of a woman's lover by her

[40] ASBo, *Torrone*, 4209, f. 23.   [41] ASBo, *Torrone*, 4228, f. 16.

husband and in-laws, which was accompanied by significant violence against the unfaithful wife.[42]

There were three homicides in April 1610, putting the month on the low end, while during May notaries were dispatched to investigate four homicides, including those of a young noble who killed a young lawyer over a gambling debt,[43] and two Bolognese *sbirri* who transported "one of those guys who castrates pigs" into Tuscan territory before killing him.[44] The one homicide shown for June is illusory, as it was accounted as a homicide by the *Torrone* but appears more to have been an accident of negligence that occurred during the procession of the Holy Sacrament, when a spontaneous horse race got out of control and a horse trampled a man of seventy.[45] The first six months of 1610, compared to 1600, were peaceful, with a total of nine homicides committed in March, April and May and no definitive homicides noted or investigated by the judges and notaries of the *Torrone* in January, February or June. The low number of homicides is suspect, but counter-balanced by the obvious dedication of involved parties to denounce, publicize and pursue justice for wrongful deaths. This assiduousness was mandated by the *Torrone*'s officials, and backed up by punishment with stiff fines.[46] Although it remains possible that the low count for the early months of 1610 reflects poor records management by the *Torrone* rather than an actual lack of violence, the weight of evidence given by the other ten years in the sample make this an unlikely scenario. This is best seen as a reminder that violence, like all phenomena, will only follow human-created patterns to a certain extent and cannot be predicted with much regularity.

The summer months of July and August brought homicides, with four and three cases, respectively. Three killings in July appear to have been murders committed during arguments over women, or in one case, the uxoricide of a wife by her husband, who was alleged to have another paramour in Modena, and who used the knife he had been given by his mother-in-law.[47] The fourth was a murder committed during an argument after the victim shot the killer's dog, which was barking at him.[48] The three August homicides were all cases of male-male conflict, all of it spontaneous, and in two cases the victim and the killer were known to each other. Included among the vicious murder of a foreigner and that of a trespasser on noble hunting grounds is a case that exposes the extreme

[42] ASBo, *Torrone*, 4220, f. 301.   [43] ASBo, *Torrone*, 4238/1, f. 22.
[44] ASBo, *Torrone*, 4232, f. 348.   [45] ASBo, *Torrone*, 4238/1, f. 168.
[46] ASBo, *Bandi intorno al Tribunale del Torrone*, "Notificazione alli massari, saltari, ministrali & altri di portare le denonce," March 27, 1690.
[47] ASBo, *Torrone*, 4240, f. 301.   [48] ASBo, *Torrone*, 4223, f. 351.

poverty endemic to rural Italy in the seventeenth century, during which two farm labourers both lost their hats. When only one hat was found, an argument ensued and one of the *contadini* died on his way home after the beating he received.[49] The absence of urban homicides made the summer of 1610 unusually peaceful. Rural homicides committed during arguments over women were prominent in July, while August contained cases typical of that time of year: arguments that took place in the course of agricultural labour or hunting.

September stands out as the bloodiest month of the year, with eight homicides noted by the *Torrone*, one of which was an agricultural accident and thus has been removed from the sample. The seven remaining cases include the double murder of two brothers who had bought land out from under their neighbours;[50] the murder of a field labourer by his noble employer;[51] the killing of a woman's lover by her jealous husband;[52] the hired killing of a pharmacist by his business partner;[53] and two cases where the killer remained unclear. In one of these unclear cases, the brothers accused of shooting their co-workers (for a local noble family) were acquitted, and the death remained unsolved;[54] in the other, no killer was ever identified in an extremely complex trial process that stretched over more than 800 folios in a self-contained *busta*.[55] This extremely violent month was followed by a peaceful October.

The *Torrone* accounted for a total seven homicides in October and November. Two are removed from the final statistical count. One of these was a clear and obvious infanticide in which an infant was found in a canal with a rope and rock tied around its neck. However, statistical consistency demands that this case be treated equal to other, murkier, cases of infanticide.[56] The other was an accident in which a cannon exploded during a ceremonial celebration, killing the unfortunate soldier tasked with loading and firing it.[57] Removing those two cases leaves five homicides between October and November, two in October and three in November. Both October homicides appear to have accompanied robberies, one of an eighty-year-old man[58] and the other of the thirty-five-year-old footman to Signore Emilio Varchetta.[59] The three November killings took place over two events. One was a double homicide, of a father and son, during negotiations over the sale of livestock.[60]

---

[49] ASBo, *Torrone*, 4254, f. 51.   [50] ASBo, *Torrone*, 4275, f. 83.
[51] ASBo, *Torrone*, 4261, f. 231.   [52] ASBo, *Torrone*, 4264, f. 175.
[53] ASBo, *Torrone*, 4273, f. 49.   [54] ASBo, *Torrone*, 4276, f. 83.
[55] ASBo, *Torrone*, 4263, *in fine*.   [56] ASBo, *Torrone*, 4290, f. 303.
[57] ASBo, *Torrone*, 4280, f. 233.   [58] ASBo, *Torrone*, 4228, f. 7.
[59] ASBo, *Torrone*, 4266, f. 397.   [60] ASBo, *Torrone*, 4284, f. 301.

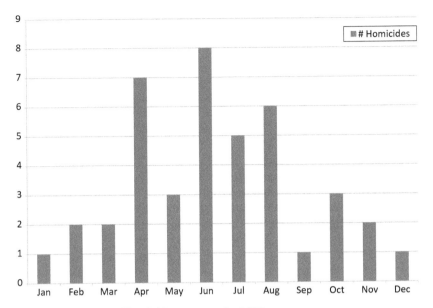

Figure 3.5 Homicides per month, 1620.
Source: ASBo, Torrone, 5025–107

The other was a shooting that occurred during a late-night argument, the causes of which are unknown.[61] These late-season homicides are typical of the time of year, when winter was approaching and resources began to grow scarce; many robberies-turned-homicides tended to occur in these months, as did disputes over agricultural property such as livestock.

With no homicides in December, 1610 ended peacefully. It had remained fairly non-violent, with a spike in homicides in September. The year 1620 featured more summertime violence, with homicides at a high level from April through August. This pattern is shown in Figure 3.5. The year 1620 was also, according to Angelozzi, the beginning of the period in which the recalcitrant nobility of Bologna began to push back against the legates' law-and-order program, which sought to curb their traditional rights to violence and prerogatives to render justice as they saw fit. Thus, following a continuation of the early-century lull in homicides, the decades after 1620 saw a rapid increase in the total scale of homicidal violence, which peaked in 1660 before rapidly falling off to levels approximately equal to rates of homicide from earlier in the century. The monthly pattern for 1620 is shown in Figure 3.5.

---

[61] ASBo, *Torrone*, 4287, f. 301.

Homicides in 1620 occurred more regularly through the summer than in 1610, with typical low levels at the beginning and end of the year. Extracting an accident leaves January homicide-free, while removing a carnival-time accident leaves one homicide in February, a pseudo-duel that nearly ended poorly for the killer before his companion stepped in and the two of them stabbed their opponent to death.[62] In March, a *sbirro* was killed by a young barber in the city,[63] and a farmer shot an employee of the Pepoli who was trespassing in his chestnut groves.[64] The year 1620 had a fairly peaceful spring before violence began to erupt in April, with six confirmed homicides.

Four of the six April homicides occurred during habitual arguments between men who knew each other and had previous enmity or friendship. In one other, a putative goat-rustler shot the owner in the mouth after being caught in his victim's stall at night. The last looked a little too much like a suicide for the *Torrone* to write it off completely as such. Both confirmed homicides in May occurred in arguments over livestock – in one case over the division of profits among cousins of the sale of some beasts, and another in which a woman guarding her sheep threw a rock at a ten-year-old girl, hitting her in the head and killing her. In all these early-season homicides, the victims were known to their killers and vice-versa. Rarely did Bolognese kill strangers, particularly at times of the year when the resources of survival could be threatened more easily by family, friends and neighbours. Social peace could be easily maintained in these conditions, especially with passers-by.

June was extremely violent, and in cases in which a motive is clear from the record (four of eight) the story is familiar. A man was killed in a case of mistaken identity by a cuckolded husband out for his wife's lover,[65] and a bailiff was killed by his footman's creditor.[66] A traffic jam on a crowded roadway ended when one carter simply pushed through, knocking another driver off his cart, beneath the wheels of another.[67] The final case whose motive is clear shows the Mediterranean pattern of combining conflict in legal arenas with more direct means.[68] Bolognese were equally willing to prosecute conflicts on multiple fronts and demonstrated this fact when a Giovan'Maria reacted to a lawsuit against him in the *Foro Civile* by murdering one of the witnesses testifying against him, who was also his opponent's cousin.[69] The other four cases from

[62] ASBo, *Torrone*, 5031, f. 303.   [63] ASBo, *Torrone*, 5037, f. 75.
[64] ASBo, *Torrone*, 5043, f. 301.   [65] ASBo, *Torrone*, 5059, f. 349.
[66] ASBo, *Torrone*, 5055, f. 333.   [67] ASBo, *Torrone*, 5051, f. 505.
[68] D. Smail, *The Consumption of Justice: Emotions, Publicity and Legal Culture in Marseille, 1264–1423* (Ithaca, NY: Cornell University Press, 2003), 89–95.
[69] ASBo, *Torrone*, 5049, f. 401.

June are murkier, due to the state of the records (in terms of both organization and preservation).

In July, the five homicides that occurred included two very similar to that of Giovan'Maria: in one, a man accused in the *Torrone* of stealing a length of canvas killed his accuser,[70] and in the other, a man killed an accused thief.[71] The month also included homicides over debt, during the arrest of two bandits taking refuge in a hostel, and a gruesome case in which a decomposed body was found strung up between trees in the woods.

The four confirmed homicides in August bring to the fore the modern concern with youth conflict, particularly bullying. Throughout the century, cases occurred in which a young boy, usually a servant to an artisan or a noble family, was killed by an older boy in the same employ, after habitual harassment and intimidation. Such a case occurred in August 1620, as did a revenge killing prompted by the theft of furniture, a roadside robbery by bandits, and the murder of one of Hercole Pepoli's retainers by the liverymen of Pepoli's brother Filippo. This was followed in September by the revenge killing of a young peasant, following a protracted conflict between two families that had already seen beatings and assaults before escalating to a public shooting on a roadside.

The remaining six homicides that occurred between October and December 1620 included two uxoricides and the murder of a husband by his wife's lover and his son. The seeming high proportion of familial homicides in 1620 should be placed against the comparative absence of urban, noble violence between the young men of the major noble clans. That kind of public disorder was precisely the target of the *Torrone*'s anti-violence program, which limited specifically the number of arms licenses granted to noble retainers and the numbers in which they could travel.[72] The "civilizing process" theory strongly suggests that certain types of violence, specifically public, male-on-male violence, observed a precipitous decline throughout modernity, while private, gendered violence such as domestic assault and murder remained relatively stable in absolute numbers, thus increasing their proportional share of the overall homicide rate.[73] The other three homicides from October–December 1620 were all of the first type: violence between young men prompted by arguments that often had precedent. In one of these cases, that of a foreigner, it is

---

[70] ASBo, *Torrone*, 5076, f. 301.   [71] ASBo, *Torrone*, 5062, f. 351.

[72] ASBo, *Bandi intorno al Torrone*, "Bando dell'Arme, con la innovation d'altri bandi, ristretto al luogo, ville e distretto di Castel Bolognese: con la rivocatione delle Licenze," December 28, 1612; "Bando in materia dell'Armi," December 20, 1616; "Bando sopra l'Armi," March 29, 1618.

[73] Daly and Wilson, *Homicide*, 284; Spierenburg, *A History of Murder*, 224.

unclear if or how he knew his slayers; but in the other two, killer and victim were obviously acquainted, if not habitual friends. Active attempts to reduce public male violence were only moderately successful.

As in 1600, the average ages of victims in 1610 and 1620 fell toward the high end of what constituted "youth." In 1610, a victim's average was thirty, and in 1620 it was thirty-three. The same patterns generally hold true for 1610 and 1620 as they did in 1600: women tended to die older than men, and as the result of planned assaults; older men died primarily by planned and organized killings; young men died in spontaneous outbursts of violence. However, the proportion of male and female victims shifted in the first and second decades of the century, such that in 1610, 9% of victims (3) were female, and in 1620, 12% were female, with male victims accounting for 91% and 88%, respectively. These are of course low numbers from which to draw any firm conclusions, but some tentative and familiar patterns emerge. The sex of killers was typically skewed toward males: male killers accounted for 95% and 98% of all killings throughout the two years, leaving 5% and 2% for females, respectively. These men killed in groups in a similar proportion to the killers from 1600. Of the total sixty-three homicides throughout the two years, twenty (32%) were committed in groups of two or more, generally made up of family or faction members whose interests aligned, at least temporarily, well enough to make group homicide a useful social strategy. The demographics of fatal violence look similar across 1600 to 1620.

Curiously, in 1610, more killers used knives than guns, though these two categories still accounted for most killings, as demonstrated in Figures 3.6 and 3.7.

In both 1610 and 1620 the large majority (53 of 63 confirmed homicides, 53 of 75 accounted by the *Torrone*; 84% and 71%, respectively) were committed with either a firearm or an edged weapon. Firearms were obvious tools of violence, and did not serve any other purpose; edged weapons were multi-use tools depending on context, and although many *bolognesi* killed with edged tools such as a hoe, men and many women were accustomed to carrying a blade, ostensibly for cutting bread or eating. That more knives than guns were used in 1610 does not mean they were a preferred weapon, as six of the killings were done with both knives and guns. Conflicts that began with knives were often finished with guns, both of which were kept close at hand. How do we reconcile this fact with the extremely tight-knit, close-bonded rural communities and urban neighbourhoods in which violence occurred? Again, this chapter stresses that violence occurred primarily within known relationships, where the victim was at the very least acquainted with his killer and

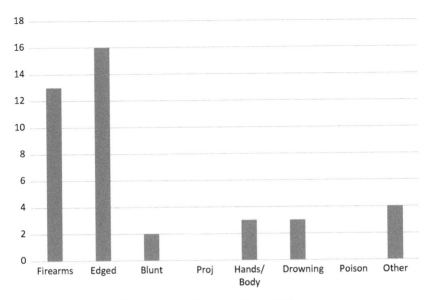

Figure 3.6 Weapons used in homicides, 1610.
Source: ASBo, Torrone, 4203–323

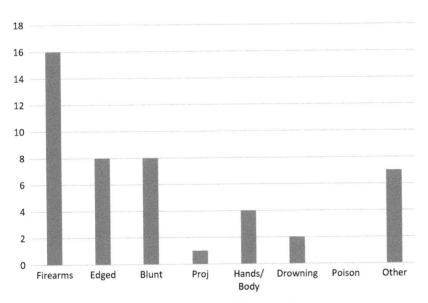

Figure 3.7 Weapons used in homicides, 1620.
Source: ASBo, Torrone, 5025–107

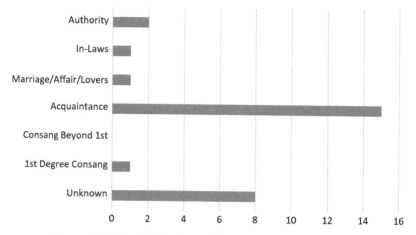

Figure 3.8 Homicidal relationships, 1610.
Source: ASBo, Torrone, 4203–323

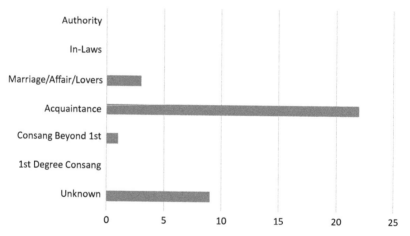

Figure 3.9 Homicidal relationships, 1620.
Source: ASBo, Torrone, 5025–107

vice versa. The relationships in which homicides occurred in 1610 and 1620 are shown in Figures 3.8 and 3.9.

As Figures 3.8 and 3.9 demonstrate, the majority of homicides occurred between people who knew each other at least by sight. The large categories in which the relationship is unclear (eight cases each year) do not contradict this: in these cases, it is primarily because the identity of the killer remained unknown that we do not know the relationship he had to his victim. In many cases, such as the robbery/ murder of Battista Parenti in Gaggio in 1620, the killers may have known their victim; indeed, they knew enough about him to judge his stall worth breaking into.[74] Familial homicides, such as parricide, occurred at relatively low rates in these two years. The one instance of homicide in a first-degree consanguineous relationship was a case in which a sixteen-year-old youth allegedly beat his sister badly enough that she took ill and died two weeks later.[75] With a smattering of homicides related to marriage (or other amorous relations) in each year, the primary category remains the amorphous "acquaintance" – a category that extends from deepest habitual friendship to a passing recognition and greeting in the road, and was often based on a shared hometown or neighbourhood. In the extremely social towns and neighbourhoods of early modern Bologna, these relationships were the field in which battles for status were fought, the theatre in which deeply felt verbal insults were acted upon, and the forum in which disputes arose and erupted into violence. Men do not, in most circumstances, murder complete strangers. The records from Bologna confirm this modern phenomenon: homicides were most likely to be committed by an acquaintance of the victim.

Although more peaceful in both indicted homicide rates and in absolute numbers than 1600, both 1610 and 1620 suffered violence characteristic of a society in which institutional and social trust was relatively "thick." Violence followed a predictable seasonal pattern with more homicides in the summer and during periods of Carnival or harvest than during winter or spring. Public male violence was present though not excessive, and domestic violence attracted the attention of authorities and communities. Easy availability of both edged weapons and guns resulted in much bloodshed, but it was largely condemned by communities, and killers often atoned. In this society, legislation such as arms bans might have encouraged some people to put away their guns, and people witnessed the court's attempts to remedy its own failings, as it did when it initiated a massive criminal process against a group of constables accused of a litany of abuses.[76] But though it may have achieved a semblance of peace in the streets of Bologna, the *Torrone* was still confronted by communities that employed violence both privately and publicly – and often fatally – to resolve their problems. More importantly, eliminating or even punishing that violence was not the goal of the criminal court. As the court's records of execution demonstrate, when

---

[74] ASBo, *Torrone*, 5040, f. 301.   [75] ASBo, *Torrone*, 4222, f. 299.
[76] ASBo, *Torrone*, 4232, process against Fuzellini brothers, 1600; 4202, process against group of *sbirri*.

committing homicides of its own, the *Torrone* was almost dismissive of criminal murderers.

General Characteristics of Homicide in 1632

The epidemic of 1630 struck the northern Italian cities harder than their Tuscan and southern counterparts. In particular, cities in the Veneto suffered the hardest, with Verona losing as much as a whopping 60% of its population, and Padua 59%; the Lombard cities also lost significant portions of their population, with Milan and Brescia each losing about 46%, and Bergamo 40%.[77] Within Emilia, Bologna got off comparatively easy with a 24% mortality rate within the city; Parma, 90 kilometres and two small cities to the west, lost as much as 50% of its population.[78] The figure of 24% for Bologna is confirmed by Bellettini's analysis of a city census undertaken in 1631, which gives a figure of 46,747 for the intramural population, and of parish censuses undertaken in 1632, which provide a total figure of 43,114.[79] These figures do not contradict one another, as the plague resurfaced in 1631 in a reduced form that accounts for the further loss of 3,000 people. Populations of the towns and villages of the countryside are not available, although Cipolla notes, from Tuscan data, that plagues tended to hit some rural settlements extremely hard while leaving others untouched, and that mortality in these cases added up to a proportional loss of population very similar to that in the urban centre.[80] The closest population figure we have for the hinterland beyond 1632 is 165,500 in 1652; in 1660, this had climbed to 177,457. Assuming the rate of population growth was relatively stable (approximately 1,200 per year) throughout this period, we can extrapolate a 1632 rural population of about 140,000, which then gives an approximate 20% mortality rate from pre-plague populations.

With these numbers we can provide homicide rates for the post-plague society. The *Torrone*'s records from 1632 included only homicides that fit within the statistical analysis. No accidents or infanticides were included in the trial records, leaving the *Torrone*'s accounting in line with this study's. In 1632, there were 16 homicides in the city, a small number compared to 61 in the hinterland, for a total of 77. This translates into homicide rates of 6.9 for the city, 43.6 for the *contado*, and 42 for the whole province. The obvious discrepancy between urban and rural

---

[77] C. Cipolla, *Fighting the Plague in Seventeenth-Century Italy* (Madison: University of Wisconsin Press, 1981), 100.
[78] Ibid.   [79] Bellettini, *La Popolazione di Bologna*, 25–27, 191–92.
[80] Cipolla, *Fighting the Plague*, 102.

homicides is a focus of Chapter 5. Here, it suffices to observe that the monthly rhythm of homicides was very similar to years prior, though there was a higher overall incidence of homicides, particularly in the first six months of the year. Figure 3.10 shows the distribution of homicides by month in 1632.

Within that rhythm, gender distributions of homicide remained similar to other years: 88% (68) of victims were male and 12% (9) female; and 98% (148) of the killers were male, compared to 2% (3) female killers. The average age of victims was 31.5, directly in line with typical early-century patterns of violence. The weaponry used, too, was in line with broader patterns of violence, with most homicides committed using either firearms or edged weapons, as shown in Figure 3.11.

Thus, the year 1632 looks ordinary in terms of the demography and means of homicide, although its homicide rates stand out as both high and disparate, with an extremely violent countryside and a peaceful city. Where it begins to look exceptional is in analysis of the relationships between killer and killed, which take a different form than in the years examined thus far. The distribution of relationships is shown in Figure 3.12.

As Figure 3.12 shows, the largest proportion of homicides occurred among people who knew each other more or less casually, through

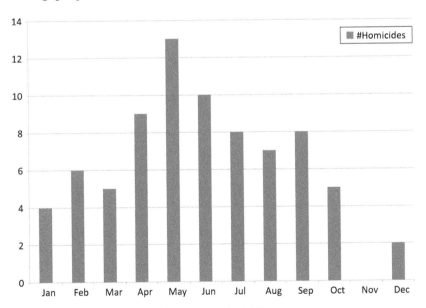

Figure 3.10 Homicides per month, 1632.
Source: ASBo, Torrone, 5806–972

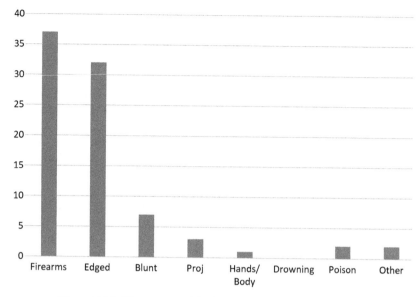

Figure 3.11 Weapons used in homicides, 1632.
Source: ASBo, Torrone, 5806–972

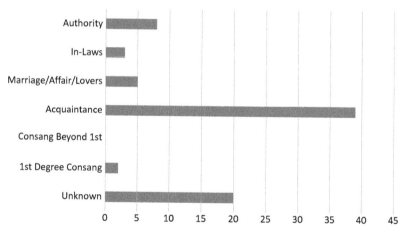

Figure 3.12 Relationships between killers and victims, 1632.
Source: ASBo, Torrone, 5806–972

friendship, a shared hometown or otherwise. This was typical of most years. Where 1632 begins to stand out is the high level of homicides in which the relationship is unknown, or does not exist, and in the high level of homicides directed vertically in hierarchies. Both these will be closely analyzed in Chapter 5. A high incidence of familial violence, particularly within marriage relationships, also draws our attention. These variations make 1632 slightly exceptional, although the reasons for this exceptionality cannot be explained without delving deeper into the social environment in the wake of the plague.

Homicides in 1640, 1652 and 1660: Civil War Brewing

As the population recovered, the social instability caused by the plague continued through the next three decades. Following a slight drop in absolute numbers and homicide rates in 1640, violence escalated rapidly between 1640 and 1660 to an extreme peak, before plummeting in the second half of the century to the lowest rates of the eleven-year sample. Bellettini's population figures do not reveal the rural population for 1640, but it can be estimated at 156,000 by assuming a fairly regular rate of growth in the post-plague era. By 1640, the urban population had rebounded to 55,911.[81] Thus, in 1640, we can estimate homicide rates of 28.2 (44) for the *contado* and 19.7 (11) *in città*. These numbers reflect a drop in rural violence, counteracted by a rise in urban violence – a pattern that characterizes much of the remaining sampled years, as urban rates first approached and then surpassed rural rates of homicide. Within those 55 homicides, 95% (53) of victims were male, while 5% were female; 97.6% of killers were male compared to 2.4% female. The average age of victims was 32.9, squarely in the range of average age of death for homicide victims across the seventeenth century. Figure 3.13 demonstrates that the annual rhythm of homicides in 1640 was much like that of 1632, with a high spike in the summer months of June through September and a bump during Carnival, and a generally elevated monthly homicide count throughout the year. The pattern shown in Figure 3.13 should be familiar to the reader, as should Figure 3.14, which demonstrates the continued dominance of firearms and edged weapons as the homicidal weapons of choice.

As shown in Figures 3.13 and 3.14, 1640 was an unsurprising year in terms of the amount and distribution of bloodshed. Its homicide rates were not extremely high, although the urban rate began to tick upward at this point, from its early-century low of 4.4 in 1620 to 19.7 in 1640. The rural rate, while fourth highest overall, was only slightly above the rural average of 27.7, while the urban rate was well below the average of 25.9. By mid-century, the *Torrone*'s hold on peace and order within the city

---

[81] Bellettini, *La Popolazione di Bologna*, 25–27.

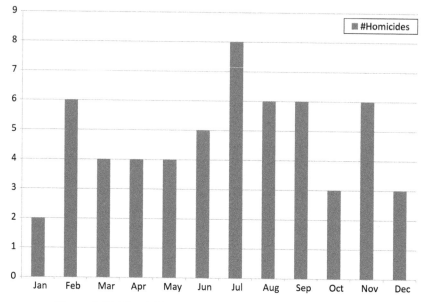

Figure 3.13 Homicides by month, 1640.
Source: ASBo, Torrone, 5606, 5634, 5946, 6001, 6206–398

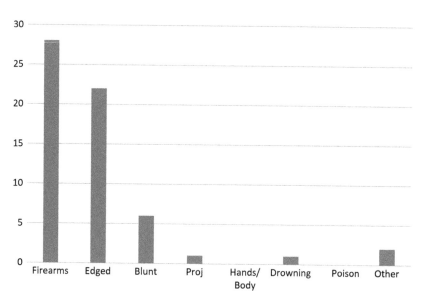

Figure 3.14 Weapons used in homicides, 1640.
Source: ASBo, Torrone, 5606, 5634, 5946, 6001, 6206–398

was slipping, but not yet to the catastrophic levels of violence that occurred in 1652 and 1660.

The relationships between killer and victim in 1640 show a high concentration of homicides among acquaintances, such as people from the same village, neighbourhood or profession. Small concentrations of in-family killing also occurred, with two homicides within the first degree of consanguinity, two within degrees of consanguinity beyond the first, two homicides within marital or other relationships, and one homicide within an in-law group. Most homicides continued to be of acquaintances of one degree or another. In only nine cases is the relationship between the killer and his victim unclear, making 1640 ripe for analysis of bloodshed within family and friend groupings. The spread of homicidal relationships in 1640 is shown in Figure 3.15.

The *Torrone*'s records for the years surrounding 1650 are damaged and waterlogged, making an analysis of 1650 impossible. However, about 75% of the holdings from the year 1652 are in good condition, and these documents allow an analysis of 1652 with a sample size of 75%. Within this 75% sample of the year 1652, there were 85 homicides; expanding this sample creates a homicide count of 108, the second highest total count next to 1660. From Bellettini's population figure for the city of 58,538 and an estimated rural population of 165,500, we can peg homicide rates for 1652 at 42.8 rural and 50.15 urban, with a total rate of 48.2. These homicide rates are radically higher than any so far, except for that of 1632, which still falls well below the total homicide rate and whose

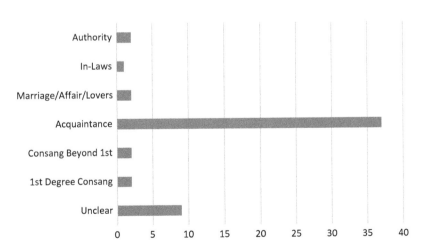

Figure 3.15 Relationships between killers and victims, 1640.
Source: ASBo, Torrone, 5606, 5634, 5946, 6001, 6206–398

urban rate is smaller by a factor of about six. The killers were 99% male, while the victims were 96% male. The average age of victims was 32.8 – once again squarely in the expected ranges.

The annual rhythm of homicides in 1652 was more or less regular, with a spike in March rather than February, and an extremely violent June (sixteen killings) next to a fairly average July (eight killings). The upshot of homicides in March is somewhat illusory. Almost half of the twelve recorded homicides from March occurred in one event: a vicious knife fight between two rival factions that left five men dead. A sixth homicide in March was a case of police brutality in which a *sbirro* shot and killed a Bolognese peasant for unknown reasons. A typical late summer/early autumn surge was followed by a diminution of violence as the year's end approached. The ten homicides that occurred in May primarily sprang from previous enmity, as well as two cases in which citizens resisted the attempts of *sbirri* to arrest and transport prisoners. Otherwise, the homicides of 1652 were not unusual in scope or style, but were part of a wave of violence that saw homicide rates skyrocket a decade later. The annual rhythm of homicides for 1652 is shown in Figure 3.16.

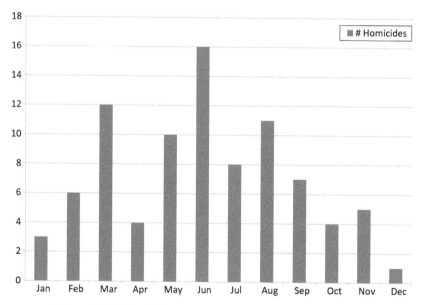

Figure 3.16 Homicides by month, 1652.
Source: ASBo, Torrone, 6505–662

As rates of violence climbed, so too did the prevalence of firearms in early modern Bolognese violence. More than half of the homicides still accessible in the preserved records of 1652 were committed with firearms, unlike previous years in which the proportion of firearms homicides fell somewhere below 50% of the total. Thus, firearms became the modus operandi of homicides by the mid-seventeenth century and played a significant role in the mid-century explosion of violence that shook the province. The other categories of weaponry played a small but significant role: edged and blunt weapons accounted for a total of twenty-five killings between the two categories; the rest were essentially negligible, with a few ill-thrown stones and a strangulation rounding off the count. The weapons distribution for homicides in 1652 is shown in Figure 3.17.

What began to change around 1652 were the social contexts of homicide and violence. The murder of the judge Pungelli was just one homicide among many in these years that emerged from conflicts between the city's elite families and their rivals among each other and the city's institutions. The collapse of order among elite classes took place amid a series of general crises in North Italy, and economic and demographic stagnation were exacerbated by an increase in violence,

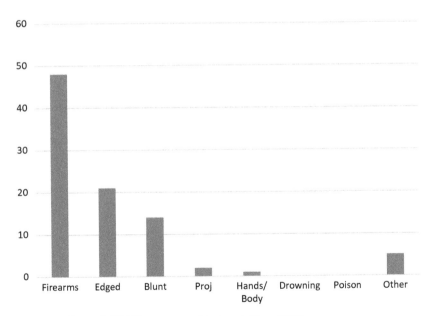

Figure 3.17 Weapons used in homicides, 1652.
Source: ASBo, Torrone, 6505–662

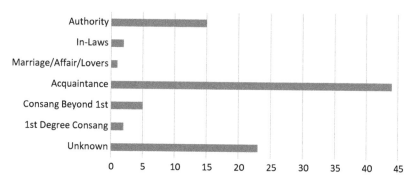

Figure 3.18 Homicidal relationships, 1652.
Source: ASBo, Torrone, 6505–662

particularly political and class-based homicides. Institutions such as the *sbirri* that may have commanded respect or at least fear prior to the plague lost their stature, and ties of blood or loyalty to one's *padrone* were disregarded under the stresses of poverty and need. The extremely fraught class tensions that played a significant role in this wave of violence were visible in the homicidal relationships of 1652, which featured more relationships of vertical authority than in any year previous. These relationships are shown in Figure 3.18.

Beyond the typical prevalence of relationships of acquaintance, the major category of identified relationships was that of authority, such as when a group of nobles shot the *sub-auditore* Giacinto Pungelli in the streets. Recall that Authority homicides also surged briefly in 1632, following the destabilizing effects of the plague. The sudden shift in the social contexts of homicide constituted the unknown civil war made visible by analysis of homicide records: for approximately thirty years, significant sectors of Bologna's nobility abandoned their allegiance to papal government and returned to the open practice of domination through violence, both against their putative vassals and against other elites, including papal officers. By doing so, they rejected the disciplining process initiated by the *Torrone* in the early century, forcing it to react with extreme measures of its own.

Thus we arrive at 1660, the year that contained the highest total homicide counts in urban areas, the highest homicide rate for the *città*, and the highest overall rate. Bellettini provides population figures of 62,284 for the city, and 177,457 for the *contado*, making a total population count of 239,741.[82] These population figures are very close to what

---

[82] Bellettini, *La Popolazione di Bologna*, 25–29.

they were in the early decades of the century before the plague, particularly the urban population of 1600 and the rural population of 1620. Thirty years after the plague, the total population had finally returned to approximately the same level as in 1620, yet the instability of the 1630s had lasting effects through the century. The *Torrone* accounted for 140 homicides throughout the year, of which four were classified as accidents and thus removed from the total count. The remaining 136 homicides, 64 in the city and 72 in the *contado*, result in massive homicide rates of 106 urban (more than twice the second highest rate, 42.8 in 1652), 41.7 rural (second to 1652), and 60.75 overall (the highest, by about 12 points). Of the 275 killers, 272 (98.9%) were males, while the remaining three (1.1%) were female. Of the victims, 131 (96%) were male, and five (4%) female. A victim's average age (31.1) was slightly lower than previous years, but it was right in line with the overall average of the century (31). Thus, the basic characteristics of homicide did not change during this wave of violence, but in fact amplified in scope and scale. This escalation is further seen in the monthly rhythm of homicidal violence, which followed the same general pattern as the years previous, but with far greater numbers of homicides. There was an unusual level of violence early in the year, particularly in January; the characteristics of these individual homicides were similar to other early-year homicides throughout the century, and often sprang from habitual encounters such as dice-playing and street drunkenness in the dark months of winter. The rhythm of homicides through 1660 is shown in Figure 3.19.

As Figure 3.19 demonstrates, 1660 had a typical if extremely bloody season of violence, stretching from May through September. July saw twenty-three homicides, making it the single bloodiest month of the century in the sample under consideration; all of the other months stack up in the high range of homicides for that time of year as well. As in 1652, the relationships between victims and slayers may tell us much about the mentality and objectives behind these killings. Additionally, the distribution of weaponry in such a violent year could indicate something about the emotional expression behind these homicides: where the *archibugio* can be considered more impersonal, fired from a distance and removed from the close-up experience of homicide, edged weapons are the ultimate face-to-face means of killing, with the exception of bare hands. The year 1660 is one of only two years in the sample in which edged weapons outnumbered firearms, as shown in Figure 3.20.[83]

---

[83] The other year, 1610, featured an unusually high number of September homicides attributed primarily to agricultural arguments between labourers, often using the tools of their trade as weapons, giving edged weapons a bump in numbers for 1610.

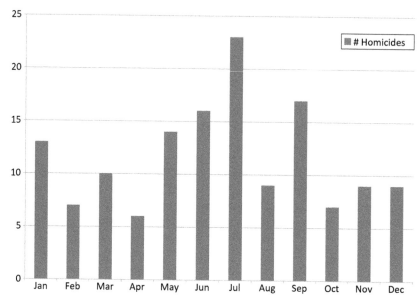

Figure 3.19 Homicides by month, 1660.
Source: ASBo, Torrone, 6755–819

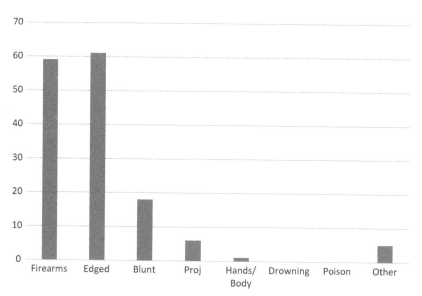

Figure 3.20 Weapons used in homicides, 1660.
Source: ASBo, Torrone, 6755–819

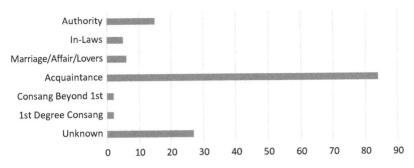

Figure 3.21 Homicidal relationships, 1660.
Source: ASBo, Torrone, 6755–819

It is significant that edged weapons outnumbered firearms, even if they did so only by two homicides (61 to 59). Violence in this year was dominated by two groups: nobles accustomed to fighting and killing with the sword, and labourers and farmhands who employed tools as weapons, being unable to purchase, or attain a license for, the highly regulated firearms that caused the lion's share of homicides in years previous. It is significant that the destabilization of social trust manifested most strongly in elite and disenfranchised networks – those who had much to gain and those who had much to lose. Similarly, the relationships between killer and killed, as in 1652 and 1640, indicate a tide of violence predicated on tension between and within socio-legal hierarchies. These tensions grew from 1630; by 1670, violence was on a clear downward track that continued until 1700. The relationships of killers and victims in 1660 are shown in Figure 3.21.

While relationships of acquaintance remained the dominant loci of homicidal violence, 1660, like 1652, featured a high number of homicides (15) that took place in relationships of vertical authority, either upward or downward. Note that this number is equal in absolute terms to the number of authority-based homicides that occurred in 1652, but accounts for a smaller proportion of total homicides. This indicates that violence between levels of authority cannot account for the entirety of the very high homicide count from 1660; however, the same destruction of hierarchical stability that led to these high numbers of authority-based killings may have resulted in the higher overall levels of violence within classes (the "acquaintance" category) as well as between them. In an environment where violence was the normative response to challenges from high levels of authority, so too did it pervade relationships between people of equal status, who may have employed violence to amplify and communicate their own status within a constrained framework, such as the sociability of the drinking tavern. The relatively high count of intra-familial homicides, particularly in the categories of marriage and in-lawship, are also part of this process in which social status was contestable between rich and poor, noble and common, or young and old.

1670, 1680 and 1690: A Sharp Decline

Following the extremely high levels of violence that shook the communities of Bologna in 1660, homicide rates began to fall in fairly regular intervals after 1680. After the highs of 1660, there was a steep drop until 1680; 1670 and 1680 had very similar homicide rates that were approximately 60% lower than those of 1660. The larger proportion of this drop came in the city, which saw its homicide rate reduced by a factor of more than four, from 105.9 to 25.2 in 1670. This extremely rapid fall has been touched upon by Giancarlo Angelozzi, who notes that the 1660s were a decade of significant, hard-nosed criminal reform by the city's papal legate and the court's officers.[84] In this decade, weapons restrictions were tightened and the private retinues of the nobility limited and disarmed. However, it is disingenuous to pin either the violence of 1660 or its subsequent decline on the nobility alone. The artisans, labourers, professionals and vagrants all participated in Bologna's "economy of violence" to advance their goals and achieve their aims.[85] What happened following 1660 must therefore bear on them as well. The remainder of this chapter traces the late-century decline of violence to draw out patterns that may shed light on the features of and reasons for this decline.

Bellettini lacks firm population figures for 1670, and estimating from the nearest year provides approximate figures of 63,500 in the city and 173,000 in the *contado*, for a total population of 236,500, about 3,000 smaller than in 1660. After 1660, the population declined for the rest of the century – particularly the countryside, which fell from 177,457 in 1660 to 165,433 by 1700. If the absolute numbers of homicides remained steady, then homicide rates would rise as a proportion of the population; nevertheless, despite the decreasing population, homicide rates continued to drop, indicating a fall in both absolute homicidal violence and in homicidal violence pegged as a proportion of the overall population. Thus, in 1670, homicide rates were 25.2 in the city, 26 in the

---

[84] Angelozzi and Casanova, *La nobiltà disciplinata*, 144–51.

[85] Cf. M. Greenshields, *An Economy of Violence in Early Modern France*, (Philadelphia: Pennsylvania State University Press, 1994), for a coherent analysis of how violence acted as a currency measuring social standing, debt and obligation.

contado and 25.7 overall. The year 1670 was also the only year in which there were no women involved in any of the killings as either killer or accomplice (as accounted by the *Torrone*; there were no infanticide trials that year); 100% of the killers were male. Of the victims, 95% were male and 5% were female, which falls squarely within the expected range for victims.

Across the year, the pattern of homicides was fairly typical, although March featured an unusually high ten homicides, including a double fratricide in a gypsy camp near Sant'Agostino di Sotto, in which two brothers both perished in a duel that their mothers blamed on an argument between their wives.[86] Otherwise, the year passed in normal fashion, with spikes in July and August that grew from a peaceful winter and spring (except March), and fell once again to a quiet autumn and December. Five homicides in each of February, April, May and October were a constant if not alarming level of violence, bookended by two each in January and November, and one in December. The pattern is shown in Figure 3.22.

As shown in Figure 3.22, the months of July to September 1670 all featured high homicide counts, particularly July and August. The pattern falls within the expected ranges, however, and the year does not present as unusual besides a high count in March, also seen in 1652.

Where 1670 does stand out, however, is in the distribution of weapons used in committing these homicides. Figure 3.23 shows the complete and total dominance of the arquebus as the weapon of choice in 1670, at a higher proportion (around two-thirds) than in any other year before or after. This may speak to the social station of the killers and victims, but not in any specific way: by 1670, firearms were easily available at least through the black market, if not legitimately through a widespread licensing system.[87]

The prevalence of firearms as the weapon of choice in 1670 is beyond dispute. As in other years, the category of edged weapons includes not just swords and daggers but also agricultural and artisanal instruments, such as the cobbler's awl used to kill an apprentice in a fight over his lethargy in repairing a pair of shoes.[88] Firearms came in primarily one type, making the *archibugio corto alla ruota* (a short-barrelled, wheel-lock musket easily available when it wasn't under extreme ban, and often when it was) the definitive weapon of choice. The reemergence of firearms as a dominant means to kill indicates that the social tensions

---

[86] ASBo, *Torrone*, 6946, *in fine*.
[87] Blastenbrei, "Violence, Arms and Criminal Justice," 75–79.
[88] ASBo, *Torrone*, 6955, fasc. 2.

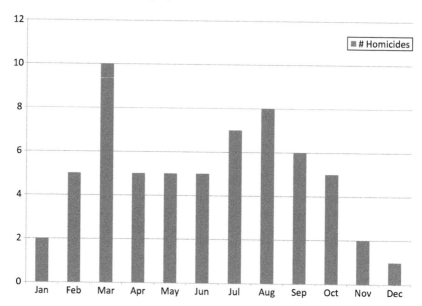

Figure 3.22 Homicides by month, 1670.
Source: ASBo, Torrone, 6930–7050

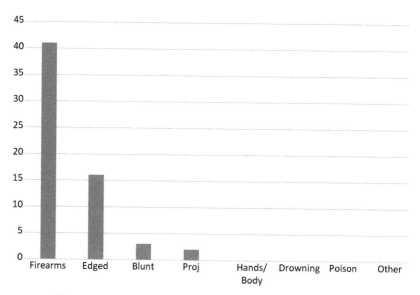

Figure 3.23 Weapons used in homicides, 1670.
Source: ASBo, Torrone, 6930–7050

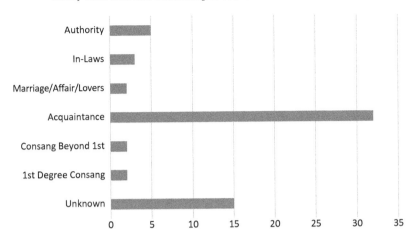

Figure 3.24 Homicidal relationships, 1670.
Source: ASBo, Torrone, 6930–7050

threatening to break class structures in the mid-century's wave of violence had begun to slacken by 1670; gone were the long blades of noble *bravi* and the daggers of aggrieved *contadini*, and the arquebus, the great equalizer, resumed its place in quotidian violence that was more easily divorced from the social and economic status of participants. This return to more normalized social relations is reflected in the relationships within which murders occurred in 1670, as shown in Figure 3.24.

Following the wave of homicides in 1652 and 1660 that were directed upward against representatives of political, legal and class authority, homicide returned to its more typical locus within families and friendships in 1670. The five authority-based homicides that did occur were primarily directed downward on the social hierarchy, excepting a farmer who killed his landlord in the course of an argument over *danno dato* (property damage) on the Signore's land, and a group of men who ambushed and killed a *sbirro* a week after he broke up their "dance party."[89] The others were judicial murders committed by constables and gate guards, in an overreach of their normal duties.

The majority (32) of the year's sixty-one homicides occurred within the category of acquaintance, which includes compatriots, friends, village rivals, business associates and a wide range of other relationships. This figure is par for the course; most homicides over the century occurred within one formulation of acquaintance or another. As in earlier years,

---

[89] ASBo, *Torrone*, 6961, fasc. 12; 6954/2, fasc. 1. The phrase here is "Festa di Ballo."

the category "unknown" does not preclude there being a relationship of some kind; it simply indicates that the records have not made clear how the killer and victim knew each other. As commonly seen in other years, homicides that occurred within the first degree of consanguinity were fratricides, while in-laws killed each other to defend the status of their womenfolk or to press their claim on the same against recalcitrant relatives.

The year 1670 thus began the decline in homicide rates that occurred toward the end of the century. However, this process was slow and did not really pick up until after 1680. The 1670s were a difficult decade, beginning with bread riots in Bologna in 1671 that saw the *Torrone* arraign multitudes of urbanites who participated in the disorders beginning in February.[90] Although this analysis does not include the years between 1670 and 1680, the homicide counts of the two years are very close. In 1680, there were 56 total homicides investigated (extracting infanticides and accidents, which account for four more). Forty of these occurred in the countryside and 16 in the city. Working from population figures derived from Bellettini of about 65,000 *in città* and 170,000 beyond the walls, the homicide rates for 1680 thus amounted to 24.6 in the city, 23.5 in the *contado*, and 23.8 aggregate. These were marginally lower rates than in 1670, but it is apparent that, following the mid-century decades of bloodshed, the real decline of violence had yet to be felt.

The legacy of this instability is seen in the monthly pattern of homicides in 1680. There were an unusually high number of homicides in the first and last months of the year, as shown in Figure 3.25. While the hot summer months of July and August both had high counts of homicide that were in line with other sampled years, May and June featured the lowest counts of the year, which is atypical. What stands out in 1680 is a high number of killings that occurred within groups of Bolognese *sbirri* and between Bolognese and Florentine *sbirri*. There were also three instances of youths playing with or cleaning their firearms and inadvertently killing either themselves or relatives; as stated above, these cases remain in the count due to the inherently violent characteristics of firearms. Beyond these two atypical features of 1680, the typology of homicides was normalized, with the majority falling into the recognized categories of both typology and relationship. The monthly count of homicides from 1680 is shown in Figure 3.25.

As we see above, in contrast to the slight bell figure that tends to occur in homicide counts across the year, 1680 witnessed a decline in violence

[90] ASBo, *Torrone*, 6951, *in fine*.

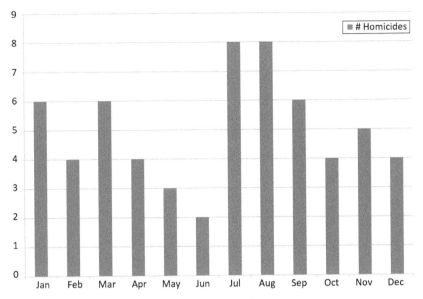

Figure 3.25 Homicides by month, 1680.
Source: ASBo, Torrone, 7144–80

over the spring months that jumped back up in July before tapering off again beginning in September. At this point, it is appropriate to introduce the element of randomness into history; there is not always an answer to the question "why," especially when considering the micro-characteristics of violence from a macro-historical point of view. The annual rhythm of homicides – that is, the pattern we have seen so far – was not dictated by some external force acting upon and constraining human behaviour. In 1680, there were simply more people who acted upon the impulses to violence in January and March than in May or June, despite (or perhaps due to?) the chilly weather and the increased difficulty of feeding one's family through the winter. Alternatively, the decline in homicides in the summer months may reflect success by the *Torrone* and its officers in controlling and reducing levels of violence; these were the months most likely to contain spontaneous, unplanned outbursts of violence in the form of brawls and assaults. Only through an analysis of individual cases can the motivations and impulses that influenced a homicide's timing be made clear in any way. However, it is still instructive to examine macro-historical phenomena to trace broad behavioural patterns, such as distribution of weapons as means to commit homicide. The spread of weaponry in the homicides of 1680 is shown in Figure 3.26.

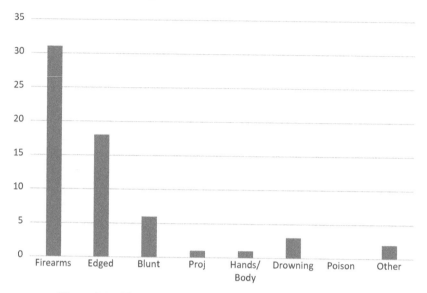

Figure 3.26 Weapons used in homicides, 1680.
Source: ASBo, Torrone, 7144–80

Figure 3.26 shows a strong preference for firearms among killers in 1680. By now, this is the expected distribution of weaponry in homicidal violence among Bolognese of both the *città* and the *contado*. Although edged weapons remain prominent in the sample of homicide cases, they still fall a distant second to firearms; this reinforces the proposition that the majority of homicides in 1660, committed with edged weapons, was a behavioural anomaly. Understanding fully who killers were, where they came from, and what their position in society was vis-à-vis their compatriots or superiors – in essence, the who, what, how, where and when of homicides – can help reveal the *why* of particular choices they made in the commission of those homicides.[91] For now, it suffices to observe the choices they did make, and conclude that firearms were the dominant mode of homicide throughout the majority of the seventeenth century.

Finally, as in the other years considered here, it is important to expose the relationships that obtained between killers and their victims. These relationships are shown in Figure 3.27, which presents a familiar portrait to the reader. As in all other years, the majority of homicides were committed by people who had an acquaintance, if not necessarily a friendship, with their victim. This included a shared hometown in which

[91] Monkkonen, "New Standards for Historical Homicide Research."

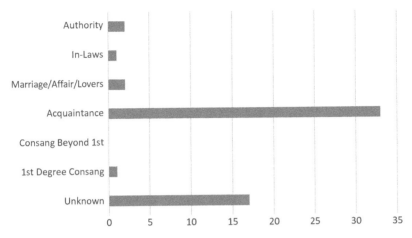

Figure 3.27 Homicidal relationships, 1680.
Source: ASBo, Torrone, 7144–80

they would cross paths frequently, friendship through social acquaintance, shared employment, or habitual rivalry and enmity. Although the category is large and encompasses a spectrum of emotional connections that range from long-term hatred to deep affection, the unifying factor of these homicides was that the killer and victim were known to each other, but not related by blood or marriage. In the intensely social world of seventeenth-century Northern Italy, these non-kin ties, and their strength, were closely connected to an individual's social status, and could draw that status up or down. Thus, this group of people was the most fertile territory for the dispute and establishment of status levels, a form of social competition that frequently led to violence and homicide. The relationships among killers and victims in 1680 is shown in Figure 3.27.

The one killing within the first degree of consanguinity was a case in which an older brother's bullying of his younger sibling went too far and thirteen-year-old Girolamo died, apparently from internal wounds sustained in a beating. In the two cases of marriage/affair/lovers, one woman was killed by her lover, and another young man by his lady love's male relatives after he had requested her hand in marriage post-defloration. Relatively stable patterns of kin-group killings couple to significant fluctuations in the acquaintance relationships, which accounts for the vast majority of spontaneous or planned male-on-male homicides. These homicides and similar assaults were the primary targets of governmental efforts to control and reduce violence among the population, as they were the most public, visible and numerous in the casebooks of the *Torrone*'s notaries. Thus, the efforts of social control were directed at and effective upon male-male social violence more than any other kind. The disruptions this process caused within the city's social structure also resulted in a temporary spike of authority-based homicides, alongside the waves of status violence that marked the resistance of elite and ordinary *bolognesi* to the state's efforts to achieve a monopoly on violence. The year 1690 continued this trend, with a lower incidence of homicide, lower rates of homicide, and a peaceful summer that flared up only in August and September.

In 1690, the city's population was approximately 64,000 and the contado's approximately 167,000.[92] In the decades on either side, the population was dropping in both the city and the *contado*, making 1690's population smaller than 1680's by about 4,000 people, and 1700's smaller still, by about 2,000. The *Torrone* accounted for 47 total homicides including accidents and infanticides. Removing those leaves a total of 43, a number well below that of 1680 and higher only than in 1610 and 1620, which, as already noted, encompassed a period of particularly harsh security action within the city that resulted in extremely low urban homicide rates. In 1690, urban homicides accounted for about one-sixth of the total count (7 out of 43); the remaining 36 took place in rural plains and mountain settlements. From this absolute count of homicidal incidents, we glean an urban homicide rate of 10.9 (less than half that of 1680), a rural rate of 21 (compared to 23.5 for 1680), and an aggregate rate of 18.6. As noted above, the annual rhythm of this year presents much differently than previous ones, more akin to the peaceful summer of 1680 but with a surge in violence in the late summer and early months of fall. The monthly passage of deadly violence is shown in Figure 3.28.

With a mere two and three homicides in June and July, respectively, 1690 had a much more peaceful summertime than the rest of the year. The homicides that did occur in these months were, as noted above, most likely to be affected by the changes to criminal law and centralization of court powers that constitute Spierenburg's modification of the civilizing process to pertain to violence.[93] The decline of violence that occurred in the seventeenth century's second half therefore affected particular types of homicide while leaving others relatively beyond the scope of government action; this phenomenon is well in line with the *longue durée* history of violence that has seen public, male-on-male

[92] Bellettini, La popolazione di Bologna, 25–29.
[93] Spierenburg, "Violence and the Civilizing Process: Does It Work?," 91–93; Blastenbrei, "Violence, Arms and Criminal Justice," 71.

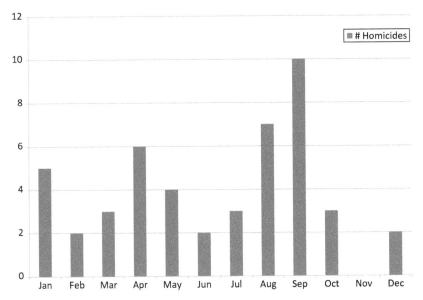

Figure 3.28 Homicides by month, 1690.
Source: ASBo, Torrone, 7344–65

violence shrink as a proportion of total homicides, to a level where it is negligible in most rural and urban areas in the West today. As levels of public, male-on-male violence have dropped, domestic homicides and familial homicides have remained at a relatively steady level, thus assuming an ever-larger proportion of total homicides committed.[94] This increasing proportion of familial and domestic violence is reflected in the relationships between killers and victims in 1690, in which the acquaintance category shrinks in comparison to the kinship, marriage and in-law categories. These relationships are shown in Figure 3.29.

Although the categories of first-degree consanguinity, consanguinity beyond the first degree, and relationships surrounding love, sex and family did not grow in absolute terms, they nevertheless constituted an increasing proportion of total incidences of homicide, at approximately 25% of all events (11 out of 43). This phenomenon may also be reflected in the distribution of weapons used to kill in this year. Although firearms remained the dominant mode of violence (25 out of 43, or 58%), they also constituted a smaller proportion than in 1670, 1680 or 1652. However, looking at the cases shows that most of the edged or blunt weapons

---

[94] Daly and Wilson, *Homicide*, 284–86.

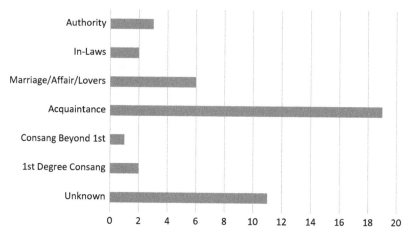

Figure 3.29 Homicidal relationships, 1690.
Source: ASBo, Torrone, 7344–65

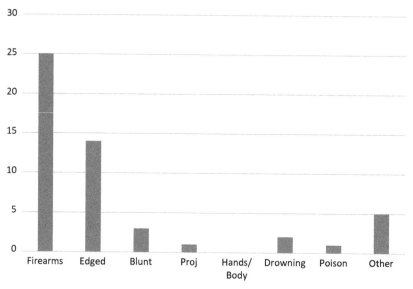

Figure 3.30 Weapons used in homicides, 1690.
Source: ASBo, Torrone, 7344–65

used were as likely to be trade tools used in arguments between artisans as they were to be domestic knives used in household arguments or family conflicts. The distribution of weapons in the homicides of 1690 is shown in Figure 3.30.

Firearms thus remained in all years sampled but 1610 and 1660 the primary method with which to kill, a fact that does not surprise given that the weapon's purpose is fatal violence. If this study encompassed non-fatal violence in its measure of the social structures and functions of violence, edged and blunted weapons would play a far larger role in this tale. This study now turns to the final year of the sample, 1700, before reviewing homicide rates across the century to adjudicate claims for a civilizing process in Bologna over the course of the seventeenth century.

1700: At Century's End

In 1700, the regular decline of homicide rates that commenced in 1670 continued, and homicide counts and rates were lower for the rural population than any other year in the sample. Urban homicide rates continued to outpace those of the century's early decades, when they reached an extreme low of 4.4 in 1620. Bellettini provides precise population figures in 1700, with an urban population of 63,346 and a rural population of 165,433. The total population of the Province of Bologna was 228,779.[95] Excluding two infanticides and four accidental drownings, the urban count for homicides was 10, the rural count was 21, and the total 31. These absolute numbers translate into homicide rates of 15.7 urban, 12.7 rural and an aggregate rate of 13.55. These rates thus bring us to the end of the statistical parabola that marks the passage of homicide in Bologna over the century. The monthly progress of homicides in 1700 was typical, with a spike in July and September that indicates the continuing role of "hot anger" in homicide tales, particularly those involving men drinking in taverns after long days in the fields or workshops. This monthly pattern is shown in Figure 3.31.

As Figure 3.31 demonstrates, the rhythm of homicides in 1700 is recognizable from analysis of earlier years in the century, despite a low overall count and low rates. As we have seen, Carnival disorder did not play an overly significant role in fatal violence throughout the century, and 1700 continues this trend of a peaceful winter and spring before homicides began to spike in July and then again in September. The homicides that occurred in the early months of the year all displayed characteristics of pre-meditated killings with a background story that involved both killer and victim, and usually a network of supporters and allies on each side. There was one exception to this, in the case of a young boy who in January was playing with his father's *schioppo*, an

[95] Bellettini, *La popolazione di Bologna*, 25–29.

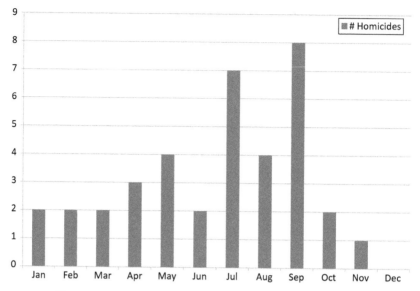

Figure 3.31 Homicides by month, 1700.
Source: ASBo, Torrone, 7515/2–7536/2

early shotgun, when it went off and killed his fifteen-year-old sister.[96] By April, this shifts to a pattern of male-male violence bred out of alcohol consumption, and to male conflict bred out of competition for the affection of women. In October and November, homicides continued to occur out of spontaneous conflicts, but these were bred by material incidents such as the theft of grapes during the *vendemmia*, the grape harvest.[97] With zero homicides in December, 1700 ended with a merciful whimper.

The use of weapons in 1700 continued the trend of 1680 and 1690, which saw the proportion of homicides committed with firearms drop, accounting for slightly less than 50% of the total homicide count (15 out of 31). The remaining homicides were committed with edged weapons or blunt force weapons such as heavy sticks and clubs, as well as with bare hands. Some weapons were not identified in the record and thus fall into the category "other." The distribution of weapons in homicide cases in 1700 is shown in Figure 3.32.

Although firearms accounted for a smaller proportion of homicides in 1700 than in 1632, 1652 or 1670, they remained the most common tool

[96] ASBo, *Torrone*, 7516/2, fasc. 25.   [97] ASBo, *Torrone*, 7528/2, fasc. 6.

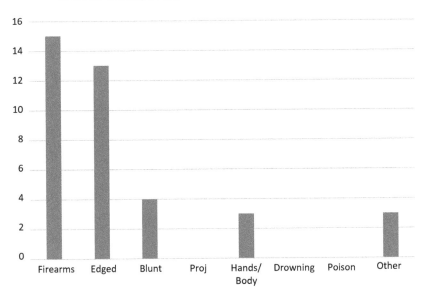

Figure 3.32 Weapons used in homicides, 1700.
Source: ASBo, Torrone, 7515/2–7536/2

for killing. There is an instrumental logic here, in which killers used the weapons most likely to cause fatal damage without risking great damage to themselves; the range and brutality of the arquebus, although extremely inaccurate beyond a short distance, make the firearm the best choice for those wishing to kill an enemy. Thus firearms killings tended toward the premeditated murder with malice aforethought, particularly as the overall proportion of firearms killings was reduced. While extremely prevalent as spontaneous weapons of murder in more violent periods, guns became more likely to be used in the prosecution of long-standing conflicts than in the sudden rise to violence that characterized much male-male homicide. When violence flared up out of hand, killers reached for their knives, their tools or other handy implements of death.

Who were they killing? As could be predicted, more than half of the killings occurred in the "acquaintance" or "unknown" category, which as noted above did not exclude the existence of a relationship, but reflects its ambiguity. The relationships between killers and victims are shown in Figure 3.33.

Here again, we see a typical configuration of homicidal relationships, with most between two men who had seen each other around town. Only two homicides occurred within families, and another three within relationships of romance, love and jealousy. Three homicides

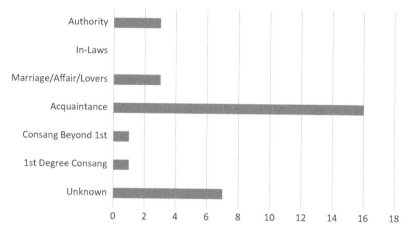

Figure 3.33 Homicidal relationships, 1700.
Source: ASBo, Torrone, 7515/2–7536/2

within relationships of authority speak to the different configurations of allegiance and authority in early modern Italy, as they involved the brutal murder of a priest by his servant, the killing of a butler by a supplicant at the door, and the shooting of a drunk in a tavern by a *sbirro*.[98] As we have seen throughout this sample, regardless of rates or absolute numbers, the majority of homicides tended to occur between men who knew each other at least by face, and were accustomed to a male culture that saw violence as legitimate recourse to challenges of status or position. Although homicide rates declined over the latter half of the seventeenth century, this characteristic remained unchanged. Efforts to curb this sort of violence reduced its proportion, but it remains the dominant form of homicide throughout the sample.

A Century Retrospective: The Parabola of Violence

This chapter has examined the incidence of homicide in eleven years that spanned the seventeenth century, from 1600 to 1700 inclusive, as made visible through the records of the *Torrone*, Bologna's centralized and monopolistic criminal court. In individual analyses of each year, it has examined the objective level of homicidal violence and transformed that into a homicide rate measured as the number of homicides per 100,000 members of the population. Further, it has broken down the homicide

---

[98] ASB, ASBo, *Torrone*, 7515/2, fasc. 12, 7515/2, fasc. 9, 7536, fasc. 31.

cases from each year in an analysis of annual patterns, determining that the hot summer months of July and August were, almost without exception, a singularly violent time of any year, while the early and late months tended to be more peaceful. Homicides that did occur in the colder months tended to involve people more closely known to each other than those from the summertime, and more likely occurred in a private space such as a home than in a public forum such as a churchyard or a *piazza*. This annual rhythm of homicides fluctuated lightly between years but still held true as a general pattern; there were more homicides in the summer months throughout the seventeenth century than in the early or late months of the year, and summer homicides likely involved young men in social competition, either for material resources in agricultural settings or for the affection of women in the many taverns and squares that dotted both the urban and rural landscape. The aggregate monthly homicides across the seventeenth century are shown in Figure 3.34, and demonstrate a clear *longue durée* pattern of annual killings. This pattern is shown again in Figure 3.35, which shows the average number of homicides per month across the century.

This chapter also analyzed the means that killers used to commit homicide, and found a strong prevalence of firearms in all but two years

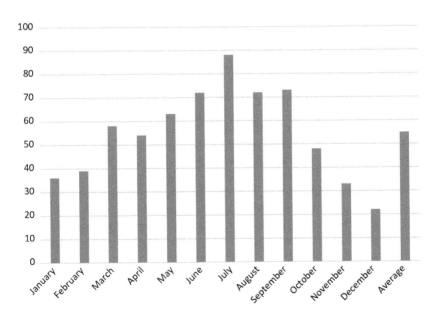

Figure 3.34 Number of homicides per month, 1600–1700.
Source: ASBo, Torrone, 3171–7532

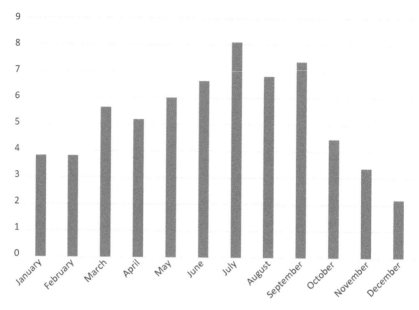

Figure 3.35 Average monthly homicides, 1600–1700.
Source: ASBo, Torrone, 3171–7532

throughout the century. In those years (1610 and 1660) where firearms did not account for the majority of homicides, they came close, falling just below the other primary category of weapons used to kill – edged and bladed weapons such as the ubiquitous dagger that almost all Bolognese men carried with them as a tool, an eating utensil and a means of self-defence and attack. The dominance of firearms as the preferred means to kill across the century is shown in Figure 3.36, which records the use of weapons across all cases throughout the century. As this chart makes extremely clear, almost all incidents of homicide throughout the eleven-year sample were committed with either a firearm or a blade. There was a strong instrumental logic here: people who killed tended to possess the means to do so, either by forethought or circumstance; the best tools for killing were the *archibugio*, with its range and utter destructiveness, and the *pugnale* (blade, of whichever sort), with its penetrative ability and infliction of serious wounds. Other categories of weaponry, particularly the projectile category (e.g., thrown rocks) and the blunt category (essentially clubs and sticks), account for very few of the total homicides, but are much more prevalent in the records of minor assaults and disturbances that pack the first 300 folios of each of the *Torrone*'s books. Poison, traditionally seen as the quintessential weapon of female killers, appeared

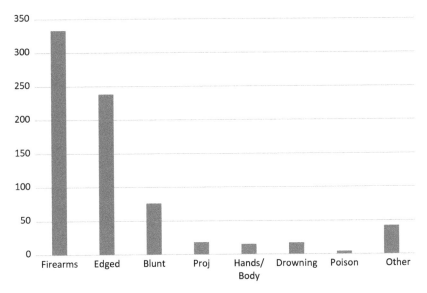

Figure 3.36 Weapons used in homicides, 1600–1700.
Source: ASBo, Torrone, 3171–7532

extremely rarely and was not in fact the dominant means of killing used by female killers, who employed more clubs and rocks than they did poison. Intentional drownings were similarly rare but not unheard of. All these patterns are shown in Figure 3.36.

We thus know the "when" and the "how" of homicides in Bologna throughout the seventeenth century. The "who," at least in terms of the killers, was more complicated, as the records did not reliably reveal the ages of killers; we do know, however, that the average victim of homicide in the seventeenth century was a male aged thirty-one, and was equally likely to be a field labourer as he was a sword-wielding retainer of a noble house. Of the eighty-two victims whose marital status was made clear, sixty-one were married. This sample of 12.3% is not, however, large enough to make claims about the broader social position of the remaining 87.7% of victims, nor is there a reliable sample indicating the marital statuses of killers.

Fortunately, we have better information for the prosopography of victims and killers than we do their marital status. Of the victims, 315 were identified by their employment or habitual occupation. The largest single bloc of victims was young men employed by households of varying rank – fitting, given what we know of noble and youth violence in this period. These were identified as *garzone* (18), *servitore* (18), *socio* (17) and *famigliare* (7), for a total of 60. The second largest bloc of victims (53) was the amorphous "*contadino*," a term that refers to the general labour required of a rural existence in an extremely agriculturally intensive area. *Lavoratori* (labourers, 9) could also be lumped in with the *contadini*, making the number of victims in these two blocs approximately equal. These two groups, the young, pampered men of wealthy households, and the labouring poor of both town and country, were thus killed in almost exactly equal numbers in the sample of 315, with each accounting for about 20% of the total. This class dispersion indicates that violence was by no means a noble prerogative, although some of the *contadini* were killed by nobility. It is also true that some of the *socii* and *famigliari* were killed by artisans and labourers. The sting of violence was felt by all classes; indeed, analysis of the remaining, more specified blocs of victims by occupation (e.g., *uccellatore*, a bird-hunter, who could equally be placed in the *contadino* category, or *dottor di leggi*, a high-ranking official from a wealthy background) reveals that labourers, artisans, professionals and nobility all suffered violence in their lives.

For the killers, we have prosopographical information for 367 individuals, out of the 1,219 total killers indicted across the century. The occupations of the killers also fell primarily into two blocs. First, those who killed professionally, that is, police and soldiers, together accounted for 54 killers. Just like the victims, the second largest group of killers was the amorphous category of *contadino*, which included 47 killers without delving into those who were identified as *contadini* who performed specific work – farmers (7), chicken farmers (1), millers (8), gardeners (2) or pig-castrators (1). The non-specific *lavoratore* accounted for another 5 killers. Beyond soldiers, police and *contadini*, the servants of respectable households played a significant role in homicidal violence, with *socii* accounting for 40 killers, *garzone* another 20, and *famigliari*, 13. These were all occupations in which the capacity for violence was a boon rather than an impediment, so it is not surprising to see high numbers of killers who were soldiers and police (the hired goons of noble and wealthy households) or rural labourers – who lived outside the safety of city walls, often near borderlands prowled by bandits and vagabonds. The urban, or at least town-based, professions that played significant roles in homicidal violence were also those where the capacity for violence was a useful characteristic. Barber-surgeons, with 9 killers, were among the most prominent of these urban *botteghiere*, along with blacksmiths (5), bakers (5) and spinners (4). Bricklayers featured as killers in 7 cases. Contrary to reputation, students did not play a more significant role in homicidal violence than any of these other groups; there were 5 student killers over the century. Other killers fell into a variety of professions and occupations, such as smugglers (4) and butchers (8). Banditry remained a problem throughout the century, and bandits who killed outnumbered bandits who were killed, with 10 and 8, respectively.

We have even better records of the origins of victims and killers than we do their occupations. Of the 658 victims in the eleven-year sample, the records make clear the hometown of 502. It is important to note here that notaries recorded not the victim or killer's current place of residence, but the town in which they were born. Often this coincided with the current residence, particularly in the cases of young men killed or killing in rural villages, but there was significant population mobility in the area, as the city's size relative to its hinterland fluctuated across the century.

The origin data for victims show that approximately 25% (127 out of 502) of the sample in which their origin is clear self-identified or were identified as being *cittadini*, city-dwellers of Bologna. Since approximately one-third of homicides occurred in the city (187), and since the origin sample was of 76% of the total homicides, slightly less than one-third of all victims had clear origins in the city; some of these victims died in the country, and some of their rural co-citizens died in town. Of the 502 victims, the remaining 375 came from the densely populated hinterland, with its myriad villages, settlements and semi-fortified towns, as well as from beyond the borders of the Bolognese *legato*.

There were fewer foreign victims than there were foreign killers: a total of 5 Modenese, 7 Florentines, 1 Milanese, 1 Frenchman, 2 *Piacentini*, 1 Piedmontese, 1 from each of Ravenna and Rome, 2 Spaniards, 2 Germans, 1 Veronese and 3 Venetians. These victims were frequently killed in the course of the business that had brought them to Bologna, whether as students, traders or soldiers. Taverns were the frequent locales of their deaths. The 348 remaining victims were scattered throughout the Bolognese countryside, with concentrations in the semi-fortified towns of Castel Bolognese (7), Castel San Pietro (6) and Castello degli Albi (4), and in larger plains settlements such as Gaggio di Piano (5), close to the Modenese border, and Cento (4), north of Bologna. Six victims came from the mountain settlement of Luminasio, and four from that of Verignana di Sopra, to the south and south-east of Bologna, respectively. Thus, some 30% of victims originated from the city of Bologna itself; about 4% (27 out of 658) were from outside the borders of the *legato*, and the remaining 66% had origins within the province's many scattered towns and villages, with concentrations in the high mountain passes to the south, the borderlands west and north of the city, and the fortified towns that served as barracks and local centres of authority.

For the origins of killers, we have data pertaining to 743 individuals, constituting 61% of the total 1,219 slayers. One hundred and eighty-four or 24.76%, originated in Bologna, almost precisely in line with the number of killings that occurred in Bologna (187) but constituting a smaller proportion of total killers; more killers came into the city to kill than left it to do so. There were more foreign killers than foreign victims in terms of absolute numbers, and a larger proportion too, at 6.5% of the sample whose origins were known. There were 1 each from Castro and Ferrara, 14 from Florence, 2 from France, 4 from Milan, 15 from Modena (often bandits involved in cross-border violence), 3 from Parma, 1 from Ravenna, 2 from the *Romagna*, 1 from Treviso, 3 from Venice, 1 from Verona and 1 from Volterra. These 49 killers all found themselves in the *legato* of Bologna, having immigrated or travelled there, when they were indicted for a homicide committed within its borders. The remaining 507 killers came from a similar spread of borderlands, mountain settlements and plain towns as did the victims: concentrations in Mogne (14), in the far southern reaches of the mountain passes; Crevalcore (8), northwest of Bologna and close to the Modenese border; and Budrio (13) and Medicina (9), both just east of the city, were the most visible markers of this pattern. Many of these killers committed their deeds in their hometowns, which resulted in high homicide counts for the mountain towns, border settlements and large agro-towns in Bologna's plain.

Armed with this information, we can assess the incidence of homicide in Bologna throughout the seventeenth century, tracing the rise and fall of homicide rates. Figure 3.37 traces the overall pattern of homicide rates, from early-century urban lows through a rapid rise in the mid-century, and finally through a diminution, particularly of rural rates, during the final forty years of the century. What stands out from this chart are the extremely low urban rates of 1610 and 1620, as compared to the years on either side; the extremely high urban rate of 1660, which surpasses all other measures across the century; and the steady fall of both rural and urban rates following the bloodbath of 1660.

Homicides occurred in all corners of the *legato*, as Map 3.1 demonstrates. The largest single proportion of homicides (182 out of 658, or 27%) occurred in the urban core, where about 25% of the total population dwelt. Homicides were roughly proportional to population, and their incidence and investigation traced the major highways of the Via Emilia and the Tuscan passes to the south. Larger population centres, such as Crevalcore to the north-west and Camugnano in the southwestern pass, saw similar counts of indicted homicides, while the fortified towns of Castel Bolognese, Castel San Pietro and Imola featured the

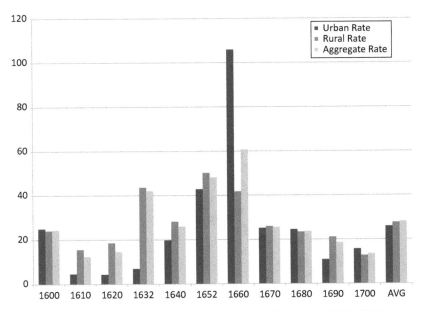

Figure 3.37 Homicide rates in the *legato* of Bologna, 1600–1700.
Source: ASBo, Torrone, 3171–7532

highest incidence of extra-urban homicide. Map 3.1 demonstrates very clearly that homicides in Bologna, if they followed any geospatial pattern, were ubiquitous in Bolognese communities across the state, affecting communities large and small and tracing roughly the lines of commerce and pilgrimage that made Bologna a crossroads for many Europeans.

Thus we have the long view of indicted homicide rates in Bologna for eleven years across the seventeenth century. In 1600, homicide rates were in the mid-twenties,[99] and there was near parity between urban and rural contexts; they then dropped sharply, particularly in the city, to among the lowest rates across the century, and the lowest for the urban milieu. In both 1610 and 1620, homicide rates in the city stood between 4 and 6 per 100,000 inhabitants, while in the countryside, with rates of 15.5 and 18.6, homicide was at its most uncommon for all years except 1700. In 1632, following the devastating plague of 1630, homicide rates in the city remained low, while in the rural murders jumped to 43.6 per

---

[99] This figure is comparable to Daly and Wilson's data for London c. 1250 and Spierenburg's for Amsterdam 1560–90. Daly and Wilson, *Homicide*, 276; Spierenburg, *A History of Murder*, 70.

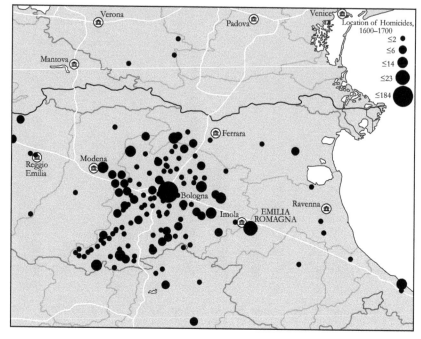

Map 3.1 Homicides by proportional dot in the *legato* of Bologna and surroundings, 1600–1700.
Map by author and Cox Cartographic Ltd.

100,000, almost exactly similar to the data Spierenburg provides for Rome in the period 1560–85.[100] Much of the violence in 1632 can be attributed to post-plague social restructuring and uncertainty regarding property rights and security in newly vacated lands, a phenomenon explored in Chapter 5. In 1640, rural rates corrected to more modest high-twenties, while the urban rate began to climb from its early-century lows. Both rates rose to above forty in 1652, which was the zenith of rural homicide rates through the century, at 50.15.

As mentioned above, the 1650s were a period of tension among oligarchic and republican factions of the nobility. This period saw these factions turn their collective ire against the officers of the *Torrone*, which sought to curtail both feudal and republican privileges to justice and violence.[101] This conflict exploded in 1660, which witnessed a wave of

[100] Spierenburg, *A History of Murder*, 70.
[101] Angelozzi and Casanova, *La nobiltà disciplinata*, 180–223.

killings that swept both the city and the countryside, bringing the urban homicide rate to 105.9.[102] The rural rate in this year dropped, however, to 41.7, making the aggregate rate for the province 60.75, still well above any other known homicide figures for the period, and indeed for the previous century. In 1670, the urban rate dropped more than fourfold to 25.2, while the rural rate fell in line with it at 26; this situation remained through 1680, when the urban and rural rates were 24.6 and 23.5, respectively. Given that the rural rate dropped to only 21 in 1690, that year's rapid drop in the urban rate of 1690, to 10.9, may reflect the final fruits of the long campaign to pacify the urban nobility. Finally, in 1700, the rural rate dropped below the urban rate to levels more in line with Northern European rates of the period – 12.7 and 15.7, respectively. Comparable Italian figures do not exist.

Thus we see parabola of homicidal violence in Bologna, Italy, as it crested and fell across the seventeenth century in an unpredicted pattern. This unexpected rise and fall of homicidal violence points the way to further analysis and indicates the phenomena that need to be explored in order to better understand the social logic behind trends in violence. What emerges from this analysis is an endemically poor and unstable society, in rapid transition between traditionally agrarian and urban-dominated modes of governance, economy and sociality. In that society, violence was not an aberrant, disease-like aspect of the human condition, nor was it necessarily seen as such by the officers of the judiciary tasked with its control, censure and, occasionally, punishment. For that reason, early modern killers often deserve the sympathy of the historian as much as do victims, for the structures of life and sociality in Bologna in the seventeenth century made violence and competition equally valuable tools of advancement as peacemaking; indeed, the two went hand-in-hand. Peace could not be made without a precondition of violence, and violence would erupt when standing peace was strained by the exigencies of social and emotional life.

It is significant that this rise in violence occurred as Bologna and the Bolognese judiciary were undergoing precisely the process of centralization and rationalization that Spierenburg and others assert as causative to the civilizing process and the long decline of violence.[103] The *Torrone*'s legislation and increased intrusion into public behaviour

---

[102] For comparison, the highest documented intentional homicide rates available for the twenty-first century are, respectively, 92, 91 and 84 per 100,000 in Honduras from 2011 to 2013. Intentional Homicide Rates, UN Office on Drugs and Crime's International Homicide Statistics Database. World Bank dataset available at http://data.worldbank.org/indicator/VC.IHR.PSRC.P5, accessed January 31, 2016.

[103] Spierenburg, "Violence and the Civilizing Process," pp. 97–99.

and particularly noble factionalism were not embraced by local elites. Rather, both nobility and commoners committed more, and more political, homicides than in the early seventeenth century, as social and institutional trust decayed rather than grew with the trappings of civilization. The sampled years from 1640 to 1660 witnessed the highest homicide numbers and rates of the century, making problematic the widely accepted conclusion of the civilizing process – that the latter half of the seventeenth century continued, indeed accelerated, a decline of violence that had been more or less consistent in a downward trend since the late middle ages.[104]

[104] Spierenburg, *A History of Murder*, p. 71; Muchembled, *Un histoire de la violence*, 66–69.

4   Gender and Homicide in Early Modern Bologna

Introduction

The large majority of homicides in seventeenth-century Bologna were committed by men, against men, and in public areas if not in broad daylight. The men of Bologna killed in a wide variety of spaces in and around the city, including churches, taverns, markets, roads, riversides, workshops and public squares. However, a significant number of homicides in seventeenth-century Bologna occurred inside homes, either between family members or in conflicts that engaged the domestic sphere. Ninety-two of the total 701 (13.1%) deaths investigated by the *Torrone*'s notaries in this sample involved relatives by blood or marriage; when infanticides and accidental deaths are removed from the tally, that figure becomes 81 out of 658 (12.3%). Homicides that occurred between two relatives either within the home or otherwise were not the norm in Bolognese violence, but they were not uncommon either. Domestic violence remained a serious threat to Bolognese women in all of the sampled years. Twenty-one women in the sample of 658 confirmed homicides (~3.5%) died at their husband's or lover's hands. Four more were killed by their in-laws, either the brother or son of a husband/lover. The city's prostitutes, or *meretrici*, were also consistently vulnerable to violence from clients, public officials and other prostitutes; the violence directed against prostitutes often occurred in their homes where they practiced their trade. Early modern Italy's continued subjugation of women through increasingly tight systems of enclosure and discipline did not protect women from homicide, nor did it afford them a cultural role that permitted significant acceptable violence of their own.

Moreover, Bolognese women committed homicide in a variety of contexts. Resource pressures in the countryside pushed some women toward violent defence of their property and foodstuffs. Women killed in more prosaic situations as well. Throughout the sample of homicides, women were investigated and prosecuted for homicides in ways that reflect medieval tropes about women and women's criminality, but at

141

the same time belied those very notions in their patterns of interrogation and punishment. Although the idea of women committing murder may have seemed particularly heinous, and stereotypes about poisoning wives and child-killing unwed mothers remained powerful psychological forces, the reality of women's homicide in Bologna showed that those tropes applied equally to men as to women. Women were, however, far more likely to face significant judicial penalty when they did poison a husband or commit a desperate act of infanticide than were men.

This chapter, then, explores the violence committed against women by their husbands and lovers, and by women against their rivals, husbands and children. It argues that the legatine government and the judges of the *Torrone*, while pursuing peace and order in public spaces, were not overly concerned by domestic violence; homicides of women by husbands and lovers were generally adjudicated lightly, even when the murder came at the end of a long period of known abuse. Women, if they wished to exercise agency in circumstances of marital violence, needed to cultivate and make use of local networks of community support, often from other women and their sympathetic husbands. In domestic homicide trials, local women often provided the necessary contextual information for the notary's investigation, and they often appeared as first intervenors or witnesses, who attempted to stop the violence by banging on the door or alerting other neighbours and the authorities.[1] Further, this chapter argues that the prosecution of women's homicide reflects these same patriarchal attitudes toward marriage: women who broke the bounds of marriage by killing their husbands or their children were a fearsome figure for Bolognese authorities to confront. In neither of these perspectives did the *Torrone*'s prosecution of homicide reflect the full involvement of women in violence, either as victims or as perpetrators. To more fully understand gendered violence, historians must look past homicide records to women's ordinary, day-to-day conflicts and the violence that accompanied them.

Gender, Honour and Violence

Over the past forty years, the relationship between Mediterranean cultures of honour and the lived experiences of Italian women have come to the fore in studies of the early modern period. These studies, such as those by Elizabeth Cohen, have demonstrated the centrality of female honour to gendered expectations of behaviour and to the norms, codified

---

[1] This phenomenon confirms that noted by Joanne Ferraro in her early work on domestic violence in Venice. Ferraro, "The Power to Decide."

or not, of Italian society.[2] Indeed, honour bears more heavily on the lives of women than of men, being more frequently cited by witnesses, accused killers and judicial officials in criminal processes involving women than those relating solely to men. To understand how gender and violence interacted in the early modern period, concepts of female honour are a useful and necessary starting point.

Much of the literature has located early modern women's honour in their bodies, and in the maintenance of a pristine sexual reputation, though this centring has also been contested using different kinds of prescriptive and descriptive sources.[3] Sexual propriety and proper relationships with men were indeed fundamental to women's standing in their communities in and around Bologna, which shared many cultural and legal approaches to women's public status with other early modern regimes both in Italy and elsewhere. Indeed, in the Roman context as in the Bolognese, homicidal violence could be excused or largely overlooked on the grounds that its victims, both male and female, had transgressed the bounds of honour in gender relations, as Thomas V. Cohen has recently shown in his exploration of a "daughter killing" near Rome.[4] In Adriano Prosperi's *Dare l'anima*, he used an infanticide trial from Bologna in 1709 to explore the many threads that linked the honour of single women, their position in Italian society, and the expected roles of maiden- and motherhood that bore on their treatment by the judiciary.[5] When women appeared in Italian courts as either

---

[2] Elizabeth S. Cohen, "Open City: An Introduction to Gender in Early Modern Rome," *I Tatti Studies in the Italian Renaissance* 17, no. 1 (2014): 35–54; Elizabeth S. Cohen, "Honor and Gender in the Streets of Early Modern Rome," *The Journal of Interdisciplinary History* 22, no. 4 (April 1, 1992): 597–625; Elizabeth S. Cohen, "The Trials of Artemisia Gentileschi: A Rape as History," *The Sixteenth Century Journal* 31, no. 1 (2000): 47–75.

[3] Elizabeth Ewan, "Disorderly Damsels? Women and Interpersonal Violence in Pre-Reformation Scotland," *The Scottish Historical Review* 89, no. 228 (2010): 153–71; Sally Parkin, "Witchcraft, Women's Honour and Customary Law in Early Modern Wales," *Social History* 31, no. 3 (2006): 295–318; Valentina Cesco, "Female Abduction, Family Honor, and Women's Agency in Early Modern Venetian Istria," *Journal of Early Modern History* 15, no. 4 (2011): 349–66; Monique O'Connell, "The Sexual Politics of Empire: Civic Honor and Official Crime Outside Renaissance Venice," *Journal of Early Modern History* 15, no. 4 (2011): 331–48; Scott K. Taylor, "Women, Honor, and Violence in a Castilian Town, 1600–1650," *The Sixteenth Century Journal* 35, no. 4 (December 1, 2004): 1079–97.

[4] Thomas V. Cohen, "A Daughter Killing Digested, and Accepted, in a Village of Rome, 1563–66," in Dean and Lowe, eds., *Murder in Renaissance Italy*, 62–82.

[5] Adriano Prosperi, *Dare l'anima: storia di un infanticidio* (Turin: G. Einaudi, 2005); this work was recently translated to English as Adriano Prosperi, *Infanticide, Secular Justice, and Religious Debate in Early Modern Europe*, Europa Sacra, volume 10 (Turnhout: Brepols, 2016).

victims or suspects of fatal violence, it was very often their reputation on trial as much as their actions.

Early modern Italy developed a significant institutional apparatus to police and control those reputations. Both elite and ordinary young, unmarried women were "enclosed" behind the walls of institutions, either religious institutions such as convents, which grew significantly in size over the sixteenth and seventeenth century, or in charitable institutions such as workhouses operating under the authority of elite-controlled municipal governing boards.[6] These walled communities sought to limit the exposure of unwed women to the men who would sully their honour and their reputations, both to protect the dowry-bound fortunes of elites and to prevent the birth of children by the unwed poor, whose labour was directed instead to local textile industries, domestic service farmed out from within the poor-houses, and the proper worship of God.

Authorities greatly feared pregnancy outside of wedlock and its potential consequences; so too did young women, and as Prosperi shows through a single case, they might turn to desperate measures to prevent the permanent reputational stain that the birth of an illegitimate child would impart. Infanticide loomed heavily in the minds of judicial authorities. In the sixteenth and seventeenth centuries laws were established around the act, moving it from sin to crime, and further laws were put in place to prevent it. Significant among these laws was a set of regulations, common across the peninsula, that required communities to report all pregnancies that occurred out of wedlock to local parish authorities; Prosperi argues that these laws and the accompanying harsh punishments for failure to report and for the new crime of infanticide were designed to "control sexual behaviour."[7] Whether these laws proved efficacious in reducing both unwed pregnancies and infanticides is difficult to judge, since the "black figure" of unknown and undetected pregnancies is potentially very large.

That the thrust of these laws surrounding young women, marriage and childbirth was directed at the women themselves rather than at men tells us something of the judicial priorities of early modern Italy. Male honour included the capacities for both violence and casual sexuality; for women, contrastingly, honour meant both sexual and physical

---

[6] Sharon T. Strocchia, *Nuns and Nunneries in Renaissance Florence* (Baltimore, MD: Johns Hopkins University Press, 2009); Nicholas Terpstra, *Cultures of Charity: Women, Politics, and the Reform of Poor Relief in Renaissance Italy* (Cambridge, MA: Harvard University Press, 2013).

[7] Prosperi, *Infanticide, Secular Justice, and Religious Debate in Early Modern Europe*, 63.

abstinence. The women who appeared as killers and victims in Bolognese homicide trials were often depicted as having violated these requirements. The treatment of their cases by the *Torrone* reflected the prevailing gender biases, focusing judicial attention on the misbehaviour of female victims or the monstrosity of female killers. One cannot understand the appearance of women in Italian homicide records, in terms of both its paucity and the frequent casual treatment of female victims, without understanding this. The links between honour, gender and violence played heavily into the record of homicides in early modern Bologna pertaining to women.

Homicides of Women

Frequent domestic violence was an undeniable aspect of early modern Italian society.[8] Bologna's society modelled an Abrahamic patriarchy, whereby a husband's authority over his wife and children included the right to beat them. There were formal and informal limits to this authority; killing one's wife would incur a legal process, if not a penalty, and communities censured and shamed those deemed to have crossed the boundaries of proper husbandly rule.[9] As noted above, the sample of uxoricides is limited to twenty-one trials. But from this small sample size we can glean some of the significant characteristics of uxoricide and its prosecution by the *Torrone* in early modern Bologna.

Bolognese uxoricide revolved around a constellation of jealousies and wounded emotions. A typical tale involved a husband who was absent either for work or because of banishment, and a wife who, in his absence, took up a lover. Upon the husband's return, the lover was discovered, and the enraged husband killed his wife and possibly the lover.[10] When no lover materialized to confirm a husband's suspicions of infidelity, even the suspicion led some men to kill their wives, as when Pellegrino Morelli murdered his father Filippo's second wife after they accused her of a previous life as a *meretrice*.[11] Tellingly, the *Torrone*'s notary insisted that

---

[8] Cavina, *Nozze di sangue*.
[9] Often communities entrusted their young men with this task. Cf. Ottavia Niccoli, *Storie di ogni giorno in una città del seicento* (Rome: GLF editori Laterza, 2000); Natalie Zemon Davis et al., *Ritual and Violence*, vol. 7, Past and Present Supplements (Oxford University Press, 2012).
[10] E.g., ASBo, *Torrone*, 5867, f. 303r, 1632. An inversion of this trope occurred in 1700 when Pasqua's lover, hearing that her husband was returning to Bologna and that she wished to end their love affair, killed her in anger. ASBo, *Torrone*, 7524/2, fasc. 9, 1700.
[11] ASBo, *Torrone*, 3232, f. 223r, 1600. A similar case occurred in 1632, *Torrone*, 5921, *in fine*.

Filippo pay a security of 400 scudi to ensure that he would not take out his rage and grief against his daughters. Again in 1600, a man named Michele di Michele accused his wife Francesca of giving him syphilis and killed her.[12] Pregnant women and new mothers seem to have been particularly vulnerable to marital violence: Catherina Scarlatti was killed by her husband two months after the birth of their child, and Cecilia Mazzoni was killed while three months' pregnant.[13] However, the majority of homicides of women by their husbands involved jealousy or suspected sexual impropriety.

These killings often concluded violent marriages. Giovanni, the man absolved of poisoning his pregnant wife, was identified by witnesses as a habitual wife abuser, accustomed to injuring her in both words and deeds.[14] In 1600, a man named Battista shot his wife Giuditta in the course of what was, by all witness accounts, a two-sided argument between husband and wife.[15] In 1660, a man named Pietro shot his wife during an argument over whether he would permit her to move into her parents' home, possibly in an attempt to escape a violent marriage.[16] Stressors that obviously had borne on a marriage for some time resulted in homicide: in 1660, sixty-year-old Giacomo Caldani killed his wife Lucretia during another argument over their son, whom Giacomo accused of being lazy and upon whom Lucretia doted.[17] Husbands killed their wives in Bologna in pursuit of jealous rage, but they also did so in the course of more prosaic arguments.

Women who died at the hands of their husbands accounted for 21 of 52 (40%) total female victims in the sampled years of homicide trials. A smaller number of fiancées and girlfriends suffered similar fates, though it is often hard to precisely characterize these relationships. The second large category of women targeted for homicide by Bolognese men was the city's sex workers, the *meretrici* who registered their occupations with the city's *Ufficio delle Bollette* and who congregated in large numbers in the neighbourhoods of Cento Trecento and *San* Mammolo.[18] These killings could be predatory: Francesca Belletta was found dead at age thirty in 1670, left beneath a portico on Via Cento Trecento after an

---

[12] ASBo, *Torrone*, 3251, f. 128r.

[13] ASBo, *Torrone*, 5867, f. 303r, 1632; 5634, *in fine*. The husband of Camilla Solomei was absolved of his wife's death by suspected poisoning. *Torrone*, 3206, f. 199r, 1600.

[14] ASBo, *Torrone*, 3206, f. 199r, 1600.   [15] ASBo, *Torrone*, 3237, f. 295r, 1600.

[16] ASBo, *Torrone*, 6776, *in fine*, 1660.   [17] ASBo, *Torrone*, 6789, *in fine*, 1660.

[18] For more on the regulation of prostitution in early modern Italy, cf. Vanessa Gillian McCarthy, "Prostitution, Community, and Civic Regulation in Early Modern Bologna" (PhD thesis, University of Toronto, 2015).

apparent assault and murder.[19] Leonora Galuzzi was murdered by her client Giacopo after refusing to leave the city walls with him to seek out a "friend" who wanted to meet her.[20] Other killings of sex workers occurred during what look like domestic disputes, as when Domenico Maria Puntani stabbed Santa "La Santavia" Mattioli out of possessive jealousy.[21] The confluence of sex work and marriage could be fatal for Bolognese women, as demonstrated by those women who were killed after their husbands accused them of prostitution.

Homicides against women in early modern Bologna revolved primarily around sex and romance: either a husband's jealousy over his wife's perceived sexual infidelities or a lover's unwillingness to accept that his relationship with a prostitute was not mutually emotional. These men killed their wives or *meretrici* because they felt aggrieved at their inability to properly enforce the hierarchies of man and woman that undergirded early modern marital relations. Male dominance was a socially accepted aspect of love and marriage in the early modern period, and homicides occurred within the romantic context when that dominance was insufficient or was credibly challenged.

Homicides by Women

In the records of non-fatal crimes, women appear frequently in the *Torrone* as instigators and perpetrators of minor assaults, scuffles and neighbourhood disturbances, and more often as witnesses, aggravators or intervenors to the violence of their husbands, sons, brothers and neighbours. In homicide trials, women were most frequently witnesses: particularly in rural areas where the *Torrone* notaries faced tightly knit, distrustful communities, women often provided the first glimpses into the history of an argument that preceded a murder.[22] As recent work has shown, early modern Italian women played important roles as experts and other participants in judicial processes; Bolognese authorities asked women for their opinions on autopsies and intervened in domestic abuse situations when asked to by neighbourhood women.[23] The legal

---

[19] ASBo, *Torrone*, 6943, fasc. 17, 1670.   [20] ASBo, *Torrone*, 6808, *in fine*, 1660.

[21] ASBo, *Torrone*, 6787, fasc. 13, 1660.

[22] For example, ASBo *Torrone*, 7349, fasc. 19, f. 306r–310v, testimony of Magdalena Roliata on the killing of her son in the village of Mogne, 1632.

[23] ASBo, *Torrone*, 4235, f. 301r, 1610, request for intervention against a violent husband by neighbours; 5904, f. 387r, 1632, trial for poisoning of Valeria *Venetiana*. On the prominent and hidden roles of women in Italian courts, cf. Joanne M. Ferraro, "The Power to Decide: Battered Wives in Early Modern Venice," *Renaissance Quarterly* 48, no. 3 (October 1, 1995): 492–512, doi:10.2307/2862872; Joanne Marie Ferraro, *Marriage Wars in Late Renaissance Venice* (New York: Oxford University Press, 2001);

anthropology of early modern Italy now accepts that women's agency in judicial processes was very real, both shaped by and challenging societal expectations and gendered behavioural norms.[24] These norms acted upon homicide trials as well. The *Torrone*'s prosecution of domestic and female homicides placed women in very clearly defined roles.

Prosecutions of women for homicide were extremely rare, accounting for nineteen trials in my 701-trial sample, or 2.5%; prosecutions for homicide of women and girls, conversely, account for sixty-four trials, or approximately 9%. The low numbers of trials against female killers probably reflects a generally low incidence of fatal violence by women, but should not be taken as the total measure of women's participation in individual, family and community conflicts and struggles. The *Torrone* thus took it for granted that female killers were an aberration when prosecuting women, particularly prostitutes and other women on society's margins, for a wide variety of petty nuisances, crimes, aggravations and assaults. The nineteen women prosecuted for homicide were mostly married and spanned the economic spectrum from peasants to urban palace servants and the wives of artisans. No noble women in my sample were accused of killing, though three female killers were the wives of men employed by noble houses.

When women were prosecuted for homicide, familiar tropes prevailed, but the seventeenth century demonstrates an evolution in judicial form and intent. Both Trevor Dean and Carol Lansing have noted a fear in medieval Bologna of the poisoning wife, who slowly killed her husband by poisoning his food, usually at the behest of her lover.[25] In the eleven-year, nineteen-case sample, only one woman was accused of poisoning her husband this way.[26] Additionally, among 551 people executed between 1600 and 1700, only two were women condemned for killing

John Christopoulos, "Nonelite Male Perspectives on Procured Abortion, Rome circa 1600," *I Tatti Studies in the Italian Renaissance* 17, no. 1 (2014): 155–74; Elizabeth S. Cohen, "Honor and Gender in the Streets of Early Modern Rome," *The Journal of Interdisciplinary History* 22, no. 4 (April 1, 1992): 597–625; Thomas V. Cohen, *Words and Deeds in Renaissance Rome: Trials before the Papal Magistrates* (Toronto: University of Toronto Press, 1993).

[24] Cohen, "Honor and Gender in the Streets of Early Modern Rome"; Christopoulos, "Nonelite Male Perspectives on Procured Abortion, Rome circa 1600."

[25] Cf. C. Lansing, "Poisoned Relations: Marital Conflict in Medieval Bologna," in G. M. Anselmi et al., eds., *Bologna: Cultural Crossroads from the Medieval to the Baroque: Recent Anglo-American Scholarship* (Bologna: Bononia University Press, 2013), 137–39; Trevor Dean, *Crime and Justice in Late Medieval Italy* (Cambridge: Cambridge University Press, 2007), 157.

[26] ASBo, *Torrone*, 7353, fasc. 18, trial of Maria Maddalena Miglioli for poisoning of Giuseppe Miglioli, butler to the Senator Melara.

their husband with their lover; only one of these did so by poison.[27] The timing of these trials is perhaps significant: the execution of a husband-poisoner occurred in 1689, and the only trial of a husband-poisoner in my sample occurred in 1690. In the seventeenth century, either the *Torrone* no longer gave credence to most accusations of wife-poisoning or Bolognese men were not making them very often. Both Dean and Lansing note that accusations of unsuccessful wife-poisoners were more prevalent in medieval Bologna, but they were rare in the seventeenth century, and trials even more so.

When the *Torrone* did investigate poisoning, it devoted unusual attention to proving the means of killing, going so far as to bring in Bologna's university medical school to assist. In most other trials, autopsies were performed, often quite casually, by the notary and two male witnesses to whom the victim was known; here, the purpose was first and foremost to confirm the victim's identity and then to create an inventory of his or her belongings. Wounds and cause of death were noted by a physician or surgeon if available, but were usually obvious and so did not occupy as much concern. In the trial of Maria Maddalena Miglioli in 1690, five surgeons and physicians from the university were asked to confirm the diagnosis of poisoning by vegetable soup. In another case from 1632, in which a disgruntled female servant was accused of poisoning her former courtesan employer, a woman was the first witness to the autopsy, before a physician was called to confirm the poisoning diagnosis.[28] This case also inverted the poisoner's trope: here, two men, one of them the putative lover of the victim, were accused of helping the spurned servant Anna to poison Valeria the courtesan. Across my sample of 701 homicide trials, four men were accused of poisoning and only two women. While the trope of the poisoning wife perhaps continued to fascinate magistrates toward the end of the seventeenth century, evidence of poisoning is extremely slim, suggesting that the medieval trope did not reflect a common reality by the seventeenth century.

More common among the sample are trials showing that violence could be a family affair. There were six trials in which women were accused of killing alongside their husbands, as both accomplices and instigators. In one case, a couple was tried for killing the wife's lover, but the wife was absolved and her husband condemned.[29] In the remaining five trials, women were condemned for joining public assaults started by their husbands, thrice delivering the final blows. However,

---

[27] ASBo, *Cronaci delle giustizie seguite a Bologna dal 1030 al 1750*, executions of February 28, 1689, and February 17, 1648.
[28] ASBo, *Torrone*, 5904, fol. 387r, 1632.   [29] ASBo, *Torrone*, 5852, f. 493r, 1632.

these homicides occurred during the daily conflicts of tightly packed urban and rural communities; for each, one finds many examples of these types of brawls that ended with bruises and cuts but no deaths. They occurred during harvest time, for instance, while the community was threshing hemp; and they tended to be public. Arguments began among men or youths, over precedence, over competition and over the stresses of endemically poor rural life. When husbands and sons began fighting, wives and mothers could either support them or join the fray, and there are examples of both situations occurring. In these trials, the court's focus was usually on the men as the instigators, and likely continuators, of the violence.

The image of the shaming wife egging her husband on to violence is familiar in both the classic anthropology of feud and modern research on early modern gender.[30] Elizabeth Cohen has documented Roman women prosecuting active grudges against neighbours and acquaintances and has shown them involving men in their quarrels.[31] For rural *bolognesi* as well, village streets and rural crossroads were contested social spaces in which slights to family status or threats to family security prompted violent encounters between whole families. Like Roman magistrates, *Torrone* judges and notaries were more concerned with deeds than motives in these cases. And they were more interested in the deeds of men than of women, placing blame on men for starting frays and for their violence. The female killer was usually treated by the court as an accomplice rather than a killer with agency, though multiple witnesses seem to have taken satisfaction in describing how, for instance, Francesca enthusiastically delivered the final blows when her husband Matteo assaulted his neighbour during a livestock dispute.[32]

There were only two trials of women accused of killing on their own outside of marriage or family ties. Both trials involved rural women who killed another woman with an unintentionally well-thrown rock during arguments over scarce resources. In part because they were so few, these trials demonstrate the significance of North Italy's endemic rural poverty for its history of violence: they are surely the tip of the iceberg of our view of women's protection of fragile family resources.[33]

---

[30] Gluckman, "The Peace in the Feud," 12; Katja Altpeter-Jones, "Inscribing Gender on the Early Modern Body: Marital Violence in German Texts of the Fifteenth and Sixteenth Century," *Early Modern Women* 3 (2008): 27–60.

[31] Cohen, "Honor and Gender in the Streets of Early Modern Rome."

[32] ASBo, *Torrone*, 6241, *in fine*.

[33] John Lynn makes the case that women were integral to the operation of an army on campaign, responsible for provisioning and caring for soldiers, and for gathering and

In one case from the spring of 1620, the young shepherdess Catterina Raimondo led her sheep to pasture too close to her neighbour's fields in the mountain hamlet of Rocca della Corneta, and Maria Cerreto drove her away with rocks.[34] One of those rocks struck Catterina hard in the side and she died overnight, leaving Maria to answer a homicide charge. In the other case, another Catterina and her neighbour Isabetta argued over "certain apples" in the agricultural village of Sant'Andrea Poggio de Rossi, during the lean times immediately following the plague.[35] As in the other case, an argument over scarce food resources led the women to violence and rock-throwing, and as before, Isabetta died the next day after complaining that Catterina had struck her in the temple with a thrown rock. The court treated these cases as arguments that went tragically beyond their original intent, since both women could plausibly deny having meant to kill their neighbour. They were not previously armed, they did not pursue the conflict to the death immediately, and they had no unusual history of neighbourhood violence. More importantly, the court judged that these homicides would not likely breed more local violence. In Sant'Andrea they were wrong, however: when the bailiff tasked Isabetta's son with guarding the prisoner Catterina until the *Torrone*'s notary arrived, he beat her with a stick and threw her off a low roof. The trial was closed with no further punishment and with assurances from all that they would maintain peace.

Infanticide

The three categories of female homicide so far discussed – mariticide, cooperative family violence, and scarcity-driven resource violence – account for ten of the nineteen homicide trials against women. As we have seen, they placed women into familiar tropes as jealous poisoners and shrieking Ladies Macbeth, but these tropes were belied by the very rareness in which the *Torrone*'s judges encountered anything resembling their reality. The remaining nine trials of women accused of killing collect another trope, and they offer some challenging questions for current research on infanticide. There are fourteen infanticide investigations, nine of which named the accused and proceeded to trial, among my decennial sample of *Torrone* records. This is a very small sample of infanticides compared to the much larger samples of infant homicide

---

managing pillage following successful sieges. John A. Lynn, *Women, Armies, and Warfare in Early Modern Europe* (Cambridge: Cambridge University Press, 2008).
[34] ASBo, *Torrone*, 5038, f. 301r, 1620.   [35] ASBo, *Torrone*, 5918, f. 301r, 1632.

trials amassed recently by Kesselring and Butler.[36] So my basis of comparison is tenuous and designed more to ask questions than to make arguments. For Italy, the argument about infanticide is largely one from absence, and both Hanlon and Hynes have mined parish baptismal records to suggest that infanticide by married couples was routine and unprosecuted.[37] Common to these writers is the argument that infanticide as a crime was thought of as a single-woman's sin, condemned most when committed by the most vulnerable. Trials from the *Torrone* suggest a more nuanced approach by Bolognese judges: infanticide as a category of homicide was prosecuted seriously by the *Torrone*; both men and women were prosecuted for it; and among those prosecuted were single women, the men who impregnated them, and married couples. This limited sample of infanticide trials – 2% of the total sampled – shows that the court investigated infanticide in the deepest reaches of the mountain passes south of the city and throughout the countryside; I have seen no complete urban infanticide trial.

The five unconfirmed infanticide investigations are an argument for the *Torrone*'s concern with infanticide as a serious category of homicide. In these cases, an infant was discovered and reported to a local bailiff, who sent for the *Torrone* and began seeking the parents. The conclusion was generally that the child had been abandoned by travellers passing through or that the child had been stillborn. All these cases occurred in the countryside, and in all cases, the *Torrone*'s notary looked to the local community to help identify the infant. Nobody could, and in the absence of any parent to link the child to, the investigations went no further. But each was duly recorded by a notary sent from the city, who included the investigation among his papers to be archived among the other homicides that arrived on his docket. Neither this North Italian court nor the communities in its jurisdiction turned a blind eye to the occasional dead baby. The act was condemned, and there are good reasons to believe its incidence did not extend much beyond what was visible in the judicial record.

The nine trials for infanticide in which the parents were identified and named span the gamut of marital configurations. In 1600, a teenaged girl named Cattarina Roversi and the boy who impregnated her were tried for killing and burying the newborn child.[38] In this case, the court

---

[36] Kesselring, "Bodies of Evidence"; Butler, "A Case of Indifference?"

[37] Hanlon, "L'infanticidio di coppie sposate in toscana nella prima eta moderna"; Hynes, "Routine Infanticide by Married Couples?" Cf. Kesselring's critique of this argument in Kesselring, "Bodies of Evidence," n. 23.

[38] ASBo, *Torrone*, 3246, f. 49r, 1600.

condemned Cattarina and not the boy, showing that the *Torrone*, like English courts, could harshly condemn infanticide by unmarried women. A similar outcome occurred in 1652, when Cattarina Zerbini was condemned for infanticide while her husband Antonio was pardoned; here, the married couple had been tried for infanticide.[39] Indeed, in four of the nine infanticide trials, either a couple was tried or a married woman was accused. Thus, four married women or couples were tried for infanticide, four single women, and one single woman alongside the boy who impregnated her, whose trial was for rape. This is hardly a large enough sample to make a meaningful argument, but it cannot be said that the *Torrone* was concerned only with policing young single women.

All available evidence points to a strong concern with investigating and determining the parentage of unidentified babies, as well as a generally low incidence of infanticide itself. This is not to say that no infanticides went undiscovered, but rather to suggest that their general absence from the judicial record should not be read as evidence of a much more widespread phenomenon, in which only single women bore the brunt of the judiciary's moralizing and violence. Married women and single women were prosecuted for infanticide in Bologna, and cases of infanticides wherein no parent could be identified were still disturbing enough that the court invested resources to investigate them. I have not assessed the sex ratios of babies baptized in Bolognese parishes as Hynes has done for Parma, but I also suggest that there are valid critiques of the conclusion that variable birth rates indicate gender-specific infanticide; a wide range of environmental stresses and physical pathologies have been noted to impact sex ratios in populations facing the type of resource-based poverty that was prevalent in seventeenth-century Italy.[40] Moreover, we

---

[39] ASBo, *Torrone*, 6605, *in fine*.
[40] Barbara A. Anderson and Brian D. Silver, "Ethnic Differences in Fertility and Sex Ratios at Birth in China: Evidence from Xinjiang," *Population Studies* 49, no. 2 (1995): 211–26; Victor Grech, Charles Savona-Ventura and P. Vassallo-Agius, "Research Pointers: Unexplained Differences in Sex Ratios at Birth in Europe and North America," *BMJ: British Medical Journal* 324, no. 7344 (2002): 1010–11; Christophe Z. Guilmoto, "Skewed Sex Ratios at Birth and Future Marriage Squeeze in China and India, 2005–2100," *Demography* 49, no. 1 (2012): 77–100; Amar Hamoudi, "Exploring the Causal Machinery behind Sex Ratios at Birth: Does Hepatitis B Play a Role?," *Economic Development and Cultural Change* 59, no. 1 (2010): 1–21; Adam Jacobs et al., "Different Sex Ratios at Birth in Europe and North America," *BMJ: British Medical Journal* 325, no. 7359 (2002): 334–35; William H. James, "Inconstancy of Human Sex Ratios at Birth," *Fertility and Sterility* 94, no. 3 (August 1, 2010): e53; William H. James, "Sex Ratios at Birth as Monitors of Endocrine Disruption," *Environmental Health Perspectives* 109, no. 6 (2001): A250–51; William H. James, "The Validity of Inferences of Sex-Selective Infanticide, Abortion and Neglect from Unusual Reported Sex Ratios at Birth," *European Journal of Population/Revue Européenne de Démographie* 13, no. 2 (1997): 213–17; S. Sudha and S. Irudaya Rajan, "Persistent Daughter

know from recent work on Italy that a wide range of abortifacients existed and were well known among medical practitioners and networks of women healers.[41] In the absence of any more evidence of infanticide, we can say only that Bolognese authorities were indeed much concerned by infanticide, and prosecuted it as a capital crime.

Conclusion

The record of women's homicide in Bologna is limited, only 2.5% of my sample of 701 homicide trials. Almost half of the nineteen trials were for infanticide, and five more infanticide investigations were cut short in the absence of identifiable parents. Among the other ten trials in which women were accused of homicides, there were women accused of killing their husbands or of killing with their husbands, and women who killed other women in arguments over food and property. Was women's homicide distinct from men's? Certainly, it was much rarer. Women were accused of killing close to home, and the victims were either other women, husbands or infants. When they were accused of killing unrelated men, it was alongside their husbands. They were executed in equal numbers (five) for husband- and child-killing, and the only other woman executed across the seventeenth century was hanged for serial theft.[42] Broadly, the prosecution of women's homicide focused on homicides that transgressed patriarchal norms. While the results of its investigations may have shown that the tropes of poisoning wives and child-killing single girls were highly nuanced in reality, its judges and notaries nevertheless remained fixated on those categories in their investigation and their punishment of women's homicide.

The limited role of Bolognese women as perpetrators of homicide, vastly outnumbered by male killers, makes sense in the context of Bologna's social hierarchies in which husbands were expected to discipline wives and were primarily responsible for the exercise of violence within the family. Indeed, more than twice as many women were killed by men than were killers themselves. Wives, lovers and sex workers were the

Disadvantage: What Do Estimated Sex Ratios at Birth and Sex Ratios of Child Mortality Risk Reveal?," *Economic and Political Weekly* 38, no. 41 (2003): 4361–69; Carel P. van Schaik and Sarah Blaffer Hrdy, "Intensity of Local Resource Competition Shapes the Relationship between Maternal Rank and Sex Ratios at Birth in Cercopithecine Primates," *The American Naturalist* 138, no. 6 (1991): 1555–62.

[41] Christopoulos, "Nonelite Male Perspectives on Procured Abortion, Rome circa 1600"; Sharon T. Strocchia, "Women and Healthcare in Early Modern Europe," *Renaissance Studies* 28, no. 4 (2014): 496–514.

[42] ASBo, *Cronaci*, execution of Maddalena di Domenico Ortolani, August 8, 1620.

most vulnerable women in *Torrone* trials. They were most likely to be killed by men in private in relationships of intimate familiarity, making their prosecution and adjudication by the *Torrone* difficult. Neighbourhood social networks aided women either by intervening in assaults by their husbands or by reporting excessive marital violence to the *Torrone* and cooperating with its notaries' investigations. The numbers of uxoricides and other murders of women in Bologna remained stable throughout the sampled years, with a few trials against femicides every year.

Women could be pushed to violence in defence of fragile family resources during lean times; women, in limited numbers, were also prosecuted and condemned for husband-killing. Their trials show court notaries pursuing stereotyped lines of questioning that were often contradicted by the atypical actions of the accused. Particularly in mariticide cases, notaries remained fascinated by medieval tropes of wives who slowly poisoned their husbands, though they prosecuted almost as many men for the same crime. More shocking and heinous to the judges and notaries of the *Torrone* were infanticides; during these trials, accused women were treated harshly by both their local communities and by the court's officers, and their trials more often led to condemnation and hanging than did parricide trials.

Bologna in the seventeenth century remained a society in which women's violence was viewed as an aberration, unlike male violence, which was largely expected and tolerated to a wide degree – even nurtured among some men. Violence by men against women also was censured more than violence between men, but Bolognese husbands retained a wide degree of latitude to discipline and violently chastise their wives. The men who patronized the city's sex workers showed little compunction about murdering *meretrici* who spent too much time with other men or whose residences were too crowded. In a period when Bologna's poor girls and women were increasingly enclosed and disciplined through institutional charity, and when both rich and poor girls were pushed toward the enclosed religious life, the failure of the *Torrone*'s law-men, notaries and judges to take a more proactive approach toward gendered homicide seems at odds with the professed counter-reform gender politics otherwise at play. With women placed in convents and reform houses in the name of their chastity and safety, their continued vulnerability to fatal violence by Bolognese men shows how gendered hierarchies remained beyond the scope of Bologna's attempts to pacify its violent population.

5 The Days after No Future
Post-Plague Homicides in Rural Bologna

Introduction

An hour before sunset on December 31, 1631, Signore Hippolito
Ravaglio rode his horse through Castel San Pietro on his way to Imola,
accompanied by a servant on horseback.[1] As a minor noble, Ravaglio was
accustomed to carrying the marks of his status: a loaded pistol, a loaded
arquebus, a dagger, and a certain amount of wealth in both cash and
jewellery. As Ravaglio and his servant passed through the town, they
encountered Stefano the blacksmith, who was visiting Giovan'Andrea, a
local reseller of used goods. According to Stefano's testimony, given the
next day from his sickbed, Ravaglio and his servant passed the blacksmith
and paused in front of the local tavern, "without dismounting," before
returning to Stefano with some pressing business. Ravaglio demanded to
know, testified Stefano, "why I did not doff my cap to him." Stefano
responded in a manner guaranteed to infuriate an already offended
nobleman: "Because I have no obligation to doff my hats." Ravaglio
drew a pistol, his servant pulled an arquebus, and the servant shot
Stefano in his right shoulder. The ball passed straight through, and
Stefano, "feeling wounded and doubting that Hippolito would not fire
some more arquebus shots," grabbed his own gun and shot the noble in
the chest. Ravaglio fell off his horse, which bolted, and he was dragged
behind it for "the length of an arquebus shot," a common measure of
distance in the seventeenth century. He died on the scene, a notary was
sent for from Bologna, and the bailiff of Castel San Pietro began investigating the murder, with the killer as his first witness, the next day,
January 1, 1632.

This murder was an ominous sign of the years to come for the judges
and notaries of the *Torrone*, years in which violence transgressed social
hierarchies and communicated strong dissatisfaction with society's status
quo in the world wrought upside-down by decades of crisis and plague.

---

[1] ASBo, *Torrone*, 5922, *in fine*.

This chapter focuses on the homicidal violence that occurred in the countryside in 1632. It does so in order to assess the impact on violent behaviour of a major societal disaster: the plague of 1630–31 that killed approximately 24% of Bologna's urban population, about 15,000 people, and up to another 30,000 from the surrounding *contado*.[2] Analyzing homicide in the immediate and long-term aftermath of widespread epidemic mortality shows the role that violence played in reconstructing the social institutions of society, redefining relationships between groups whose circumstances had shifted radically, and recalibrating the options available for those seeking to modify their station in life. It is also an opportunity to test the hypothesis put forward by Roth that homicide rates – and violence more generally – respond to changes in levels of societal trust in and support of governmental, judicial and social institutions.[3]

Were it unique in the year 1632, the murder of a young noble by a blacksmith would have raised eyebrows but appeared otherwise unremarkable. However, the seventy-seven homicides that occurred in 1632 collectively displayed a breakdown of the stability of local governments, judicial systems and social hierarchies. The plague cycle that struck the state of Bologna particularly hard from May 1630 to February 1631 destabilized social norms and obligations to a degree visible in the fatally violent crime that occurred as the city and countryside pieced themselves back together in 1632.[4] Not only did homicide rates – particularly the rural rate – spike in 1632, to an aggregate of 42 per 100,000 (the third-highest of the sample), but the quality of homicides changed as well. The few urban homicides (16) represented in the *Torrone*'s trial records show the reinvigorated presence of deadly rivalries between the noble clans of the city. These rivalries reemerged following a period of

---

[2] C. Cipolla, *Fighting the Plague in Seventeenth Century Italy* (Madison: University of Wisconsin Press, 1981), 101. Cf. Population figures for Bologna in 1632 in chap. 3.

[3] Randolph Roth, *American Homicide* (Cambridge, MA: Belknap Press of Harvard University Press, 2009), 3, 16–26.

[4] Guido Alfani has done much on the demography and economics of seventeenth-century plagues in North Italy. He argues that the 1630 plague, specifically, initiated a period of long-term economic decline for the North. While property structures in areas such as Ivrea remained stable compared to medieval plague experiences, cities that experienced both the 1576–77 plague and the 1629–30 plague entered a protracted demographic decline through 1800. Bologna, like other cities primarily hit by the 1629–30 plague, had a relatively rapid demographic recovery. G. Alfani and M. Percoco, "Plague and Long-Term Development: The Lasting Effects of the 1629–30 Epidemic on the Italian Cities," Working Paper (IGIER (Innocenzo Gasparini Institute for Economic Research), Bocconi University, 2014); S. K. Cohn Jr. and G. Alfani, "Households and Plague in Early Modern Italy," *The Journal of Interdisciplinary History* 38, no. 2 (October 1, 2007): 177–205; G. Alfani, "The Effects of Plague on the Distribution of Property: Ivrea, Northern Italy 1630," *Population Studies* 64, no. 1 (March 1, 2010): 61–75.

relative calm that was shattered by the epidemic. Rural homicides emerged from conflicts over basic provisions, land, and employment. In both town and country, robbery and revenge homicides broke hierarchical borders. The plague reduced an already fragile trust in institutions and communities and led to the destabilization of traditional norms of authority and deference. This reshaping and contestation of social norms was visible in the many homicides that crossed those traditional boundaries.

In the fifty years prior to the 1630 outbreak of plague in North and Central Italy, Bologna's population fluctuated between approximately 62,000 and 70,000, averaging about 67,000 within the city walls. During the same period, the rural population was more changeable, with a low in 1600 of about 145,000 people, and a high in 1617 of nearly 172,000.[5] When the plague of 1630 first struck in the late spring and summer, it ignited an epidemic that saw the population of the city reduced by about 25%, such that in 1632 the population of the city was 43,114.[6] Carlo Cipolla argues that the rural provinces of Italian city-states seem to have experienced mortality rates similar to those within the cities, despite a long-held notion that urban dwellers fled to the *contado* during times of plague because of its comparative safety.[7] Cohn and Alfani note further that for Nonantola, a small commune between Bologna and Modena, the mortality count of the 1630 plague was 760 of a population of 3,439, a mortality rate of 25% after adjusting for deaths of infants under five.[8] We can thus estimate, conservatively, that the plague killed some 20% of the rural population overall, with mortality rates varying between villages. Thus, although no official figures exist for 1632, we can extrapolate a rural population of about 140,000 in that year. The significant decline of both the urban and rural populations amplifies the homicide rate, although there were also more homicides in absolute numbers in 1632 than in the sampled years on either side. With so many people dead during the passage of the plague, the potential for significant social, economic and political tensions among survivors was high.

The World Turned Upside-Down: Bernardino Spada's Failed Efforts to Combat the Plague, and the Expansion of the *Torrone*'s Authority

The plague did not strike Bologna suddenly or without warning. Nor was this North Italy's first encounter with virulent contagion: plague had

---

[5] A. Bellettini, *La popolazione di Bologna dal secolo 15 all'unificazione italiana* (Bologna: Zanichelli, 1961), 25–27, 48.
[6] Ibid., 191–92.   [7] Cipolla, *Fighting the Plague*, 100–110.
[8] Cohn and Alfani, "Households and Plague in Early Modern Italy," 201.

struck with some frequency since the fourteenth century.[9] As early as 1627, the legate of Bologna, at the time Cardinal Bernardino Spada, began issuing a series of announcements (*bandi*) that warned citizens of plague in nearby cities and placed bans – on pain of death – against anyone seeking to transport "persons, animals, goods, monies, letters and any other thing that comes or may be transported" from infected cities, which at this point were primarily in the north, in France and Germany.[10] Twenty-five days later, on January 12, 1628, he expanded his list of infected areas, based on information he had received, to include more Swiss towns, and reiterated the ban on importation of goods into the city.[11] During the plague, Spada issued a continual series of *bandi* in an attempt to prevent the plague from reaching Bologna, and failing that, to control its virulence within the city through strict curfews and security protocols.

Spada's initial attempts to ward off the plague took the form of commercial and travel embargoes. On January 14, 1628, he simply closed the city gates to any person not bearing a declaration of good health written and signed in their town of departure; he also made these "*fedi di sanità*" available to *bolognesi* at no cost.[12] These *fedi* covered humans and their animals and goods and were an attempt by early modern city governments to coordinate their responses to the plague and minimize its epidemic reach, without paralyzing the dense commercial networks at whose crossroads Bologna laid. A *fede di sanità* allowed *bolognesi* to continue their commerce with the inhabitants of surrounding cities and provinces, and vice versa. Spada continued to release announcements tracing the passage of the plague as it approached North Italy and began to cross borders into it. Ultimately, he closed the city to Milanese traffic in October 1629.

The quarantine was the civil government's first, though not its only, means to prevent the outbreak of plague in Bologna. As early as 1557, Italian medical and civil authorities had recognized the need for directed government policy to maintain the well-being of city populations; medical authorities argued that the therapy of individual patients was the

---

[9] The most recent major outbreak to affect Northern Italy was in 1575–77. Plague struck with distressing regularity: 1452, 1468, 1483, 1502, 1523, 1556–57, 1570–76, 1597–98. Cohn and Alfani, "Households and Plague in Early Modern Italy," 180–82; O. J. Benedictow, "Morbidity in Historical Plague Epidemics," *Population Studies* 41, no. 3 (November 1, 1987): 402; Alfani and Percoco, "Plague and Long-Term Development," 5.

[10] Bernardino Spada, *I bandi di Bernardino Spada durante la peste del 1630 in Bologna*, ed. Pietro Malpezzi (Faenza (Ravenna): Casanova, 2008), *Bando* of December 19, 1627, p. 32.

[11] Ibid., 33.   [12] Ibid., 34.

realm of physicians, while the responsibility to "provide for the collect-ive" lay with city leaders.[13] In reality, Cipolla notes, this separation was in fact too neat. Medical men influenced civic policy and advocated for preventive measures against the plague, and also recognized the modern medical notion that effective prevention was much preferable to the need for therapy.[14] Possessing an internally consistent scientific account of the plague, the miasmatic theory, medical authorities collaborated with governments to institute policies and practices that would ward off a contagion that travelled primarily through human contact, and spread, according to their understanding, by "venomous atoms" that poisoned the air and created plague-bearing "miasmas."[15] In Florence, this included the division of the city into six *sestieri*, each under the authority of notable men from the *Compagnia di San Michele*, a charitable confra-ternity. These men determined that filthy mattresses were a leading cause of plague in poor households, and arranged for both the distribution of 1,347 new mattresses to still-healthy households and the preventative burning of the old.[16] These preventative measures were well known by the time plague erupted in Bologna in 1630.

Armed with the best available knowledge about plague and its trans-mission, Spada adopted a proactive approach to plague control in late 1629, when it became clear that Northern Italy was without doubt stricken by the plague. He noted in a *bando* on November 4 that the *fedi di sanità*, employed by many of the cities in the region, failed to check the spread of the plague; he therefore determined to "decree and order the following provisions in addition to those already done."[17] Existing *fedi di sanità* were respected, and citizens were admonished again not to admit into Bologna any persons, animals or goods that lacked this guarantee of health. All other mail, goods, people and animals were banned from the province. Gypsies, vagabonds, cripples, the enfeebled and tinkers were all forbidden entry to the city, on pain of the lash and imprisonment if Spada judged it appropriate. To enforce the ban, Spada established a citizen's brigade to guard the city gates, made up of "gentlemen, citizens and artisans" who would follow the instructions and orders nailed to the gates. He set strict schedules for the guards, posting them in pairs at the gate and mandating that at least one remain if the other needed to leave to eat.[18] Anyone opening the door without the express permission of these deputies or in their absence would be subject to three lashes.

---

[13] Cipolla, *Fighting the Plague*, 7.   [14] Ibid.   [15] Ibid., 10–15.
[16] Ibid., 15; N. Eckstein, "Renaissance History and the Digital Turn," Plenary Address, Renaissance Society of America, New York, March 28, 2014.
[17] Spada, *I bandi di Bernardino Spada*, 48.   [18] Ibid., 48–49.

These harsh penalties for non-compliance were resisted by residents of Bologna, who through disobedience and distrust subverted the legate's attempts to control the plague.

The legate knew that there were risks inherent in this sanitary regime. Recognizing the strain that plague put on his population, and the dangers of establishing citizen militias to control access to the city, Spada finished these provisions by admonishing citizens of Bologna not to "harass [the gatekeepers] with injurious words, evil wills, dishonesties or threats ... and even less to forcefully enter the city, [or] do any uncivil or indecent act against the guards."[19] He sought to close the entire province to foreign travellers, sending groups of soldiers to the province's borders to prevent entry into Bologna along the major highways; nine days later, he expanded their mandate to include enforcing quarantines of castles and walled settlements.[20] Even as the plague rapidly approached, Spada maintained hope that prudent action and collective precautions could ward off the pestilence that was striking down the peoples of France, Germany, Switzerland and much of the Italian peninsula. At the same time, he was well aware of the potential for interpersonal violence emerging under fear of the plague, as demonstrated in his orders not to assault civil authorities.

Spada continued to publish decrees regularly throughout April, both expanding the scale and intensifying the scope of regulations on commerce and travel while displaying an increasing frustration with "many drivers who through their own interest and greed to profit have introduced and continue to introduce foreign beasts into the province."[21] On May 6 he instituted a new sanitary regime in Bologna itself, as the threat of plague was now imminent and immediate measures needed to be taken were the city to remain free of contagion.[22] All inhabitants and corporate bodies of Bologna, without exception for religious status or social privilege, were required to clear their properties of all trash and filth. Those practicing dirty jobs – tanners, paper-makers, and certain butchers – were additionally required to transport their waste outside the city walls every evening. Fishmongers faced tightened sanitary regulations that monitored the state of their warehouses and goods, and were required to dump their refuse into the river once a week. As the plague drew closer to Bologna, Spada employed all the power of his office to prevent Bologna from becoming infected.

However, Spada's hopes to keep Bologna free of the plague depended upon the complete and total cooperation of the local populace.

[19] Ibid., 49.   [20] Ibid., 52.   [21] Ibid., 67.   [22] Ibid., 68–70.

The frequent repetition of the basic elements of preventative sanitation – commercial quarantines, exhortations to inhabitants not to assault and disobey the citizen guards at the city gates, and strict controls on the maintenance of city streets – in Spada's many decrees from 1628 to 1630 make clear that these measures were not followed to the letter. The fear of contagion was not enough to overcome the fear of poverty and destitution for residents of the city whose livelihoods depended on trade in animals or goods with persons outside Bologna. Spada's efforts in fact reduced the trust of the populace in the institutions of civil government. Despite having their freedom of movement and commerce severely restricted during the plague's approach, many *bolognesi* lost friends and family in 1630. The legatine government failed to protect Bologna, and it paid the price in the shocking disillusion of societal norms that produced the homicide spike of 1632.

When the plague struck, regulations on movement were tightened further and the legate brought in more authorities from the city's court and medical college. The first case of plague was officially reported on May 6.[23] By June 1630 Bologna was in the grip of epidemic, and Spada shifted his attention from prevention of an outbreak to the management of a plague-stricken city, with an eye to minimizing the spread of infections and protecting healthy neighbourhoods. Immediately, he instituted strict regulations on the movement of people and goods within the city and gave responsibility for enforcement of curfews and enclosures to the constables and notaries of the *Torrone*.[24] On June 13, Spada's Health Magistrate (*cancelliere di sanità*) issued a direct order to "all the doctors" that they were required to meet in their guild halls the next morning to discuss emergency measures for sanitation and medical treatment.[25] The doctors were a central part of Spada's plans for containing plague, as they were able to maintain detailed records of illness and death in the city's two plague hospitals, the *lazzaretti*.

The legate also shifted some responsibility for controlling the plague to citizens themselves and gave the criminal court responsibility for enforcing this responsibility. All inhabitants were required to report any suspected cases of plague in their households, providing doctors with the plague-stricken victim's name, length and quality of illness, parish and residence; doctors then prohibited people from entering that place, conversing with the victim or removing goods of any kind from the house. Deputies were appointed to provide food and care to victims who remained in their homes and to report these cases to the director general

---

[23] Benedictow, "Morbidity in Historical Plague Epidemics," 406.
[24] Spada, *I bandi di Bernardino Spada*, 73–74.   [25] Ibid.

of the *lazzaretto* outside the parish of San Mamolo.[26] A general curfew was imposed, with strict regulations on the movements of bodies and goods that were possibly infected with plague. By restricting movement and activity within the city, Spada hoped to track the progress of the plague, maintain detailed records of its incidence in terms of both overall prevalence and mortality, and reduce the potential for unchecked infection. He relied on the *Torrone* to assist in enforcing this curfew by transferring criminal jurisdiction over these matters to its judges and notaries.

The emergency measures engendered particular challenges for the judges of the *Torrone*. The records of the plague year contain a great number of denunciations and trials for breaking and entering into houses emptied by plague – either by relatives of the deceased hoping to retrieve their patrimony before it was inventoried, inspected for plague and possibly destroyed, or by opportunistic thieves curious to see what goods and monies might lie behind the white-washed cross that indicated a plague house.[27] The court also prosecuted *bolognesi* for insulting and harassing the officers of the *Torrone* and the *Sanità* as they went about their duties, and it enforced the regulations on women that restricted them to their houses under the authority of their *padrone*.[28]

Two recurring problems stand out from the other *Torrone* priorities of 1630, both of which reveal the population's rejection of the logic of curfew, their privileging of individual activity over collective regulation, and an overall class-based hostility to city regulations that severely restricted the lower classes' abilities to feed and support themselves but allowed wealthy *bolognesi* to carry on with little disruption. Throughout the plague, the *Torrone* prosecuted multiple women, usually prostitutes, for walking around the city in defiance of enclosure regulations and dressed as men to avoid the notice of officials.[29] This gender role-reversing by some of the city's most vulnerable, yet independent, women was explained by the women themselves as the only strategy they had available to survive during the plague: they needed to practice their trade outside, and dressing as a man was the only means to do so without being arrested or harassed.

A more sinister crime also came under the *Torrone*'s purview in 1630: smearing the doors and windows of houses and buildings with mysterious ointments, *unzioni*, in what officials considered attempts to infect

---

26 Ibid., 77.
27 A. Pastore, *Crimine e giustizia in tempo di peste nell'Europa moderna* (Rome: Laterza, 1991), 77–81.
28 Ibid., 82–98.   29 Ibid., 99–101.

houses with the plague.[30] Not dissimilar to poisoning wells, this crime was viewed as particularly heinous by the *Torrone* and prosecuted with vigour whenever possible. This practice was not restricted to times of plague only: in 1671 there was a rash of incidents in which someone applied "a suspicious yellow material" to all of the doors in the town of Budrio; the *Torrone*'s denunciations note that this had been occurring all over Lombardy and officials were at a loss to explain it or to catch the culprits.[31] Smearing of doors with pestilential ointments, or with human or animal effluent and feces, was not an uncommon means to ostracize someone from the community, to sow dislike and distrust against rivals, or, in the case of the plague of 1630, to attract the unwanted attention of civic officials and to disrupt a household's activity by bringing the fear of contagion upon it.

Because these matters occupied the *Torrone* throughout 1630 and into 1631, the archival record of homicide during the plague itself is spotty; it is impossible to tell with any conviction how many homicides occurred as the plague ravaged the population. It is possible that a great many killings were committed under the shadow of pestilence, when a mounting death toll may have provided cover to killers enacting revenge or seeking material gain. Although local physicians had a good idea of the visible, physical symptoms of the plague, the sheer volume of dead *bolognesi* cannot discount the idea that some of the plague victims were in fact victims of a more human pestilence. Further, interpersonal violence and homicides were not the *Torrone*'s primary concern during the plague: if a peasant murdered his neighbour deep in the mountain passes, logistical problems likely prevented the court's discovery of the crime, let alone its investigation and prosecution of a culprit. Throughout 1630, the *Torrone* focused its activities on the maintenance of civil order and sanitary restrictions in Bologna proper; the *contado* was very much left under the authority of militias and groups of soldiers responsible for protecting the borders and enforcing the quarantines of walled towns and other settlements. The visible representatives of order in the *contado* were capricious and unregulated bands of armed men, whose presence could only serve to reduce general societal confidence in the legitimacy of social and governmental hierarchies.

For these reasons, 1632 is an opportune year to investigate homicides in Bologna. By a year after the plague, whose last infection was reported

---

[30] Ibid., 102–8.

[31] ASB, *Torrone*, 6951, *in fine*; for an Alpine comparison, cf. William G. Naphy, *Plagues, Poisons, and Potions: Plague-Spreading Conspiracies in the Western Alps, c. 1530–1640* (New York: Palgrave, 2002).

in Bologna on January 31, 1631,[32] the *Torrone* had returned to business as usual, while the inhabitants of the city and country struggled to piece together the lives, and livelihoods, that had been shattered by the deaths of family, friends and business associates. The plague's destabilizing social effects were manifested in revenge, robbery and status-based homicides, and in a resurgence of intra-class violence perpetrated by the city's nobility. Homicide trials from 1632 display these destabilized social norms; the words and deeds of witnesses and killers show that as *bolognesi* rebuilt their lives, they attempted to build stronger foundations by killing in the pursuit of material gain, social status and local power.

Post-plague Homicides in the Bolognese *contado*: Poverty, Disillusion and Revenge

Within the city's walls, the homicide rate jumped from 4.4 per 100,000 in 1620 to 36.9 per 100,000 in the span of twelve years. This is not significant in itself: homicide rates could change dramatically in a very short time, and without further research into the archives of the *Torrone*, it is impossible to determine exactly when and how the rate began to rise.[33] The homicide rate in the walled towns, villages and mountain hamlets of the countryside also increased over this period, from 18.6 per 100,000 to 43.6 per 100,000, as similar forces shaping violent behaviour in the city acted upon the countryside. Recall that the *contado* endured similar mortality rates from the plague as did the urban *enceinte*. Rural inhabitants were even less protected by the city's preparations for plague than were those within the walls: indeed, without walls, they had no concrete, or even wooden, means to control the flow of goods and people passing through their territory and possibly carrying the deadly pestilence. The impact of widespread rural mortality was qualitatively different than in the city, however. Families dependent upon the labour of all members could see their livelihoods evaporate with the death of the patriarch, or the mother, or even the children. This was particularly true for tenant labourers and small sharecroppers. These peasants killed, in 1632, in ways that reflect both the abject poverty of the hinterlands and the fear and frustration that attended plague recovery. Artisans found themselves with heightened status and sought-after skills and in turn broke social hierarchies by murdering nobles and each other. Members of each of these groups at times also rejected the hierarchies that

---

[32] Benedictow, "Morbidity in Historical Plague Epidemics," 406.
[33] On the rapid mutability of homicide rates, cf. Roth, *American Homicide*, introduction and chap. 1.

governed social relationships in and around Bologna by murdering judicial officials and employers. Rural nobility changed their stations by using violence, including homicide, to procure land that had been made available by the plague. All these groups also committed revenge homicides in high numbers, a phenomenon common to periods of distrust in societal institutions.

Rural violence was inescapably coloured by the extreme poverty in which most people lived. Families had very few possessions or clothing; food supplies had to be carefully managed to sustain villagers through the winter; and money was dealt in quattrini and soldi, the smallest denominations of local currency. At the best of times, one bad winter could mean an extremely lean and possibly deadly year for a sharecropping family of five. As Cohn demonstrates in the case of Milan, the plague struck disproportionately those whose material resources were already stretched to their limits, turning poverty into destitution for many families.[34] After the plague, those whose already difficult rural lives were made harder and more uncertain by the deaths of family members used homicidal violence to ensure the security of their families and goods. Items of clothing and food – a hat, an apple – were fatally contested by peasants for whom a hat meant relief from sunstroke in the August heat, or whose apples would sustain their children through the winter. Resource homicides – that is, instrumental violence used to ensure the killer's continued physical well-being – became prevalent among rurals following the plague.

Most obviously, material poverty translated to violence in a series of killings involving highway robberies and rural thefts that occurred in 1632. In each of these cases, the killers, or witnesses, attributed the violence to extreme poverty and the need to sustain themselves. On February 6, 1632, Andrea Sinibaldi, a farmer, left his wife at home in Castiglione to take some animals to Bologna to sell. On February 7 he was found dead in a ditch, beaten to death and stripped of the 30 ducatoni he carried in his coin purse.[35] According to his wife, he must have been robbed by a local youth named Giovanni di Claudio, because he knew her husband "usually carried money with him." Giovanni was a poor youth who lived in the house of Marchino Romanino, Andrea's neighbour and travelling partner. Giovanni knew of Andrea's habit of carrying money, and witnesses said he killed Andrea for it. Giovanni had recently moved to Castiglione to find work. While we cannot know for sure what happened to Giovanni during the plague, his

---

[34] Cohn and Alfani, "Households and Plague in Early Modern Italy," 194.
[35] ASB, *Torrone*, 5840, f. 389r–440v.

relocation suggests that his network of family and community support was destroyed by the epidemic. In another case, while driving his cart through Castel San Pietro to sell his hemp at market, Vincenzo d'Astorre and his son Giovanni were waylaid by robbers who attacked the cart, bashing Vincenzo on the head and taking his goods.[36] These robbery killings indicate the strong pressure that poverty could exert to push men toward violence when they had little faith in official poverty-relief programs that saw women as more appropriate targets of charity and poor relief.[37]

Poverty also drove people to kill in other ways. There was at least one killer in 1632 hired by someone to eliminate an enemy. On January 7, Bartolomeo Razani, a local *ciavattino*, or cobbler, shot Vincenzo Bennini in the village of San Giovanni.[38] Vincenzo and his friend Giacomo were passing time beneath an arcade outside the house of the Loratelli family when Bartolomeo arrived and, without a word, shot Vincenzo. Vincenzo died on January 23. Before he died, he told *Torrone* judges that Bartolomeo must have been hired to kill him, since Bartolomeo was a "poor man," to whom Vincenzo had "never done any displeasure"; Vincenzo would not, however, name the enemy who had hired his killer. While the investigation never revealed the money behind the crime, Bartolomeo was sentenced to an ignominious death as a hired killer. He was not executed, however, and he instead entered exile as a contumacious bandit. The chance to lift oneself out of poverty drove at least one man to kill for money in the Bolognese countryside in 1632, while three other cases of killings display the predatory and non-personal markings of hired killings.

In the seventeenth century, material poverty meant much more than simply a light purse, particularly in the agrarian economies of cities' rural hinterlands. Reading homicide trials in the wake of a plague makes vivid the desperate situation in which many peasants, robbed of labour resources and facing difficulty with their food supply, found themselves in 1632. On October 21, in Bagnarola, Giacomo Cantelli and Angelo Bettinozzi argued over "a gram of hemp," useful both for rope-making and as a grain.[39] Angelo denied that he had stolen some grain from Giacomo, who responded by smashing him in the head with a hoe.

---

[36] ASB, *Torrone*, 5867, f. 456r–479v.
[37] N. Terpstra, *Cultures of Charity: Women, Politics, and the Reform of Poor Relief in Renaissance Italy* (Cambridge, MA: Harvard University Press, 2013). Terpstra demonstrates that Bolognese charity was organized principally around care for women in vulnerable life stages, such as childhood or widowhood. Young men were considered able to work to earn a living, and therefore lacked consistent access to poverty relief.
[38] ASB, *Torrone*, 5832, *in fine*.   [39] ASB, *Torrone*, 5878, f. 409r–436v.

After killing his customer during this argument over a trivial amount of hemp, Giacomo took to the fields and was sentenced to three years' galley slavery in contumacy. The economic and material fallout of the plague left Giacomo in a position where killing a possible threat to his well-being was a viable option, in a system in which Giacomo had no reason to trust the forces of official order to protect his station. In another food-related killing, two women argued in Sant'Andrea Poggio de Rossi on September 26, 1632. Caterina de Poggioli accused Isabetta of taking some apples from the barrel in which she kept her winter's supply.[40] Although no immediate violence ensued, Isabetta was found the next morning sitting leaned up against her house, bleeding from a head wound. When asked by the bailiff what happened, Isabetta said that following the previous day's argument, Caterina threw a rock at her, hitting her in the temple. The bailiff sent Isabetta's son Giovanni to find and detain Caterina; when Giovanni found her, he dragged her to the top of her house, beat her about the shoulders with a heavy stick, and dangled her by her ankles over the ledge before dropping her from the roof. Isabetta died two days later, and the bailiff set a guard on Caterina's sickbed to ensure no more retaliatory violence would occur. In both these cases, violence emerged from conflict over the management of the winter's food supply, any interruption or damage to which could mean a lean and dangerous season ahead.

This poverty and fearful planning for the future was also apparent in post-plague killings that arose from disputes over land ownership, borders and field maintenance. The plague left much land untended, and in the immediate aftermath, peasants and landowners alike moved to procure more land or to modify the boundaries of their fields. *Danno dato*, damage caused by livestock to others' land, was a perennial cause of conflict and violence between peasants.[41] In the period following the vicious plague of 1630, these conflicts were sharpened by the diminution of the labour force and the concomitant rise in anxieties for the seasons ahead, which, as shown above, made the management of food supply a matter of one's own life and someone else's death.

More land was available for a smaller number of farmers after the plague. This did not lessen competition and conflict over the control of arable farmland, however. On September 8, 1632, Gemignano Fabbri and Dominico Fabbri argued in the commune of Vigo, and Gemignano

---

[40] ASB, *Torrone*, 5918, f. 301r–391r.
[41] G. Hanlon, *Human Nature in Rural Tuscany: An Early Modern History* (New York: Palgrave Macmillan, 2007); A. Dani, *Il processo per danni dati nello Stato della Chiesa (secoli XVI–XVIII)* (Monduzzi, 2006).

ended up stabbed, dying from his knife wound on the spot about two hours before sunset.[42] The recent plague had left a piece of land bordering Domenico's property empty and available for purchase. Gemignano, a labouring farmer, had hoped to raise his station by cobbling together the resources to purchase the small plot. Domenico, a physician, preferred to expand his land holdings further and stabbed Gemignano when negotiations soured. In another case, two neighbours, Domenico Ascorri and Bartolomeo Toschi, argued over the boundary between their fields near Medecina.[43] When they met at the church of San Michele di Sanzanigo on February 22, they first exchanged words before Bartolomeo grabbed his dagger and stabbed Domenico in the arm and shoulder. Domenico died of his wounds. Bartolomeo was sentenced to ten years' galley service but was pardoned when he made peace with Domenico's family and the conflict over land was resolved.

Girollamo Scozzeri, a member of a family with land near Sant'Agata, accused Biagio Mattioli of cutting down some sheaves of wheat.[44] The Mattioli brothers were outside the town church on May 3, 1632, when Girollamo and his brother Pierino showed up armed with farm implements. Girollamo stabbed Biagio with a boar spear (*ronca*) while Pierino wielded a pitchfork. Biagio died on May 5. Similarly, Paolo Stadiera was fed up with his enemy's employees habitually pasturing their beasts on his land and confronted them the night of June 19, 1632, in his fields near Ceniglio.[45] When Paolo demanded they remove the beasts, one employee, Niccolo Borsi, replied, "Let them stay, or we'll shoot you"; the argument ended when he did just that. The impact of plague on land tenure, management and ownership was manifested in the tense and often violent negotiations over the distribution of land left untilled by plague deaths. Whether they were attempting to procure more land, expand the holdings they already possessed or ensure that their land was productive enough to survive the upcoming winter, rural *bolognesi* killed their townsmen and neighbours in the uncertain times following plague. Most of these killings were committed with short blades or farm tools, a fact that speaks to both the combatants' generally low or middling status and the relatively spontaneous nature of their violent acts.

---

[42] ASB, *Torrone*, 5915, f. 444r–490v.   [43] ASB, *Torrone*, 5850, f. 301r–320v.

[44] ASB, *Torrone*, 5895, f. 612r–*fine*.

[45] ASB, *Torrone*, 5895, f. 337r–394v. This case speaks further to the fraught social economy of plague and post-plague North Italy. During the plague, upon the death of the incumbent, a new miller was brought to Ceniglio. Distrustful of this outsider and the contagion he might bring, Paolo and a group of villagers surrounded the mill and attempted to enforce a quarantine on the newcomer.

It was not only poor shareholding farmers who resorted to violence to protect the viability of their land. By reducing the available labouring population, the plague of 1630 also shook up the labour market in the villages around Bologna. Employers poached each other's tenant labourers, who were drawn by promises of higher wages and better treatment, and who eagerly exploited the labour shortage to improve their lots. This shift in the labour market drove both employers and employees to kill laterally and vertically, although cases of employee-employee murder appear much like those above, as cases of defence against *danno dato*. The farm labour market was based on the *mezzadria*, or sharecropping system, and it thus depended on a surplus of labour to sustain the economic relationship between landowner and tenant farmer that defined the rights and responsibilities of each.[46] When this surplus became a dearth, peasants moved more freely between landowners, allowing their employers to resolve the ensuing conflicts between them.

Landowners reacted with violence when other landowners employed their tenant farmers. Unlike the peasants described above, these landowners displayed a degree of premeditation in their killings. When Rizio Balzano went outside to get a chicken for dinner at his home in Longara on September 7, 1632, Gabrielle Lombardo, who had been lying in wait with an arquebus, shot him in the back and fled.[47] It transpired that one of Lombardo's tenants had recently taken employ with Balzano, under the false pretence that he had received permission from Lombardo to do so. Rather than initiate a protracted legal suit in the *Foro Civile*, which would have drained resources and precious time during the harvest season when all hands were required in the fields, Lombardo put an end to their argument by resorting to fatal violence.

On May 24, Armisio, the farmhand of a landowner named Giacomo Riatti in Fiesso, arrived with his brother from the fields where they had fed Riatti's animals; Armisio told his boss that the two of them had found one of the labourers for land owned by the monks of Santa Maria Nuova dead in a ditch on Riatti's land.[48] Riatti was indirectly responsible for the death: two weeks before, the young man, whose name was Giacomo Sgarzi, came to Riatti and told him he wanted a new employer; his current boss, Giacopo degl'Atti, was starving him and mistreating him. Riatti was unable to employ Giacomo Sgarzi, but did send him to a friend who would employ him at the farm belonging to Santa Maria Nuova. Giacopo degl'Atti was condemned for stabbing the boy to death. In killing his employee who had fled his abusive service, degl'Atti may have

---

[46] C. F. Black, *Early Modern Italy: A Social History* (London: Routledge, 2001), 43–48.
[47] ASB, *Torrone*, 5911, *in fine*.   [48] ASB, *Torrone*, 5885, f. 347–372.

been warning other employees and employers: if they left his service or employed those who had, retribution would surely follow. It is difficult to tell how premeditated this killing was, but the fact that the employee was found in a ditch may indicate that he had been ambushed. A third man, Sabbatino Buzzeri, was killed in Vergnana di Sotto on June 21, 1632.[49] While no one was ever processed for this homicide, the dead man's companions all alluded to their employer's responsibility without saying why or how the man might have wanted to kill his employee.

While the unstable market for employment contributed to homicides between employers and employees after the plague, the uncertainties of inheritance after so much unexpected death could have fatal consequences for families. Younger sons, formally dispossessed by a system of *primogeniture* and perhaps finding their father dead intestate, sought to gain a share of the family patrimony. One particularly vivid homicide makes the case that the plague left in its wake disputes between brothers over family holdings; without mediation, these disputes could turn violent and even fatal. Fratricide was uncommon: in the sample of 658 homicides here considered, there were nine fratricides; six occurred in the course of drunken disputes, and the remaining three, in 1632, in 1640 and 1660, were the results of arguments over the division and sharing of land.

The case from 1632 stands out because the belligerents, the brothers of the Piatesi family, were high-status nobility with roots in the city and extensive holdings in San Venanzo. On March 3, 1632, Francesco Piatesi was shot and killed while walking with his brother Ippolito.[50] Ippolito immediately ran to Francesco's house, where he informed the servants that a third brother, the Count Carlo Piatesi, had been the gunman and had killed his own brother. The murder emerged from a dispute over a small piece of the family land. The first witness called, a servant named Jacopo Fabretti, revealed that the family had divided into two factions: on one side, Francesco and Ippolito; on the other, Carlo and Alessandro, the fourth brother. About a month earlier, Ippolito had sold his brother Alessandro a small house on the family land, in exchange for some rich red textiles. Alessandro wanted to tear the house down, and rebuild it in another location, along with Carlo; the two younger brothers wanted to manage their own affairs free of the interference of the older pair. Francesco refused to allow them to tear the house down, and on the day in question, he confronted Alessandro and Carlo about their desires to part ways from the family patrimony. A witness stated that Francesco and

---

[49] ASB, *Torrone*, 5916, *in fine*.   [50] ASB, *Torrone*, 5857, f. 299r–366v.

Ippolito initiated the altercation, but that Alessandro committed the first insult, calling his brothers "*can'becchi*," cuckolds. The argument escalated from words to deeds, and Carlo shot Francesco in the head, killing him immediately. Thus did a family argument over land, controlled by the eldest brother after his father's passing during the plague, end with a fratricide resulting from the younger siblings' desires to exercise independent control over their wealth and the elder brothers' refusal to break up the family patrimony.

The Piatesi were radically destabilized by the death of their father, and resentments that may have seethed beneath the surface while the patriarch lived quickly found an outlet when Count Alessandro felt slighted by his share of the patrimony and wished to strike out on his own with his brother. In a noble culture that emphasized clan and kinship ties above all other loyalties, keeping the family patrimony intact was a priority for noble families. The Piatesi demonstrate well the effects of widespread plague mortality on family and social structure during the recovery. With the death of the family patriarch, the ties that bound the brothers together were broken; the younger brothers were in a position to amplify their social status by appropriating a larger and more independent part of the family holdings than their father's testament had given them.

This chapter has reviewed the effects of plague on the ways that plague destabilized social and economic relationships in the countryside, leading to conflicts over land and labour. This destabilization affected more than the ability of landowners and farmers to manage food supplies and ensure adequate harvests. Practices of authority broke down as well, and *contadini* murdered judicial officers. Peasants and townsfolk killed *sbirri*, the rudimentary police force responsible for arresting and bringing prisoners to the city for trial. An atmosphere of distrust in government officials – especially those who had been tasked with enforcing the hated quarantine measures during the plague – alongside their generally poor repute among the population made these law-men targets when villagers found their interests in direct conflict with those of the central court.[51] The *sbirri* in 1632 were stand-ins for the frustrations of rural poor who received no support from the central government during their recovery from North Italy's deadliest plague.

As Steven Hughes demonstrates, law-men perhaps deserved their reputation, given they were specifically and intentionally recruited from among people only "one step removed from the criminals they captured."[52] On March 6, 1632, sixty-five-year-old Giacopo Ariento,

---

[51] Hughes, "Fear and Loathing in Bologna and Rome the Papal Police in Perspective."
[52] Ibid., 97.

who may have acted as a local court informant, sat down for dinner with Capitano Francesco Incontri, a constable of the *Torrone*, in Camugnano.[53] Francesco had sent a man to Bagnano to fetch Giacopo because he wanted to discuss matters in Camugnano. When the two argued over the character of an unnamed man, Francesco grabbed an implement from the hearth and struck Giacopo with it; as Giacopo stood up and tried to flee, Francesco shot him in the back. Giacopo's son told the court that the Capitano "is a person completely at home committing homicides, who will kill someone for anything, just like he did my dad."[54] Like other *sbirri* who killed, Francesco was not convicted or condemned. Not all law-men were serial murderers like Francesco. Nevertheless, the peasants of Bologna in 1632 were not misplaced in venting frustrations against *sbirri*, whom they viewed as the violently intrusive agents of an authority that did not succour the inhabitants of the *contado* during the plague.

This seething resentment boiled over on the night of October 30, 1632, in the fortified town of Castel Bolognese.[55] A group of *sbirri* led by Felice Lorenzini and Domenico di Silvio, the gatekeeper of the town, were on patrol outside the town hall when they encountered a group of ten men led by Giovan' Battista Marcolini, between two and five hours after sunset. Marcolini accosted the *sbirri* with the words: "You are here to spy on us, to tell the Lord Commissioner that we go about armed at night."[56] According to the denunciation made by the bailiff of Castel Bolognese, Domenico di Silvio replied quite civilly, given that "spy" was a serious insult that conjured up associations with inquisition and oppressive social control: "I am a *sbirro*, but I do not spy." Incensed, Marcolini turned words into deeds: he first whipped Lorenzini in the face with the butt of his pistol before shooting him in the shoulder. In the ensuing firefight, in which a witness recounted that she heard "seven or eight shots, fired in two or three rounds," Marcolini's father and brother came to his aid, and another *sbirro* was wounded. Lorenzini fell to the ground, and he survived long enough to give a statement from a sickbed before dying of his wounds on November 1, 1632.

In his statement, Lorenzini noted that the men had been drinking; they carried arms and were becoming rowdy, and so he and his officers

---

[53] ASB, *Torrone*, 5898, f. 352–387.   [54] Ibid., f. 356r.
[55] ASB, *Torrone*, 5943, f. 299–*fine*.
[56] Bans on loitering, particularly while armed, in groups of more than four to six were frequent in the later sixteenth and seventeenth centuries, as a means to reduce incidences of street gang violence. Cf. ASBo, *Bandi*, Series I, No. 3, *bandi* of June 19, 1559; Series I, No. 4, *bandi* of June 30, 1574, May 12, 1576, June 24, 1578, August 12, 1579; Series I, No. 6, *bando* of July 25, 1591.

interrupted their party. Lorenzini also noted that before interrupting, he did in fact attempt to inform the town's commissioner about the group, but the man had gone to bed and his house was locked. Lorenzini insisted that his *sbirri* were convinced the men were up to no good: "we doubted that they had not committed some evil and were fleeing." On its surface, then, this homicide occurred during a botched arrest. However, the altercation that preceded the homicide, particularly the accusation that the *sbirri* were spies, indicates that the drinkers did not acknowledge, let alone respect, the authority of the law-men to interfere in their social lives. The measures taken by the civil authority to control the spread of the plague had failed to prevent it from killing thousands of *bolognesi*; and the *sbirri* were a visible, physical representation of those failures. Their continued intrusion into the activities of Marcolini and his companions – who were probably not total innocents – was met with the violent rejection of their authority to do so.

That this altercation occurred outside the town hall reinforces this point: in 1632, the representatives of civil justice had lost their legitimate authority to police order. Having failed to prevent the deaths of thousands, the *sbirri* bore the brunt of frontline frustration as survivors sought to rebuild and to improve their stations in life. Marcolini and his fellow revellers may indeed have been up to no good; witnesses could only recount that they had been drinking in a tavern operated by a woman named Bianca, and that they had continued their revelry outside. Marcolini's brother Riciotto, who was also involved in the firefight and who was subsequently caught and taken prisoner, insisted that neither he, nor his father, nor any of his brothers, had ever "been investigated, condemned or processed in any way whatsoever" and that they were all licensed to carry firearms in the Castello. Another witness, one of Marcolini's party, noted that the *sbirri* had been drinking all night in the same tavern. While *sbirri* were never held up as paradigms of virtue to be respected at all times, this case indicates that they were positively reviled in 1632.

Nobility were killed by common folk, too, when they acted as representatives of law and order. Alessandro Marsilii, the Provedere della Fortezza of Castel dei Britti, tried to arrest Gironimo Sacchetti on the night of July 5, 1632.[57] Gironimo shot him dead and fled. In contumacy, Gironimo was sentenced to perpetual galley slavery, but the casebook notes his fate as *interfectus* – killed. How this happened is unknown, but his crime speaks to the same tensions displayed in the shootout with *sbirri*

---

[57] ASB, *Torrone*, 5885, f. 444r–*fine*.

described above. As the inhabitants of the Bolognese countryside rebuilt their lives after the plague, they rejected the authority of the *sbirri*, and thus of the secular court, to practice the sort of social control that had, in fact, been relatively successful in controlling violence and arms possession in the 1620s.

The diminution of trust in and respect for the ability of institutions and officials to resolve conflicts also led people to settle old scores. Revenge homicides and homicides proceeding from minor obligations such as card-playing debts featured heavily in the judicial record. These homicides indicate that in times of societal stress, *bolognesi* looked first toward the protection of their interests and their families' safety, appropriating the obligation to react with violence to slights – perceived or real. These public homicides served to advertise the killer's status to witnesses and others around town, and to ensure that this status was respected by the killer's co-vivants. Pier Francesco Zini was killed on October 9 in a roadside ambush near Sassadello by four or five members of the Linguerni family, his enemies.[58] Egidio Vernizi and his accomplices – eighteen or twenty of them, according to witnesses who saw them flee – shot and killed Stefano Fabri after his nephew, Egidio's farmhand, had tried to kill his employer a few days prior.[59] Stefano was also a known cattle rustler. After Giovan Battista beat up his son while guarding his father's fields, Sabbatino Galli went to teach the fourteen-year-old youth a lesson. When Sabbatino and his brother arrived in Giovan Battista's field, heavily armed, the boy shot Sabbatino and fled.[60]

Killings that broke official peace accords provide acute evidence that revenge killings in 1632 demonstrated a breakdown of centralized judicial order. These *paci* were registered documents included in judicial procedure that enabled offenders to receive pardon and brought ends to judicial processes.[61] In Bologna, they were a feature of a judicial system that ultimately sought to mediate violent conflict rather than punish it;

---

[58] ASB, *Torrone*, 5972, *in fine.*   [59] ASB, *Torrone*, 5892, f. 299r–429v.
[60] ASB, *Torrone*, 5883, *in fine.*
[61] Natalie Zemon Davis, *Fiction in the Archives: Pardon Tales and Their Tellers in Sixteenth-Century France* (Stanford, CA: Stanford University Press, 1987); Nicole Castan, "The Arbitration of Disputes under the Ancien Regime," in John Bossy, ed., *Disputes and Settlements: Law and Human Relations in the West*, pp. 219–60 (Cambridge: Cambridge University Press, 1983); Claude Gauvard, "Les clercs de la Chancellerie Royale Française et l'écriture des lettres de remission aux XIVe et XVe siecles," in K. Fianu and D. J. Guth, eds., *Écrit et pouvoir dans les chancelleries médiévales: espace français, espace anglais*, Textes et études du Moyen Âge, 6 (Louvain-la-Neuve: Fidem, 1997), 281–91; A. Logette, *Le prince contre les juges: grâce ducale et justice criminelle en Lorraine au début du XVIIe siècle* (Nancy: Presses universitaires de Nancy, 1993); O. Niccoli, *Perdonare: Idee, pratiche, rituali in Italia tra seicento e cinquecento* (Rome: Editori Laterza, 2007); C. Nubola, "Supplications between Politics and Justice: The Northern and Central

in doing so, this system was designed to prevent outbreaks of revenge violence, precisely like the one seen in 1632, from further damaging Bolognese communities. Breaking an official peace was an act that defiantly rejected that system's goals in favour of an individualist approach to justice in which insults and attacks required equal or greater retribution to vindicate the offended parties.

Domenico Cisa took such retribution against Leone della Strada in Figareno on September 29, 1632.[62] The two had been in a swordfight in Crovara the previous year, after which a peace was forged and the two made to swear not to offend again. However, Domenico refused to abide by it and attacked Leone during Mass, shooting him in the church. The location, the weapon and the timing ensured that this public and premeditated killing would be advertised broadly throughout the neighbouring villages, restoring Domenico's reputation as a hard man who was not to be trifled with. Enemies reticent to forge a peace killed to prevent its implementation. Giovanni Angelini was on his way to Mass in Mogne on May 16, 1632, when ten members of the Sechi clan, long-time enemies of his family, ambushed him with guns from the house of Battistino Olivieri, after repeating taunting his mother with threats that her "son [was] going to be dead soon!"[63] Previously, Giovanni had been seeking to forge a legal peace between the two families. Men also killed in order to escape a judicial process entirely, as when Pierino Giorgi cut Angela Gabrielli's throat and shot at her husband, after she refused to renounce the quarrel she registered against him for house-breaking.[64] Through their violence, all of these killers advertised their rejection of the court's mechanisms for resolving conflict and maintaining peace in communities. High numbers of these killings in 1632 link them to the challenges faced by central governance after the destruction of the plague.

While many killers avenged wrongs done to themselves, many others killed in defence of their family members' safety or honour, particularly those of their female relatives. Pierino Smiraldo, a servant of a gentleman from Scadenari, killed Sabatino Comellino after the latter joked that the pimples on Pierino's sister's hand were the result of her life as a woman of loose virtue.[65] In another public revenge killing, Marco Gualandi and an accomplice first tried to shoot and then stabbed Angelino Paiazolo as he was leaving mass in Castel d'Aiano, following the rape of Marco's

---

Italian States in the Early Modern Age," *International Review of Social History* 46, Supplement 9 (2001): 35–56.
[62] ASB, *Torrone*, 5901, *in fine*.   [63] ASB, *Torrone*, 5879, f. 301r–519v.
[64] ASB, *Torrone*, 5878, f. 317r–381v, 396rv.   [65] ASB, *Torrone*, 5865, f. 299r–343v.

cousin Margherita two months before.[66] On August 2, Pietro and Antonio Brigame avenged the March kidnapping of Pietro's daughter by publicly, and in broad daylight, shooting Mariotto di Grillino and Lorenzo di Rinardo in the town square of Monterenzio.[67]

Conversely, men expressed their own frustrations by killing unfaithful or unwilling women. Biasio Compatelli killed his wife Sabatina di Rosso on October 8, 1632, because she had begun working as a prostitute in the city during and after the plague.[68] Matteo Costa killed Gentile de Cavalieri, his lover, in her pear orchard in San Lorenzo in Collina, after she had refused to move away from her family and live with him instead.[69] Oliviero killed his wife Catharina when he allegedly found her in flagrante delicto with Giovanni Vaglia, two months after their child had died and she had become depressed.[70] All these killings took place at a time when heightened societal tensions caused by post-plague demographic and economic pressures made recourse to retributive violence a prevalent option for Bolognese *contadini*.

In this atmosphere of quick recourse to violence to protect one's reputation and status, games and Carnival revelries could sow fatal resentments or erupt into deadly violence. Francesco Stanzini, a twenty-three-year-old labourer from Crespellano, threw gravel at Carlo Olmi during the February revelries; the two began to fight and were separated, registering a quarrel with the *Torrone* through their local bailiff.[71] On May 22, 1632, Carlo's brother Paolo Olmi accosted Francesco on his way to Vespers. Paolo bashed Francesco with a club, and gave him a few more after he fell to the ground. Francesco died on May 29 after giving an account of his history of conflict with Olmi to the notary of the *Torrone*, Santi Martini. When Antonio Vicinelli and Antoni Fanti argued during a card game in Caprara sopra Panico on September 3, Vicinelli's brother Domenico arrived and smashed Fanti's head with a rock.[72] Vincenzo Righi, called Il Barbiero, and Gimignano Carole clashed over Righi's debt to Gimignano from a game of *bocci* on April 28.[73] Il Barbiero stabbed Gimignano in the stomach, killing him.

In the absence of a working structure of conflict resolution, gaming could also bring resentments and grudges to the fore. One homicide aptly demonstrates the connections between public competition, weak social and central control of conflict, family structures, and homicidal violence. Two cousins, Giovan'Battista and Zaccaria Lolli, were playing

---

[66] ASB, *Torrone*, 5874, f. 387r–445v. [67] ASB, *Torrone*, 5922, *in fine.*
[68] ASB, *Torrone*, 5921, *in fine.* [69] ASB, *Torrone*, 5901, f. 300r–323v.
[70] ASB, *Torrone*, 5867, f. 303r–332v. [71] ASB, *Torrone*, 5881, f. 301r–375v.
[72] ASB, *Torrone*, 5915, f. 44r4–490v. [73] ASB, *Torrone*, 5863, *in fine.*

a game of lawn bowling in Castel Fiuminesi on May 1, 1632.[74] The outdoor public area provided the scene for Zaccaria to revenge himself against Giovan'Battista, who had shot at Zaccaria a few years before. As Giovan'Battista bent to throw his ball, Zaccaria shot him in the thigh; his second shot missed, and Giovan'Battista grabbed his own pistol and shot Zaccaria in the face. Both men subsequently died. Before the plague, the fragile peace within the Lolli family had contained this vengeance within a community structure of reconciliation and communal responsibility for conflict resolution. Following the plague, weak structures of judicial and social control allowed the individualist emotions of revenge and retribution to triumph over peace. Families were rent by violence as competing branches sought to improve their station at the expense of their relatives' positions in society.

Finally, noble conflicts occurring within the walls did not leave the countryside untouched. In addition to the fratricide committed by the younger Piatesi brothers and the killing of nobles by artisans, rural nobility settled scores and eliminated enemies in the weak judicial environment of the Bolognese countryside. On August 24, Count Ramazzotto Ramazzotti left the church of San Bartolomeo with two companions after hearing Mass in Castel San Pietro, and headed toward the nearby Borgo San Pietro.[75] As a witness told it, as he passed "outside the gate, near the gatehouse, five shots were fired from inside a workshop at the said Count," which hit him, killing him immediately. It was a brazen daylight assassination. His enemies from the city, Stefano della Fisca and several members of the Pignattarini clan, had removed themselves to this rural hamlet to eliminate their rival. They were all declared capital bandits and had fled the Bolognese territory. While the institutions of centralized justice were weak, their large armed group had escaped the attention of authorities. The destabilization of judicial and social processes after the plague allowed planned revenge killings such as this to flourish among both urban and rural nobility.

Conclusion

Throughout 1632, the social impact of the plague on violence was manifested both quantitatively, in the elevated homicide rates that year compared to sampled years on either side, and qualitatively, in the prevalence of factional, robbery and revenge killings, coupled with an unusual degree of violence toward judicial officials. The characteristics of

---

[74] ASB, *Torrone*, 5883, *in fine*.   [75] ASB, *Torrone*, 5878, f. 457–*fine*.

homicide in the plague's aftermath varied between the city and the country. In each setting, members of social groups who previously had maintained a degree of peace – urban nobles and rural artisans – killed in pursuit of individual goals; in doing so, they broke structures that had provided mechanisms, such as the peace accords and pardon letters, through which violent emotions could be displaced, and conditions of peace imposed upon individuals and communities. People killed both along and against the grain of social and economic hierarchies, murdering their employees or fellow employers, killing nobles in a defiant rejection of obligations of deference, and slaying priests or shopkeepers in their places of prayer and work. Families were rent by the plague, too, as tensions that previously may have been suppressed under the authority of a still-living patriarch suddenly came to the fore, as in the case of the rural Piatesi family discussed above. The homicides of 1632 reflect the breakdown of trust in communities and governments to resolve conflicts and improve people's stations.

In the city, this breakdown was most visible in a rash of noble killings that swept through the streets following the plague of 1630 – this is explored further in Chapter 6. The high levels of violence between the young men of elite noble clans indicate that the fragile system built by the Pope and the legates – in which Bolognese nobility ceded their traditional rights to justice and vengeance, in exchange for an active and important role in the administrative and legislative governance of the city – was strongly challenged by the chaos that accompanied the *Torrone*'s attempts to maintain order in the city throughout 1630. The effects of this challenge reverberated through the century, as the legates and the *Torrone* continued to face resistance from the elite noble clans who, after the quiescent early decades, fought in the 1640s and 1650s for the reinstitution of the traditional elite privileges that had been curbed by the *Torrone*. Noble violence continued, accompanied by political challenges to and movements against the court's monopoly on justice, frustrating the court's efforts to reduce hostilities among the city's leading families until at least the 1660s.

Outside the city, a similar pattern existed: individuals resorted to violence instead of submission to legal process or community means of peacemaking. As this chapter's opening narrative suggests, structures of hierarchy and submission were severely compromised by the plague-borne reality that death was the great equalizer. That nobles and peasants suffered equal pain and death from the plague made human distinctions of status obsolete. In the period of recovery following the death of 25% of the population, people lashed out against the hierarchies that governed their daily lives. Employees sought to change employers to improve their station, and either they or their new employers often faced homicide as the price of economic mobility. Groups of drunks engaged in fatal shootouts with groups of law-men who were ostensibly keeping the peace. Neighbours killed over petty land border disputes, and brothers killed for the opportunity to separate their financial futures from oppressive older siblings.

At the same time, country dwellers used the overall lack of order as cover to prosecute vengeance and gain satisfaction for both significant and petty quarrels. Men killed to avenge wrongs done to their female relatives, such as rape or kidnap. Conversely, they killed these women when their obedience and the relationship's stability were in question. They killed to avenge quarrels that had taken place years earlier. In some instances, petty arguments over gaming brought these conflicts to the fore, while in others, insults and aggression during games or Carnival festivities were left to fester until an appropriate moment presented itself for the offended party to take his revenge.

All these killings occurred in an atmosphere in which structures of conflict resolution were severely compromised, both by the morbidity of the plague itself and by the inability of central authorities such as the *Torrone* to assert their legitimacy both during and after the plague. The plague presented a challenge to the growing centralization of justice and peace in Bologna, and allowed ancient patterns of kin solidarity, factionalism and individual defence of status through violence to reemerge in the brave new world that awaited survivors.

6 It's Good to Have Land
The Defence of Noble Privilege through Violence

Introduction: The Death of a Judge

For Giacinto Pungelli, September 8, 1652, began as inauspiciously as any other Sunday in the busy northern capital of the Italian papal states. Giacinto was a *sotto-auditore*, or assistant judge, of Bologna's powerful criminal court, the *Tribunale del Torrone*. He made his way from the court's offices in what is now Bologna's city hall in the majestic Piazza San Petronio, and followed the pointing hand of Giambologna's Neptune fountain south toward the Piazza dei Celestini. There, he attended mass in the Celestine Convent, now the seat of the *Archivio di Stato di Bologna*. It would be his last Mass. While Pungelli was in the church, a group of men, led by two petty nobles named Filippo and Mario Stefanini, gathered in the piazza outside with arquebuses and knives. When the judge, his servant and a notary of the court left the church, the Stefanini descended on the group, separated Pungelli from his companions and shot the thirty-eight-year-old judge repeatedly before fleeing the scene. Pungelli's friends rushed him to the home of lawyer Giovanni Coragli, where he received medical treatment from the surgeon Rinaldo Battaglia, but he died of his wounds the next day.[1]

Pungelli's murder took place at a time when recalcitrant factions of Bolognese nobility were reasserting their traditional privileges against the papal legates who governed the city. The noble families of Bologna had endured diverse fortunes in the century and a half since the papal conquest. Branches of many of them adapted to papal rule and, by working within the systems of marriage, cronyism and patronage familiar to the papal court, had risen in stature and joined a broad North Italian elite, consolidating the goals and finances of the papal state.[2] Men of the Paleotti and Ghisilieri saw the benefits of the papal state's negotiated

---

[1] ASBo, *Torrone*, 6612/1, f. 1r–38r.
[2] Carboni, "Public Debt, Guarantees and Local Elites in the Papal States (XVI–XVIII Centuries)."

absolutism, which tended to leave local government structures and hierarchies intact. On the other hand, powerful rural nobility of the oligarchic period, such as the Malvezzi and Barbazza, had suffered humiliation at papal hands, and had seen their power and presence in city politics reduced to the right to participate in the Senate of Forty (at this point, made up of fifty men, though the old moniker remained), and their old judicial privileges stripped away.[3] The restriction of those judicial privileges had been a focal point of papal policy toward Bologna beginning with Julius II.[4] The *Torrone* – perhaps the most effective Italian criminal court of the seventeenth century, and certainly the most professionally developed – was the means by which the legates gradually drew artisans, merchants and other former clients of noble courts into the legatine fold by promising a better, more reliable means of conflict resolution and redress for wrongdoings.

As we have already seen, the crises of the 1610s and 1620s and the plague of 1630 interrupted this process, which until then had been relatively successful at reducing the nobility's public violence within the city. However, following the plague, radical elements within Bologna's nobility abandoned the fragile peace that had held earlier in the century, continually frustrating the attempts of legates to transform the Bolognese nobility into a Tuscan-style service class.[5] In 1640, 1652 and 1660, public violence such as the Pungelli assassination marked this resistance, and communicated both rejection of Rome's jurisdiction over Bologna as well as a revived claim to traditional rights of vendetta, violence and judgment. In this context, much like in absolutist France, public noble violence retained its place as a political and social strategy, as various

---

[3] On the ways that Bolognese nobility adjusted to, accepted or rejected papal rule, cf. J. deSilva, "Ecclesiastical Dynasticism in Early Modern Bologna," in N. Terpstra et al, eds., *Bologna: Cultural Crossroads from the Medieval to the Baroque: Recent Anglo-American Scholarship* (Bologna: Bononia University Press, 2013), 182–85; N. Reinhardt, "Quanto è differente Bologna? La città tra amici, padroni e miti all'inizio del seicento," *Dimensioni e problem della ricerca storica* 2, pp. 107–46; N. Terpstra, "Republicanism, Public Welfare, and Civil Society in Early Modern Bologna," in Terpstra et al, *Bologna: Cultural Crossroads*, 205–16.

[4] G. Angelozzi and C. Casanova, *La giustizia criminale in una città di antico regime: il tribunale del Torrone di Bologna, secc. XVI–XVII* (Bologna: CLUEB, 2008), 1–25; G. Angelozzi and C. Casanova, *La nobiltà disciplinata: violenza nobiliare, procedure di giustizia e scienza cavalleresca a Bologna nel 17. secolo* (Bologna: CLUEB, 2003), chap. 2.

[5] Cf. John K. Brackett, *Criminal Justice and Crime in Late Renaissance Florence, 1537–1609* (Cambridge: Cambridge University Press, 1992), chap. 1. Brackett's work places in stark relief the organizational and professional differences between Florence's *Otto della Guardia*, in which untrained civil servants acted as citizen-judges in order to exercise patronage and win influence, and the *Torrone*, in which a professionally trained staff of judges and notaries instituted a hybrid inquisitorial system that relied heavily on regularity and indifferent justice to win plaintiffs from private courts.

branches of noble families adjusted – or failed to adjust – to new legal realities over the course of the sixteenth and seventeenth centuries. The upshot was a general increase in fatal violence, much of it directly or indirectly related to noble agitation.

Reading the Pungelli case is difficult, as the accused and their witnesses actively dissembled and fabricated truths throughout their interrogations. That dissimulation itself reveals the strength of the animus between legatine justice and the noble clans, and demonstrates how illusory the seeming success of the early century had actually been. Some conspirators downplayed their roles in the plot to kill Pungelli and shifted the blame to uninvolved persons; others clogged the process with legal objections and technicalities discovered by their lawyers; still others flatly refused to cooperate, even under torture. The first three witnesses each gave entirely incompatible descriptions of the men who had attacked the judge, frustrating the notaries' attempts to penetrate their dissemblance. The case became extremely complex because of the status of both the accused and victim, and the level of investigation that status necessitated. Compared to an average homicide trial, which comprised around fifty folios for a thoroughly investigated killing, the *Torrone* dedicated a great deal of time and resources to investigating the murder of Pungelli: a total of ninety-seven witnesses, relatives, concerned parties and local authorities were interviewed or interrogated, bringing the case's total size to well over 1,200 folios. The formidable powers at the heart of the conspiracy appear to have escaped unscathed. Nevertheless, what we can learn from the plot to kill Pungelli reveals a great deal about the embattled position Bolognese nobility found themselves in by the middle of the seventeenth century.

From Mario Stefanini's confession, which was extracted about halfway through the process and in which he denied his active role in the killing, we can glean some basic facts about the case. On the Friday previous to the killing, September 6, Mario's cousin Filippo Stefanini arrived in Bologna, banned from the state but in possession of a *salve condotto*, a guarantee of safe conduct granted to exiles to allow them to seek a peace accord from their victims and the pardon that accompanied it.[6] According to Mario, Filippo told his cousin that the true purpose of his visit was to arrange the killing of the judge Pungelli, for which the Count Astorre Barbazza had given him some money.[7] Filippo had brought with him some men to do the job, who were hiding in his family house; he asked Mario to help him hide their presence until Saturday night, when the plan would be put into action.

---

[6] ASBo, *Torrone*, 6612/1, f. 496r.   [7] Ibid., 496v.

Already we see signs of a conspiracy among elite nobility, including hereditary magnates with the highest honorifics. Even without knowing the deeper context, it is apparent that there existed a large divide between the legatine judicial apparatus and some remnants of Bologna's magnate class, who continued to exempt themselves from the judicial regime. This gap helps contextualize the judge's murder, and the story that Mario wove for the *Torrone*'s notary, Anselmo Mainardi, reveals the noble mentality that persisted well past the moment when the Papacy's effective control over Bologna was beyond dispute.

According to Stefanini, Pungelli was marked for death because he had disrespected the powerful Barbazza clan by exiling a young cousin of the Barbazza count, Luca Tonelli, for his role in the murder of the priest of the twin communes of Vigo et Verzone.[8] Tonelli was a lackey in both these plots, a minor player among more powerful men. The priest was killed because the leaders of Tonelli's group, several men of the Parisi clan, held him responsible for the murder of a Parisi cousin. The priest's murder took place in June, three months before Pungelli was killed, during which time the Parisi party had fled into contumacious banditry while the *Torrone* investigated the killing, ultimately sentencing five members of the Parisi to hang.[9]

In those three months, Mario's cousin, Filippo Stefanini, and Luca Tonelli made contact with Astorre Barbazza and began plotting to murder the judge who, in their eyes, had wronged the clan by interfering in its private vendetta. The underlying political implications of the plot to kill Pungelli are clear. Directly challenging the authority of the central court of the *Torrone*, the Stefanini and their accomplices attacked a central pillar of papal rule, the curbing of noble privilege in its most literal sense, the practice of private law. The *vendetta*, an ancient code that structured obligations and debts of blood throughout the Mediterranean, took on the role of political protest, and its victims expanded to include not just the parties involved in the noble conflict, but those who sought to tame its explosive violence: the officials of the new criminal

---

[8] Ibid., 6607, *in fine*. In fact Tonelli was not sentenced de jure to exile, but rather incurred it de facto by fleeing the legation and receiving a death sentence *in contumacia*. Equally important, his exile was a legal fiction: Tonelli was present at the murder of Pungelli, having broken his exile and entered the city to avenge himself on the judge. Both urban and rural nobles in Bologna continued to harbour bandits and exiles as clients and *famigliari*.

[9] As was frequent, these death sentences were not carried out, according to the records of the comforting confraternity of Bologna, the *Compagnia di Santa Maria della Morte*. ASBo, *Cronaci delli giustizie seguito a Bologna 1050–1797*. Note too that at this late date, 1652, contumacious bandits represented a violent threat to rural security, countering the notion that banditry was effectively banished at this point.

law, whose work in pacifying the nobility proceeded only in starts and stops.

The public nature of Pungelli's death sent a clear message: certain noble families rejected the legate's criminal jurisdiction. As the recent magisterial work by Sarah Blanshei makes clear, the Bolognese nobility of the fourteenth and fifteenth centuries had enjoyed a large degree of judicial power, which they used to protect clients and attack enemies, exercising it from their neo-feudal estates with papal blessing.[10] The grand project of the reinvigorated papal authority of the sixteenth and seventeenth centuries was the elimination of the nobility's remaining quasi-feudal powers, a process that focused inevitably on the need to contain, control and ultimately reduce the public violence by which nobility advertised their exceptionalism. Pungelli's death was a flagrant attack on court authority, but it occurred in the context of partisan rivalry and anti-papal feeling. It was, in fact, one attack in what should be considered a low-level civil war fought in Bologna from approximately 1630 to the 1660s. Angelozzi labels this a period in which the Bolognese nobility was "disciplined," but the record of violence shows no such thing.[11]

The three decades after the plague of 1630 proved traumatic for the citizens and judiciary of early modern Bologna. Although the overall homicide rate dropped between 1632 and 1640, the proportion of homicides that occurred within the city walls grew by a factor of six between 1632 and 1660. After 1640, the next two sampled years indicate a surge of urban violence, particularly among the retainers and liverymen of noble families anxious to preserve traditional and hereditary prerogatives of violence and justice. The year 1660 inaugurated a shift in the geographic patterns of violence when, for the first time since 1600, the urban homicide rate was greater than the rural one. Urban rates were greater than or equal to rural rates for the rest of the century, with the exception of 1690. The traumatic urban violence of these years was the last effort of Bolognese elites to assert their privileges through murder and coercion.

Nobility, Redefined: *Torrone* Legislation on Factionalism and Weapons

The Bolognese chronicler Francesco Antonio Ghiselli, who began writing his chronicle of the Bolognese nobility in 1666, was curiously silent about the decades of violence that preceded his taking up the

---

[10] Blanshei, *Politics and Justice in Late Medieval Bologna*; Robertson, *Tyranny under the Mantle of St Peter*.
[11] Angelozzi and Casanova, *La nobiltà disciplinata*, 289–321.

pen.[12] Although broadly critical of the decadence of Bologna's nobility, he reported neither the quantity nor quality of homicides that occurred in the sampled years, except for the Pungelli affair. This curious fact might reflect Ghiselli's particular concerns, which focused much more on the evolution of noble ambition toward courtly advancement through social climbing, spectacular festivity and courtiership.[13] But the resurgence of noble violence manifested as a low-level civil war whose sides were murky and unstable, even within kin groups. Noble clans and families divided into loose factions dominated by old family names – Pepoli and Barbazza in particular, as well as Malvasia and Malvezzi. These factions fought each other and they fought the *Torrone*'s efforts to control or sanction their violence. During this period, the legatine government and the *Torrone* both responded with legislation and police action to improve public order and to mitigate violence in Bologna's streets and villages. Laws regulating expenditures, public gatherings, and weapons were the pillars of public order legislation.

As we have seen, early-century legislation tried to improve the *Torrone*'s presence and position in rural areas, and arms regulations frequently exhorted ordinary *contadini* to either take up or put down their guns. Beginning after the plague, however, and in line with the *Torrone*'s increased presence in daily life in 1630, *bandi* sought to regulate the city's streets in a much more significant manner. This was in large part because of the nobility's renewed zeal for armed bravado, travelling in groups, and reaching for weapons at the slightest challenge.

Increased weapons regulation inside city walls preceded more explicit legislation on factionalism in the 1680s. A 1637 *bando* by Legato Cardinal Sacchetti aimed to reduce the amount of weapons in the city, making their public use a capital crime and giving detailed instructions to gate-keepers and *sbirri* on how to manage transgressors bringing in weapons.[14] Guns were banned from all churches and cemeteries in the district, on pain of an immediate fine of 50 scudi to be paid to the arresting *sbirro*. Between 1637 and 1640, three people were executed for firearms infractions, one for firing his gun and the other two for

---

[12] F. A. Ghiselli, *Memorie antiche manuscritte di Bologna raccolte et accresciute sino a'tempi presenti* (Bologna : Biblioteca Universitaria, ms. 770), vols. 30–34.

[13] Noblemen like Ghiselli are at the heart of the "civilizing process" approach to violence, and representative of elements of Bolognese nobility who advanced their fortunes through accommodation of new political realities. Not all members of Bologna's elite were violent oligarchs, and not all were docile courtiers: civilizing processes are contingent upon the participation of elite populations. Spierenburg, *A History of Murder*, chap. 3.

[14] ASBo, *Bandi e Notificazioni*, Series I, No. 7, unnumbered *bando* of July 13, 1637.

possessing one.[15] The capital ban on firearms was obviously not so effective that only three people contravened it in this period; rather, the books of the *Torrone* are packed with summary citations by *sbirri* who, during their rounds, handed out fines and confiscated weapons from multiple people on a daily basis. Like all legislation, repeated firearms and weapons bans indicate their ineffectiveness. Weapons bans were repeated in January and March 1638 and upon that model for at least fifty years.[16]

Firearms were particularly dangerous to city officials, given their ubiquity by the mid-seventeenth century and their availability to all members of the civic body, but long-bladed weapons were the particular preserve of noble factioneers. Among the privileges retained by the nobility of the senatorial class was the right to bear swords in the city, and the right to license certain of their servants and retainers to carry long blades as well.[17] The March 1618 decree revoked the right to carry arms on a broad social levels (wishful thinking, yet again) but excepted from its provisions a massive number of civic officials and notables, beginning with the *Anziani* and the *Tribuni delle Plebe*, and including "The Counts, and Knights privileged in their persons only, because they are Noble, and lead knightly lives, but they should not train with them, and their other privileges are elsewhere described and admitted, but beyond these limits and uses they should not be suffered."[18] A 1640 decree promulgated by the archbishop of the city on behalf of an absentee legate stipulated further conditions under which nobles were allowed to carry blades in the city: daggers were forbidden to anyone carrying a sword who was not licensed to do so. Blades were required to be at least ten inches long, revealing a concern on the legate's part about concealed blades, assassination and predatory violence. Moreover, all blades were to be blunted with an "olive" on the end.[19] Following the plague, urban authorities sought to quell the influx of weapons into the city and to control their distribution among the population. The continued ubiquity of firearms bans, license revocations, and night-time bans on weaponry demonstrates how ineffective this legislation was, despite the high numbers of

---

[15] ASBo, *Cronaci delle Giustizie*, executions of June 6, 1637, January 22, 1638 and February 8, 1640.

[16] ASBo, *Bandi e Notificazioni*, Series I, No. 7, *bando* of January 15, 1638; ASBo, *Bandi intorno al Torrone*, "Rinnovatione del Bando...," August 13, 1688 (republication of *Bando* of March 24, 1638).

[17] ASBo, *Bandi intorno al Torrone, Bando sopra l'armi*, March 29, 1618. [18] Ibid.

[19] ASBo, *Bandi e Notificazioni*, Series I, No. 7, *bando* of December 17, 1640. The "olive" referred to was perhaps a carved ball of wood stuck to the tip of a sword, rather than an actual olive, which would not be much help in blunting a pointed blade.

citations given out every day for unlicensed weapons. To add to this difficulty, nobles were generally licensed to carry arms as a symbol of gentlemanly status, either through their participation in civic office or because of their hereditary titles.

Armed groups displaying their weapons in public were a threat to public order and safety. The *Bando Generale* of 1550 subjected the raising of armed groups of seven men or more, or unarmed groups of ten or more, to a fine of 50 gold scudi – a fee large enough that the targets of this legislation were undoubtedly the elite nobility who practiced factional violence.[20] Seventeenth-century firearms regulations generally included stiffer fines for carrying weapons while in a large group, a *conventicola*. Factionalism had never disappeared from the early modern scene, as we now understand, and its role in politics continued to plague the efforts of centralizing governments to bring nobility more firmly under control.[21] Bolognese legislation variously defined a *conventicola* as a group of between seven and ten men, in particular if they wore livery of a certain family, or badges, or even had their beards cut in a particular way.[22] The anti-factional legislation of the sixteenth century was still in force in the mid-seventeenth, though there are few records of its prosecution.

By 1652, the *Torrone* was again preoccupied with urban violence and disorder. Prominent among this disorder were the misdeeds of nobility. In the decade following the plague, factional divisions between old oligarchic and republican families reemerged. Sometime in early 1638, Signore Giovanni di Giovanni Lucatelli hired two peasants from Pepoli territories to murder and rob the Cavaliere Leggiere Benedetto della Torre.[23] In September 1644, two men were executed for the murder of the Senator Andrea Angelelli one year previous, though the nobleman who employed them remained anonymous in the execution record.[24]

---

[20] ASBo, *Bandi e Notificazioni*, "Bando generale publicato in Bologna a dì III di Zugno MDL," June 3, 1550.

[21] Gregory Hanlon, "In Praise of Refeudalization: Princes and Feudataries in North-Central Italy from the Sixteenth to the Eighteenth Century," in Nicholas Eckstein and Nicholas Terpstra, eds., *Sociability and Its Discontents: Civil Society, Social Capital, and Their Alternatives in Late Medieval and Early Modern Europe* (Turnhout: Brepols, 2009), 213–25; Angelo Torre, "Feuding, Factions, and Parties: The Redefinition of Politics in the Imperial Fiefs of Langhe in the Seventeenth and Eighteenth Centuries," in Edward Muir and Guido Ruggiero, eds., *History from Crime: Selections from* Quaderni Storici (Baltimore, MD: Johns Hopkins University Press, 1994), 135–70.

[22] ASBo, *Bandi e Notificazioni*, Series I, No. 6, August 25, 1591.

[23] The actual *processo* is not here examined, but the murder is noted both at the execution of Gasparo Spini, one of the *contadini* (ASBo, *Cronaci*, execution of March 2, 1638), and in a *bando* seeking information about his accomplice (ASBo, *Bandi e Notificazioni*, Series I, No. 7).

[24] ASBo, *Cronaci*, two executions of September 10, 1644.

Around the same time, Franco-Spanish conflicts in North Italy released large numbers of soldiers into the cities and countrysides, and they too caused many disorders; the *Torrone* executed twenty-nine of them between 1640 and 1644. The *Torrone* policy of the time was to present a firm hand of justice within the city to quell rebellious instincts and prevent threats to the state.

Alongside noble factions, the Torrone had to deal with deserted or deserting soldiers. In 1644, an unknown number of soldiers from Bologna's fortress deserted their posts and headed south to the service of the Grand Duke of Florence, committing many crimes along the way. According to the records of the comforters' confraternity, the *Auditore del Torrone* set a meeting with the comforters and declared that four of these men had to die.[25] The group was duly arrested in Mirabello as they fled south, and, again according to the *Confortatori*, the group was forced to play dice to determine who would be hanged. In the end, only two of the soldiers were hanged – two others had hanged in 1643 for deserting to the Duke of Parma.[26] Most of the soldiers were executed for desertion or fraudulently claiming pay. The *Torrone* continued its policy of executing institutional threats rather than executing the participants of interpersonal violence; these categories blended in the noble violence of the time, though execution numbers continued to fall. It is significant that the *Torrone* appeared to be losing the fight: in 1660, when the city's homicide rate was 106 per 100,000, only three people were executed, none for homicide.

This is not to say that the *Torrone* did not react to the disturbances. The legates of the late 1630s were active in investigating and tracking down killers, and publishing *bandi* about individual incidents that called on citizens to provide information. The legates offered both carrot and stick incentives to those who knew, for instance, who killed the butcher Giovanni Francesco as he was closing up shop on February 9, 1638.[27] To anyone who could turn the killer in for torture or condemnation, the *Torrone* would give 300 scudi, a significant sum, as well as the free remission of a similar or lesser crime. If any of the presumed conspirators turned on their accomplices, they would receive immunity from prosecution and anonymity as well. On the other hand, anyone who did not take the opportunity to inform would be considered an accomplice and therefore guilty. The legate Sacchetti was trying to create a prisoner's dilemma among Bolognese citizens.

Legates and judges used a combination of threats and enticements to gather information from the criminal underworld; many informants

---

[25] Ibid., executions of June 6, 1644.   [26] Ibid., executions of August 29, 1643.
[27] ASBo, *Bandi e Notificazioni*, Series I, No. 7, *bando* of February 11, 1638.

show up in trial documents as a "friend of the court" who wished to remain anonymous. They used more extreme measures as well, when they deemed it necessary. On October 10, 1638, Sacchetti encouraged Bolognese priests to break the confessional seal and report the murderer of Domenico Mainardi in a *bando* that appears as though the judges were otherwise at a loss: the *Torrone*'s officers had apparently found no evidence and were looking for "clothes, weapons, or cloth" that anyone might have recovered in the vicinity of San Petronio. In the late 1630s, order was already breaking down in the city, and the legate had to request information on the murder of Giacinto del Bono, the Barigello's *Cancelliere* and an officer of the court. The people of Bologna were not forthcoming with information, despite the proffered 200 scudi and free remission of two crimes: this *bando* was renewed two weeks later with an emphasis on the penalties for non-compliance.[28]

The *Torrone* was a daily presence in Bolognese life during these decades, represented by *sbirri* at the gates and in the streets, *massari* in rural villages, and declarations plastered on walls across the state. By its own self-promotion, the court represented centralized papal government and promised an impartial justice untarnished by factional allegiance and violent enforcement of arbitration. The "civilizing process" theory of violence and its reliance on a Weberian state apparatus here begins to fall apart, since seventeenth-century *bolognesi* had a very real alternative that persisted in the face of the *Torrone*'s administrative prowess. The building of the centralized state in Bologna was not welcomed peacefully by a nobility who saw the benefits of courtly politics, nor were all of its nobles content to channel their undisciplined vendetta into ritualized duels. Rather, sections of Bologna's senatorial class – branches of prominent families – continued to practice private warfare and revenge politics. The *Torrone* policed these actions as best it could.

The Pepoli family, one of the city's most ancient lineages and descendants of medieval tyrants, had active senatorial branches and appeared to defend a republican position from within the papal government, with prominent members developing civic charity schemes, for instance.[29] Members of the Pepoli family also continued the elite tradition of comforting the condemned, an activity that reinforced the justice of the *Torrone*.[30] At the same time, the clan refused to relinquish its traditional

---

[28] ASBo, *Bandi e Notificazioni*, Series I, No. 7, *bandi* of January 26 and February 9, 1639.
[29] Terpstra, "Republicanism and Civic Welfare," 205–17.
[30] Two Pepoli Counts and one Marchese comforted condemned prisoners across the seventeenth century, indicating that the highest-ranking nobility continued to see this charity as an important demonstration of their piety. ASBo, *Cronaci*, executions of January 29, 1661, October 20, 1666, and January 14, 1693.

noble identity that was rooted in violence and the legitimacy of that violence.[31] Younger members of the family continually appear in *Torrone* records, usually in cases connected to the violent deaths of their retainers.[32] They also pursued large-scale vendetta well into the seventeenth century.

In April 1640, Count Odoardo Pepoli revived an old disagreement with the Marchese Onofrio Bevilacqua in their neighbouring territories near Ferrara.[33] Using Pepoli lands in La Palata as a staging ground, Odoardo called upon his relatives in the city: his brother, the Count Uguccione Pepoli; the Count Alessandro Maria Pepoli; the Marchese Girolamo Pepoli; Girolamo's brother, the Count Camillo Pepoli; and Count Francesco di Giacopo Pepoli. Odoardo asked them for aid and armed men, and the five nobles gathered eight or ten men each before marching out of the city in a brazen violation of public order. Alessandro Maria and Francesco were singled out for "passing on horseback through the public square in front of the Palace of the Most Eminent Cardinal Legate with eight or ten men on horseback, each armed and heading towards the Porta San Felice," which would lead them toward La Palata.[34] The others left through the Porta Sant'Isaia. In total, some sixty armed men reconvened for a Mass in La Palata, where Odoardo welcomed them with open arms and his own small host of men. An anonymous "servant of the court" reported all this activity as the "debt of his office" and because the Pepoli's call-to-arms was "against the law ... as much as to provide against the disorders that might grow between the Pepoli and the Marchese Bevilacqua and his family who will arrive to help him."[35]

The legate himself became personally involved in the *Torrone*'s process against the Pepoli, and the court acted fast to prevent the Pepoli's misbehaviour from inspiring any other "scandals." The case against the Pepoli noted that calls to arms of this type were often the pretext for homicides and other violence, and it threatened banishment to the Veneto against the contumacious nobles. Witnesses at the city gates all supported the denunciation, having seen the Pepoli men riding out of the city; public rumour spoke of a rivalry between Bevilacqua and Pepoli, and of the murder of two anonymous Venetians by Pepoli servants in Modenese territory. These two homicides came as a surprise to the

---

[31] S. Blanshei, "Habitus: Identity and the Formation of Hereditary Classes in Late-Medieval Bologna," in Terpstra et al., *Bologna: Cultural Crossroads*, 143–58; Lansing, *The Florentine Magnates*.

[32] For instance, when Francesco Gilio shot Francesco Zannibono in an argument over irrigation at Count Edoardo Pepoli's house. ASBo, *Torrone*, 6610, *in fine*, 1652.

[33] Ibid., 6243, *in fine*.   [34] Ibid., denunciation of April 15, 1640.   [35] Ibid.

Torrone and were added to the charges against Odoardo. In June, Odoardo gave in: he drafted a petition to the legate, begging forgiveness for having raised the *conventicola* to attack Bevilacqua. He denied any involvement in the murder of the Venetians, though rumours persisted that he ordered their killings.[36] He begged for the cancellation of any process against him and his relatives. The legate pardoned both crime and punishment for all except Alessandro Maria Pepoli, who had strayed too close to the legate's palace for it to be a coincidence. However, even papal grace did not guarantee a peaceful end for the Pepoli family: Girolamo Pepoli was murdered two years later in 1642.[37]

The Pepoli were just one of many noble clans to become embroiled in factional troubles over these decades, challenging the authority of both the papal government and the *Torrone*, and radically and violently destabilizing Bolognese society. Harbouring bandits was an evocative challenge to the court's jurisdiction, and the nobility of Bologna did so often. As Ghiselli recorded, in June 1659, Fabbio Bolognini was accused by the legate of sheltering bandits in his urban palazzo, though he denied it publicly.[38] According to Ghiselli, the legate sent "the whole of the constabulary with orders to capture Fabbio, and to burn down his house if he did not want to turn himself in." They duly set fire to the building, and Fabbio jumped naked from a window, using the flames to shield his retreat toward the countryside but leaving his dog behind. Even when he returned for the dog, he was again able to slip out of the city, aided by his cousin.[39]

Noble violence was predictable only in its unpredictability. As Ghiselli related, on August 20, 1659, noble rivalries and arguments ruined what otherwise would have been a pleasant evening at a local fair. Count Antonio Gioseffo Zambeccari and "many knights and ladies" arrived at the festivities a couple hours after sunset.[40] When Zambeccari saw Giacomo Malvezzi, whose family was allied with the Pepoli at the time, he slapped Malvezzi across the face with a glove, recently having become angry at Malvezzi's associate, Marchese Guido Pepoli. Swords were drawn on both sides as Malvezzi's men rushed Zambeccari, but fortunately further violence was avoided. There are, in *Torrone* archives and Bolognese chronicles, countless episodes of this petty violence, much of which ended before bloodshed as everyone backed down to save face, but

---

[36] On petitioning and violence, cf. Davis, *Fiction in the Archives*; Claude Gauvard, *De grace especial: crime, etat et société en France à la fin du moyen age* (Paris: Publications de la Sorbonne, 1991); Rose, "'To Be Remedied of Any Vendetta.'"
[37] ASBo, *Torrone*, 6289, *in fine.*   [38] BUB, *Cronaca Ghiselli*, vol. 33, 50–51.   [39] Ibid.
[40] Ibid., 53.

some of which became homicidal. Many of the rivalries that divided noble houses were the stuff of public record and played critical roles in the *cronache* of the time. Ghiselli notes that following the death of Count Odoardo Bargellini, his brothers intensified their enmity with Count Rinaldo Ariosti and his brothers in late 1660. The resulting homicides, according to Ghiselli, destroyed all chances of any reconciliation and "finally achieved the ruin of the branches of these two families."[41]

The *Torrone* reacted to the resurgence of noble violence with both carrot and stick, including firearms legislation and emergency *bandi* that sought information on particular crimes or criminals. The *Torrone* judges also worked with a newly established government council to promote and enable peace between conflicting families. This body, the *Assunteria dei Liti e dei Paci* (The Council on Conflicts and Peace Accords) emerged first in documentation in 1658 and apparently existed until at least 1672 – it was evidently a failed initiative. Its extant documentation includes two peace processes mediated between the Bentivoglio, the Ghisilieri and the Malvezzi, which concluded with no resolution and which comprised fewer than fifty folios of documentation.[42] The legatine government was apparently unable to effectively mediate violence between Bologna's noble factions through its own official channels. The destruction of social and institutional trust initiated by the crises of the early century had riven beyond repair any ties between noble factions and papal overlords; as a result, factionalism and revenge became prominent features of Bolognese politics at the time.

Urban Homicides in the Wake of the Plague: The Nobility React

Bolognese urban violence in 1632 reflected continuing tensions between elements of local nobility who had revived the republican and oligarchic factions of the medieval period. Homicides in the city of Bologna were dominated by killings and fatal brawls between the young men employed as enforcers by these families. Homicides were much reduced in the record in the decades leading up to the plague (1600–1630) when compared to the 1632 homicide records. While the goons of nobility killed each other infrequently, or nobles killed insolent servants, these noble homicides formed a minority of the 114 homicides recorded in 1600, 1610 and 1620. Thus, the resurgence of noble fighting in 1632 – practiced, of course, by young employees and not the clan leaders, who

---

[41] Ibid., 250.
[42] ASBo, *Assunteria dei Liti e dei Paci* 1, *Atti dell'Assunteria dei Paci*, 1658–72.

thus gained a crucial bit of plausible deniability – showed the extent to which plague could break down the established patterns of society, particularly one as fragile as an informal noble peace. The government's efforts to eliminate the casual violence of warring clans had not eliminated the long-held rivalries that spurred them to violence, and they rose with vigour in the wake of the epidemic.

Thus, on the evening of May 23, 1632, Battistino, a corporal of the Baroncello's rudimentary police force, arrived breathless at the *Torrone*'s offices in what is now the Palazzo Comunale to report a murder.[43] Battistino did not know much, as he had come running as soon as he heard; all he could report in his initial denunciation was that someone had been killed outside the doors of the Church of San Francesco, in the city's west end. The court sent Santi Martini, a notary, to investigate, and he found a young man, "with his first beard … about the age of 25 or so" dead on the ground with a stab wound through his left breast – surely a swordsman's blow, given its expertise. Two witnesses, both members of high-status families, attended the autopsy and confirmed its finding. Giorgio Paoletti and Pietro Landi also identified the young victim as Marc'Antonio Acciarini, a young servant of Count Alessandro Bentivoglio. As the investigation progressed, it transpired that Marc'Antonio had participated in a swordfight in the streets of Bologna, a public conflict that transgressed and sought to undo the conditions of peace that had hitherto muted public factional violence.

The first witness called to give information was Silvestro Gherardini, the man who had first seen the conflict and, according to his own dubious report, ran to separate the fighting parties. Silvestro's report is checkered with the marks of a man giving unwilling testimony, who feared for his safety as he did so. He refused to name the companions he stated were in his company, and when pressed to provide their names so the court might also interview them, he denied even knowing them in the first place – they were simply his friends, but he did not know their names. His hand was wrapped in a bandage, and he claimed he received the wound while attempting to make peace between the combatants. It is more likely that he had acted as a second to one party or another, for what he told the court indicated a duel in fact if not pure form.

Silvestro told the court that as he had been returning from dinner, walking past San Francesco on his way to Sant'Isaia, he "saw two who were giving the question [*questione*, a challenge and resulting duel], and being armed with a sword I ran towards that doorway, and I grabbed my

---

[43] ASB, *Tribunale del Torrone, Atti Processuali*, 5880, f. 409r.

sword and shouted 'stop! stop!'"[44] Silvestro's heroic tale of running in between the warring parties, laying his sword on theirs, and receiving a wound to his hand in the process may have impressed the court, but his actions still failed to prevent the combat being fought to the death. Silvestro was careful to note that he did not see the fatal wounding, and he claimed that the wound must have been given before he intervened, because he saw one of the parties fall without witnessing the wounding itself. As Silvestro described the scene, he gave an account of the fight that distanced himself from any responsibility while making it clear that this brawl flowed from hatred between the Bentivoglio and Ruina families.

Silvestro could not provide any information about the fight's participants or origins, except that the killer was Pier Andrea, "who was a man of the Lord Marchese Ruina." The next day, the *mestrale*, or bailiff, of the parish of San Marino provided a list of names of men who had been present and needed to be examined, and the court dispatched summons for the four men he listed.[45]

What interested the court more than any other fact of the case was the position of both killer and killed as minor players in the households of very powerful families. How long had Marc'Antonio been employed by the Marchese Bentivoglio? He had lived with Bentivoglio for ten months, said his brother Ludovico.[46] After brief and fruitless interrogations of the witnesses provided by the *mestrale*, and of two neighbourhood women who heard the scene and watched from their windows, the court summoned the Marchese Ruina to give testimony. A high-ranking servant (his *ordinario*) answered his summons and submitted to interrogation because "the Marchese is not in Bologna and since Christmas I have served in his place in the household."[47] The *ordinario* provided more information on the killer, who had been in the Ruina household since January; but like the witness before, the *ordinario* was unable or unwilling to answer the question of why the two men had duelled in the first place.

Excepting the brief biography, provided by the *ordinario,* of Pier Andrea, the witnesses collectively had very little useful information for the judge. None of them knew the origins or cause of the conflict; none of them knew how Silvestro involved himself as the professed peacemaker; none of them had even seen the fight begin – everyone just heard the shouting and ran to investigate. Nevertheless, the witnesses all agreed that Marc'Antonio of the house Bentivoglio had been cut down in the street during a *questione*, and that Pier Andrea of the house Ruina was the

---

[44] Ibid., f. 412v.   [45] Ibid., f. 415rv.   [46] Ibid., f. 420v.   [47] Ibid., f. 430r.

killer. For a court more interested in tamping down outbursts of violence than in exposing the roots of social conflict, this was enough. Pier Andrea was condemned and sentenced to the galleys for seven years, where he was sent upon the process's close.[48] He did not write a petition for pardon, indicating either his death on the galley or his inability to receive sponsorship for his good behaviour following a pardon. The sentence of seven years' galley service was a severe penalty for an otherwise innocuous street battle between two servants, and the absence of a petition was also unusual. On such sparse information regarding the murder's cause or potential to have social repercussions, the judge of the *Torrone* had thrown the book at Pier Andrea.

The status of the belligerents and their social milieu helps to explain that harsh sentence. The two men involved in the killing – the victim, Marc'Antonio, and the killer, Pier Andrea – were representatives of two of the city's greatest noble houses: the Bentivoglii, oligarchic tyrants who had been expelled from Bologna by Julius II in the early sixteenth century; and the Ruine, who in the approximately 120 years since 1506, had grown to be principal members of the city's republican vestige, the Senate and its affiliated bureaucratic magistracies. The murder took on a character beyond that of two young men engaged in status conflict, exposing the streets of Bologna to dangerous networks of alliance and loyalty, of obligation and expectation, and the ultimate possibility of igniting a feud between two large and powerful clans. In its bid to reestablish and re-cement the authority of both the papal legate and the secular central court, the law came down harshly on the young man who had risked civil war in the pursuit of a conflict with factional origins.

Not knowing the full course of the homicide – the social context of the initial encounter, the words that led to deeds, whether it took place entirely at San Francesco or had its initial outbursts elsewhere in the city, and, not least importantly, whether the two young men were drunk at the time – does not prevent us from placing it into a lucid context. As noted above, the noble infighting for which the Bolognese elites were famed had been largely repressed early in the seventeenth century, and there were no equivalent duels or *questioni* in the sampled years leading up to 1632. Contrastingly, in 1632, the *Torrone* reported and prosecuted eight armed brawls resulting in deaths in the city; six of them involved young nobles, their attendants and hangers-on, or the soldiers of their houses. The outburst of public violence by the young men of noble houses can be understood in the confluence of social, political and

---

[48] Ibid., f. 436r–437r.

economic fallout from the 1630 plague. Natural disasters have been examined in diverse contexts, and a frequent finding is that dominant social paradigms – of social capital, of the right to rule, and of the relative status of groups and individuals – fluctuate rapidly and unpredictably in the immediate aftermath of societal crisis.[49] Factional violence often had its roots in competition for control of the local environment and its resources.[50] The nobility witnessed their customarily high status threatened by artisanal classes who yearned for a greater place in society, and lacking other avenues to achieve success, were willing to fight for it. The resurgence of public noble feuds, particularly of formal, ritualized duelling, was the response of a group under threat; they were reacting to perceived reductions of their social power by lashing out in very traditional acts of violence that emphasized their houses' historical skill at and responsibility for retributive violence within the city and rural lands.

With the Marchese Ruina out of town, and the Marchese Bentivoglio unaccounted for, the young men were the public representatives of their families, and had to maintain the prestige of noble clans at a time when the very bases of that prestige were being undermined by both the lower classes and the papal overlords.[51] The consequent responsibility that fell on these young men's shoulders resulted in a quick turn to public violence in response to even minor slights, even if the cost of that violence was an effective death sentence of a seven-year galley term. The remaining five brawls involving the young men of noble houses should be considered in this light. Following the plague, Bolognese nobles, or their retainers, fought to maintain their traditional places within a rearranged social structure that had dampened the nobility's influence on daily life in the streets of Bologna.

On April 7, 1632, a similar brawl took place on the Riva di Reno, north of San Francesco and in the city's west end; the incident demonstrates how the reassertion of noble status took place not just between families,

---

[49] Charles F. Walker, *Shaky Colonialism: The 1746 Earthquake-Tsunami in Lima, Peru, and Its Long Aftermath* (Durham, NC: Duke University Press, 2008); *The Lisbon Earthquake of 1755: Representations and Reactions* (Oxford: Voltaire Foundation, 2005); Diana K. Davis, *Resurrecting the Granary of Rome: Environmental History and French Colonial Expansion in North Africa* (Athens: Ohio University Press, 2007); Brian M. Fagan, *The Little Ice Age: How Climate Made History, 1300–1850* (New York: Basic Books, 2000); *Natural Disasters, Cultural Responses: Case Studies toward a Global Environmental History* (Lanham, MD: Lexington Books, 2009); *The 1755 Lisbon Earthquake: Revisited* (Dordrecht: Springer, 2009); Peter Sahlins, *Forest Rites: The War of the Demoiselles in Nineteenth-Century France* (Cambridge, MA: Harvard University Press, 1998).
[50] Carroll, *Blood and Violence in Early Modern France*; Muir, *Mad Blood Stirring*.
[51] Angelozzi and Casanova, *La giustizia criminale*, chaps. 1–3.

but within them as well.[52] As with the death of Marc'Antonio above, there were few witnesses and very little information available as to how exactly the death of Giulio Paci, the young son of Giovan'Battista Aquilini, came about. Giulio was found with a stab wound in his chest – here again, the mark of a trained swordsman. His body was identified by Giovanni Trevisani, who noted that the victim was a member of the *Compagnia di San Bartolomeo*, a local confraternity of notables. As the *Torrone* investigated, beginning by interviewing the dead man's parents and siblings, it emerged that Giulio and his stepbrother, from his father's second wife's first marriage, had found themselves on opposite factions of the city's nobility, Agostino joining the retinue of the Marchese Girolamo Pepoli, and Giulio that of the Zambeccari. On the evening Giulio died, he had encountered Agostino in a bottega, said one witness; another added that for eight years, Agostino had resented Giulio's presence in his home.

The young men were both around the age of twenty when Agostino killed Giulio in the street, and both had made names for themselves as young nobles attached to more powerful families. The circumstances surrounding the death are hazy, as witnesses once again were unable to provide details of the immediate event itself. One witness, the keeper of the shop where Giulio and Agostino had first encountered each other, went so far as to say that he could not tell what he knew because he was "afraid that they will kill me." There was an argument, and a swordfight, and Giulio was left dying in the street as his adversaries and his companions fled.

In cases of noble homicide, witnesses were often loathe to provide any information that would incriminate the predictably violent knights and elites who formed the upper tier of the city's domestic social hierarchy. As Angelozzi makes clear, the most powerful clans of Bolognese elites (Barbazza, Malvasia, Pepoli) continued to operate throughout the century in ever-reduced spheres of influence – private courts that adjudicated both civil and criminal matters between artisans and peasants, on whom these nobles pressed their authority with threats of violence and dispossession.[53] The efforts of papal legates to reduce and eliminate this practice may have been responsible for the massive spike in violence that occurred in 1660.

How, then, should we consider the testimony of witnesses to noble violence, who were for good reason afraid to say too much, knowing that their words would very likely make it back to the imputed killer and that

---

[52] ASB, *Torrone*, 5861, *in fine*.

[53] Angelozzi and Casanova, *La nobiltà disciplinata*, 36–41.

they might become the next target? It is crucial to separate the knowable and established facts – the name and age of the victim, the location of the crime, the date and time of the murder, the weapon used to kill – from aspects of the case that are more subject to vagaries of memory and strategic witnessing, such as the identity of the killer, the motive for the crime, or the past histories of both victim and killer that pushed them to their fatal encounter. Often, the facts are enough to establish an understanding of the social dynamic at play in a fatal encounter. When they are not, as in the case above, much can be gleaned from the common threads of resistance among various testimonies. What questions did witnesses continually refuse or fail to answer to the judge's satisfaction? Did multiple witnesses refuse to answer a given question from the notary's standardized list? Were statements that seem to have been evasive verified by other witnesses, or by other documentary sources from the *Torrone* and elsewhere? This is a perennial problem for historians of crime: for many reasons not always explicit, people – victims, witnesses, criminals – lied to judges, whether intentionally, through omission or simply because of a misunderstanding of facts. When an uncle claimed that his nephew had never before had any encounter with the law, this can be disproved by finding the relevant process in the *Torrone*'s documents. But when a statement concerned the social situation leading up to a murder, it is more difficult to assess its validity or parse its truth.

The first five witnesses – the father and stepmother of the victim, his younger brother, and two learned men who were in the area at the time – interviewed in the homicide of Giulio Paci make clear that the *Torrone* judges were confronted with hesitancy, an unwillingness to speak or impart crucial information, and fear of what might happen if word got around that witnesses had leaked secrets to the ecclesiastical government. None would go further than to confirm the time and the place of the death; that Giulio was a partisan of the Zambeccari, and his brother Agostino of the Pepoli; and that no one had seen Agostino since the morning of the murder, although witnesses took pains to assure the judges that this was not an indication of Agostino's guilt. They maintained these stories through repeated interrogations. The court was aware that it was not receiving all the information and imprisoned some of the witnesses, who continued to hold back.

Finally, on June 1, 1632, a witness was convened who admitted to being in Giulio's company the evening of his death. Niccolo Poggiali recounted how he dined with Giulio at Giulio's father's house in the evening before setting out around the city in his company, along with Girolamo Nanni, who had failed to provide this information during his previous testimony. Niccolo left them shortly while he entered a pharmacy outside the house of the Count Ruina and came outside to find Giulio alone, with the other two having headed toward the butcher's market in Galiera. According to Niccolo, he and Giulio went to the butcher's market and rejoined Agostino and Girolamo. Together, the four of them headed in the direction of the palazzo Zambeccari, where Giulio expected to find some friends. Outside the palace, they encountered a large group of people walking underneath the portico. Niccolo said to Giulio, "These must be Agostino and Girolamo's gang of lunatics" on patrol.[54] The group's members were armed, and Niccolo said that as they passed, he turned to see a man with a bared sword, who tried to cut Niccolo's face but missed. Niccolo escaped the crowd, drew his sword to defend himself, received two cuts from his attacker – and he was sure to say that he gave four for his two – and forced the man to drop his sword. During the fight, Niccolo heard Giulio cry out, "I am a friend! I am a friend!" before going silent. Niccolo went home and checked to make sure he was not injured before going to seek out Giulio at his home. When Niccolo asked where Giulio was, his brother Paolino responded, "A bad year; follow this portico here to go to San Bartolomeo and see it to believe it." Niccolo pressed on, asking, "Was he wounded?" and Paolino responded, "He is dead."

Although he provided the clearest account of the brawl yet, Niccolo still avoided the crucial issues for the judge and notary investigating a homicide: Who had killed Giulio, and how and why? Believing Agostino to be somehow involved, because of earlier testimony about the young men's respective allegiances, the *Torrone* pressed Niccolo on Agostino's involvement. After prevaricating over whom he knew and how much they knew, Niccolo admitted that a friend had told him that Agostino and "the sons of Giovanni [Battista Aquilini, Giulio's father]" were behind the attack but refused to say how he knew. Sabbatino added that Agostino had fled the city, which was supported by Niccolo's affirmation that he had not seen Agostino or Girolamo Nanni since the fight. Niccolo did note, however, that he had heard from the priests of San Giorgio that Agostino and Girolamo had taken refuge in their church after the killing, to avoid prison; he also admitted to having gone straight to the church of Santa Maria Maggiore immediately after learning of the killing, for the same purpose.

The judges were closer to an answer but were still facing a reticent witness. When asked the standard and crucial question of whether Giulio had any habitual or long-term enemies, Niccolo gave the standard denial

---

[54] ASB, *Torrone*, 5861, *in fine*; "dissi a Sig. Giulio devano esser questi matti d'Agostino et di Girollamo."

that Giulio had never been enemies with anyone, anywhere. His inter-view concluded with the judges not much further ahead than they had begun: a story was emerging of a brawl between groups of youths in the street, but no one would identify anyone, except for the young priest who attacked Niccolo, whom Niccolo had happily fingered as the first man to draw a sword. Still, Niccolo could not or would not explain why the fight had begun, who its principal instigators were, or who had given the fatal wounds to Giulio. The investigators now had the whereabouts of Agos-tino, at least; they arrested him at the church of San Giorgio and interro-gated him on June 2.

Agostino's interview took the case in a whole other direction. The documentation and the course of the interrogations thus far had made it clear that the authorities considered Agostino the prime suspect. However, he happily cooperated in the interrogation, telling the notary and judge about his family, the farm he and Giulio shared in Sant'Anto-nio di Savena, and the girl Giulio had kept there, who had left since Giulio was killed. He then gave a string of information about the killing – date, time and place – and said he knew all this because he was with Giulio at the time. His story confirmed that told by Niccolo Poggiali: that the four men (Giulio, Agostino, Niccolo and Girolamo Nanni) were out on an evening stroll and had stopped at an apothecary's shop before continuing to the butcher's market to buy some meat, when they encoun-tered a group of four or five armed men outside the convent of San Bartolomeo. Agostino denied that the group was known to him, and said that this group had in fact challenged his own. Somewhere in the ensuing scuffle, Giulio was wounded and fell to the ground; Agostino and his group returned home and searched Giulio's room, retrieving a sword before going to find a confessor. When they saw the large crowd, and saw the victim's father Giovan Battista and his brother Paolo being arrested, the group dispersed for fear of being arrested themselves. Still, the court was left not knowing who had given the fatal blow, nor what grievances had anticipated it. Agostino was not as forthcoming as he pledged to be, and lacked these crucial bits of information.

The frustration of the *Torrone*'s investigation, by repeated witnesses who failed to answer the most pertinent parts of the examinations, is worth dwelling on, because it confirms this chapter's argument. In 1632, two years after the plague had demonstrated the central government's inability to respond to a massive crisis, the urban population of Bologna was unwilling to participate in justice on the court's terms. Factions arose among local nobility, who instead turned on themselves to pursue and resolve conflicts. The code of silence that seemingly operated within the trial records is part and parcel of the pattern that saw homicide rates, and the number of homicides prosecuted by the *Torrone*, jump significantly between 1620 and 1632. It is not surprising that Girolamo and Niccolo were extremely reticent to speak to the court, even though their friend had been killed in front of them by people they likely often passed in the street. They believed that there would be better justice available if the details and facts of the crime remained within their specific social group – in this case, the violent young men of noble houses.

The case occupied the *Torrone* into the autumn of 1632, with the initial sentence given on October 1. In six months, the court had failed to amass enough evidence to pin the murder on Agostino directly. He and Girolamo were not convicted of the crime, but were made to undertake a pledge not to offend on pain of a 50-scudi fine. Agostino's mother, Giovan Battista's new wife Giulia, was also declared non-culpable in this sentence. On November 6, however, the notary copied into the investigation a letter from Domenico Benedetto, a local priest who claimed he knew how the death of Giulio Paci had come about: his father had arranged it, at the behest of his new wife and her children. The principal characters, including the father now accused of procuring his son's death, had already signed pledges to keep the peace and had been made to ratify their pledges in person. The *Torrone* concluded the case without any further sentencing or investigation.

Between witnesses' refusal to give candid testimony and the generally confused nature of the events, it is tempting to write off this case as a private matter between families and as a failure of justice for the murdered member of that family. However, this case reflects issues specific to its timing, in a period after the plague when the papal government was beginning to assert its judicial and legal presence more strongly by ramping up the *Torrone*'s activities. The plague itself had challenged the relationship between the "despotic" papal government and the "republican" nobility that still fantasized of Bolognese liberty, free of the papal yoke. There was no trust to be had between these two groups, and the plague had underlined this fact. The *Torrone* had attempted to maintain public safety in Bologna during the plague, only to be rebuffed at every turn by the groups of nobility who refused to obey curfew, continued to transport goods and stock into and out of the city, or harassed gate watchers. The state had failed to achieve its purpose during the plague, and whatever thin contract had kept the nobility more in line during the early decades of the century quickly dissolved. Given what we know with certainty about the above case – Giulio Paci was killed; his father had recently remarried a woman with a son of about the same age; and Giulio and the son, Agostino, were engaged in litigation over the terms of their parents' marriage – the homicide presents as a not-uncommon form of family homicide. This homicide was likely committed to prevent Giulio from receiving the inheritance that would now pass to Giulia and Agostino. The other possibility is that Agostino and Giulio had indeed found themselves on opposite sides of a growing factional conflict, between the Pepoli and the Zambeccari, and had pursued that conflict within the realms of marital kinship.

It remains unclear whether Agostino killed his brother as part of a factional conflict or colluded with his mother and stepfather to have him killed in order to seize Giulio's share of family wealth. In either case, however, this homicide must be placed within the context of a weakened judicial apparatus colliding with a population that preferred to resolve conflicts internally, that practiced a form of justice specific to the privileges of class, and that resented and rejected the court's efforts to increase centralization and assume responsibility for maintaining peace in the city. The relationship of a state to its population, and vice versa, has strong effects on the type and frequency of homicides in that state. In Bologna in 1632, the state had a weak relationship with a population that could not trust it to preserve the security of the city or of persons, whether physical or financial, or to prevent an epidemic from rapidly killing 25% of the city's inhabitants. The Aquilini/Cheldi clan operated in an environment of low political trust; the institutions available to them for conflict resolution, such as the civil court and civil litigation, were unsatisfactory to their needs and strategies, and could not preclude the possibility of violence resulting from the results of litigation. In such a circumstance, Agostino Cheldi arranged and possibly enacted the death of his stepbrother as the best option available to him to ensure that the conflict resolved in his favour. The collective refusal by witnesses to denounce Agostino during the 312-folio trial make clear that this dislocation from the machinery of government was not an individual phenomenon; indeed, in 1632, members of all social castes saw the legate's government and court as a distraction, possibly useful for leveraging concessions out of conflicting neighbours and acquaintances, but unable to provide real remedies for injustice.[55]

The pressing social and economic problems that resulted from the deadly passage of the plague all confronted both urban and rural *bolognesi* in 1632, whether in the form of estate division, the production of food

---

[55] The mixed use of court systems both to prosecute criminals and to put pressure on rivals to resolve conflict is explored thoroughly in D. Lord Smail, *The Consumption of Justice: Emotions, Publicity, and Legal Culture in Marseille, 1264–1423* (Ithaca, NY: Cornell University Press, 2003). A similar dynamic existed in early modern Italy, in which litigation was part of a continuous spectrum of methods of conflict, including interpersonal violence.

with a significantly reduced labour force, or the relative status and position of community members following the deaths of prominent citizens. After their recent experience with the state's ineffective crisis management, the young nobility of Bologna reintroduced a violent factionalism to the city's streets, in which the quick recourse to violence was a necessary and useful trait for survival. Of the sixteen homicides that occurred in the city in 1632, nine were public killings done by young employees of high-level families, usually in small groups of four or five and against the young employees of their *padrone*'s rival. Compare that to 1620, when not one of the three victims of urban homicides were noble. The destruction wrought by the plague, coupled with the widespread destabilization of the Thirty Years' War and the economic stagnation spreading across the region, ushered in an era in which there were no means for people to rely on the government for help in solving conflicts; in environments such as Bologna in 1632, homicidal violence between unrelated males would tend to spike *as a result of* the process by which the court sought to increase its presence and importance in the daily lives of early modern *bolognesi*.

Thus, in Bologna in 1632, in addition to the duel and the unsolved killing of Giulio Paci above, there were seven other killings of servants of nobles in brazen public attacks. These killings were all reflective of a noble class rejecting the pretences of their foreign overlord – the Pope himself – to police law and order in the city. The tyrannous republican oligarchy that had ruled Bologna until the beginning of the sixteenth century, and whose members continued to dominate its internal politics throughout the seventeenth, renewed their claims to the individualist justice and kin-based systems of loyalty that made recourse to public violence a means to broadcast and resolve their conflicts. Remembering Julius II's expulsion of the Bentivoglio family from the city 126 years previous, leaders of Bologna's noble houses remained careful not to engage directly in public violence themselves. They instead granted their servants – *bravi, socii, servitori* – a great degree of latitude to pursue both their own and their houses' enmity with public violence in Bologna.

These other killings largely followed a very similar pattern to those above, in which little legal satisfaction was gained after extensive investigation to determine the circumstances of the homicides, and in which young men targeted specific individuals for assault and murder, intentional or otherwise. Signore Alessandro Ariosto led a group of young men, including Giovanni Leoni and Livio Accorsi, who ambushed two servants of Signore Giovanni Grimani, and killed Orazio Donati in the Strada Santo Stefano three hours after sunset on September 2, 1632. Rather than face sentencing for their crime, which was widely and publicly denounced by witnesses, the killers all fled into contumacious exile, where one died. Ariosto and Livio Accorsi wrote supplications and forged a peace with the Grimani family that allowed them to return home on the payment of a 200-scudi fine, each.[56]

Giovan'Battista di Medico, a thirty-five-year-old lawyer, was shot in the middle of the night while walking through Piazza San Petronio with a *sbirro* on May 20; although a suspect was identified, there was insufficient evidence for a conviction, and Giovanni Giacopo Algardi was absolved.[57] The killing of a noble scholar at the *Collegio di Spagna*, Signore Don Giovanni di Sandovali, by a mixed party of Bolognese nobility that included members of the Landini family and Paris Maria de' Grassi, was preceded by a full day of brawls in the city. The conflict began with insults and minor offences during daylight and continued at various points throughout the city until two large crowds, one of young Bolognese and one of students from the college, engaged in a night-time battle outside the Palazzo Pepoli that resulted in the Spaniards fleeing while leaving Sandoval behind to die at the hands of the *bolognesi*.[58] In that case, the Landini, Alberati and Miserali who were formally charged were all sentenced to death in contumacy, while de Grassi and others were absolved for not having delivered the killing blows. In 1632, when trust in government functions was low and the legitimacy of a foreign ruler was highly contested, the noble families of Bologna prosecuted their own grudges and rivalries and rejected the authority of the legate, through a series of targeted killings of other nobles, through brawls between their servants, and through attacks on judicial officials.

Not all of the noble homicides of 1632 displayed the calculated violence visible in the ambushes and battles noted above. Fabio Roverso, a forty-five-year-old servant of Marchese Girolamo Pepoli, was cut down after dinner by another mixed company that included members of the Grotti and Colonna families and servants of the Marchese Ruina, in what was likely a drunken argument that brought residual angers and resentments to the fore.[59] While the specific conflict in this case was spontaneous, the fact that one of the killers – Achille di Roverso – was the victim's cousin suggests a long history of antagonism between factions of the Pepoli and the other families involved. As Roth notes, homicides between related males are extremely rare, except in circumstances wherein institutions governing family continuity and property were severely compromised.[60] This killing, as well as the killing of Giulio Paci,

---

[56] ASB, *Torrone*, 5910, f. 402r–479r.   [57] ASB, *Torrone*, 5864, *in fine*.
[58] ASB, *Torrone*, 5902, f. 455r–651v.   [59] ASB, *Torrone*, 5884, f. 301r–*fine*.
[60] Roth, *American Homicide*, p. 109.

possibly by family members in a dispute over inheritance, demonstrates this tendency well: fratricides were extremely rare, except in 1632, when those two cases occurred among high-status people of the city; lesser family homicides occurred in the city as well, alongside rural noble fratricides.

Another spontaneous killing took place in the Borgo Polese, in the city's northwest corner, near the banks of the Reno canal. On July 4, 1632, a brawl occurred between the servants and soldiers of Francesco Santacroce, a military captain, and of Alessio Filiani, a Doctor of Laws.[61] Benedetto, Santacroce's butler and the eventual victim, was leading his party through the neighbourhood when they passed the brothel run by Franceschina, a local *meretrice*. One of Franceschina's employees, Lucia, insulted them by calling them *becchi fottuti* (fucked goats) and other indignities as she lounged against the wall outside. The group of men began arguing with her, drawing Franceschina and a client outside. This client, Matteo Bartolini, a servant of Alessio Filiani, upbraided Benedetto and his friends for their behaviour. The argument became physical, and Matteo ran Benedetto through with a sword. While not obviously connected to an ongoing rivalry or conflict between houses, this killing nevertheless demonstrated how the crisis of the plague had amplified the male impulses toward status and the defence of individual reputation that created fertile conditions for fatal violence. These homicides, both spontaneous and planned, reflect the Bolognese nobility's rejection of the civil society envisioned by the papal government, in which nobility were to function as high-level administrators and abandon their traditional rights to justice, violence and the public resolution of private conflicts.[62]

Changes in homicide rates were driven primarily by changes in the number of killings between unrelated males. As multiple studies of homicide have confirmed, in times of societal pressure – after warfare, following famine and other natural disasters, and during times of economic crisis – social hierarchies are destabilized and relationships of respect or friendship during stable times can be rocked by violence.[63]

---

[61] ASB, *Torrone*, 5876, f.396r–429v.

[62] G. Signorroto and M. A. Visceglia, *Court and Politics in Papal Rome, 1492–1700* (New York: Cambridge University Press, 2002); I. Polverini Fosi, *Papal Justice: Subjects and Courts in the Papal State, 1500–1750* (Washington, DC: Catholic University of America Press, 2011).

[63] Roth, *American Homicide*; P. Spierenburg, *A History of Murder: Personal Violence in Europe from the Middle Ages to the Present* (Malden, MA: Polity Press, 2008); P. Spierenburg, "Faces of Violence: Homicide Trends and Cultural Meanings: Amsterdam, 1431–1816," *Journal of Social History* 27, no. 4 (July 1, 1994): 701–16; M. Eisner, "Long-Term Historical Trends in Violent Crime," *Crime and Justice* 30 (January 1, 2003): 83–142; M. Eisner, "Killing Kings: Patterns of Regicide in Europe, AD

This occurred in Giulio Paci's family described above: bonds between a father and his new wife broke those between father and the son, who died as a result. Similarly, non-noble homicides that occurred in Bologna after the plague exhibited a powerful disruption of hierarchical relations and standards of behaviour. A priest was murdered in his San Salvatore cell during a vicious night-time robbery by a student of the *Collegio di Spagna*;[64] two brothers-in-law, operators of a family pigeon business, had a quarrel over management practices that ended in twenty-year-old Carlo Ravi's death at the hands of Giacinto Mazzini;[65] Annibale Cesare was accused of murdering his wife, Margherita, after her autopsy revealed the effects of poison.[66] The killers inverted relationships that in stable times could have provided support and comfort, making victims of religious figures and close relatives in the pursuit of material or social gain.

The *botteghe* and *osterie* of Bologna were sites in which hierarchies were publicly manifested in relationships between employers and employees, and keepers and customers. In these meeting spaces, seniority of both age and profession provided order and continuity in times of general stability. Following the plague, they could be poisonous. A shocking assault committed on December 6, 1632, makes this clear. Petronio Pratoni, a local good citizen, heard a great noise four hours after sunset and went outside to find a crowd outside the inn of Bastiano Mariani, a sixty-year-old from Milan.[67] Pratoni sent a boy for the *massaro*, who duly arrived with his *sbirri*; finding the door locked, the group procured an iron bar and duly smashed out the door frame. They encountered a gruesome scene, which Pratoni described with seeming relish. A struggle was taking place: "in front of the fire on the ground was the said Bastiano, who is an old man, thrown there by a certain Domenico Magnano, a youth of about twenty, and the said Domenico had the handle of a short, bare knife in his hand, and the said Bastiano held it by the blade, and both of their faces were bloody." Bastiano said that Domenico had "robbed him and wanted to take his money."[68] The heroic Pratoni and the *massaro*'s men grabbed Domenico, tied him up,

600–1800," *British Journal of Criminology* 51, no. 3 (May 1, 2011): 556–77; J. B. Given, *Society and Homicide in Thirteenth-Century England* (Stanford, CA: Stanford University Press, 1977).

[64] ASB, *Torrone*, 5887, f. 301r–625v.   [65] ASB, *Torrone*, 5880, *in fine*.
[66] ASB, *Torrone*, 5876, f. 432r–453v. Another case of poisoning, with a female victim and three suspects – one female, two male – took place in 1632 as well. In this case, the killer was the fired servant of an elite courtesan named Valeria, whom Anna the servant killed. ASB, *Torrone*, 5904, f. 387r–468v.
[67] ASB, *Torrone*, 5900, f. 301r–363v.   [68] Ibid., f. 302v.

and took him to prison. Bastiano died six days later, on December 12, and Domenico was hanged on December 18.[69]

That he was hanged at all shows how transgressive this homicide was: there were six executions in 1632, and only Domenico was hanged for murder, while one other man was hanged as a bandit after committing multiple homicides.[70] Before dying, Bastiano told the judge that Domenico was a frequent patron, who would often come to drink and take a room, and that he "couldn't believe he wanted to kill me, for anything else than to take some of my money."[71] For his part, Domenico said that Bastiano had "begun to speak villainies to me" and that he had first met the old man about a year previous.[72] Domenico had come on hard times: "I have no money of any sort to secure me."[73] According to Giacopo Bardiani, a co-worker, Domenico had lost his job "two or three months" earlier.[74] Societal crises such as plague could exact extreme pressure on young men with small or nonexistent support networks; Domenico's mother and brother could not help him. With no job and no money, Domenico overturned the hierarchical relationship of age over youth and shopkeeper over client to express his otherwise impotent frustrations. Domenico's execution reflects the severity with which such violent transgression was discouraged.

Two other urban homicides in Bologna further demonstrate the destabilizing effects of plague on the normal course of business and social relations. Giacopo Camedoli stabbed the baker Giovan'Battista Maestri, alias Quinquini, while robbing his shop on March 26, 1632.[75] Robbery homicides were generally more common in the Bolognese countryside, where waylaying travellers or breaking into sheds and barns was considerably easier and more fruitful than breaking and entering into a merchant's shop in hopes of finding cash or goods. When robberies did happen in the city, they tended to be either petty incidents of pickpocketing gone terribly wrong, or, as in this case, aggressive invasions of property, often by more than one person. Giacopo, like Domenico above, was poor and needed money to eat, so he robbed Giovan'Battista and killed him while doing so.

Another workshop killing demonstrates how public spaces could be fraught with new status competition in the wake of a plague that, while killing swaths of the population, paradoxically created new social and

---

[69] ASB, *Cronaci*, execution of December 18, 1632.
[70] The timing of this execution was also significant. Winter months often coincided with a spike in executions of young, dispossessed young men whose cadavers were given to the University's Anatomy Theatre for their last act of public service.
[71] ASB, *Torrone*, 5900, f. 303v.   [72] Ibid., f. 311v–314r.   [73] Ibid., f. 314r.
[74] Ibid., f. 316r.   [75] ASB, *Torrone*, 5864, f.301v–337v.

romantic opportunities for survivors. Francesco Dorino, a thirty-year-old carter, had his heart set on the same woman as did his employer's son, Giovanni Battista Bucchi. On July 9, 1632, the two quarrelled outside the workshop owned by Giovanni's father, and Giovanni stabbed Francesco in the head and arm, from which wounds Francesco died the next day. The status hierarchy among these two is unclear. As the employer's son, Giovanni could claim a superior status to Francesco; as the older of the two, Francesco perhaps had more social capital, which nevertheless failed to save him. Francesco had recently married a woman named Francesca, with whom Giovanni was in love; Giovanni lashed out when he heard the news and killed his romantic rival. In more stable times, killings of this sort – romantic rivalries and other conflicts stemming from the sexual and romantic choices of women – were likely to take place out of the public eye, either within homes or outside the city walls. That Giovanni Battista walked up to Francesco at the hour of sunset and slashed at his head with a sword speaks to the level of societal distrust and the erosion of social mores begat by the plague. With a reduced population, a government recently proven incapable of protecting citizens from death, and an attitude of superiority over his father's employee, the circumstances were ripe for Giovanni Battista to lash out and to advertise his romantic conflict for the public to judge.

The year 1632 was thus a dangerous one to be within the walls of Bologna. Most importantly, a rash of homicides committed by and against the young men of the city's elite houses demonstrated the fragility of the government's program to reorient Bolognese nobility toward good governance in the early seventeenth century. While the levels of intra-noble homicides were quite low in the first three sampled years, they spiked in 1632, following the devastation wrought by the plague and the pressures this put onto society's economic, governmental and charitable resources. The nobility fought, via their young proxy retainers, to gain status and improve their clans' positions relative to each other and to the foreign overlords who controlled the legate's office. These fights could be public, to advertise a conflict to the entire community, or they could be clandestine, like the lawyer shot in the piazza, to redress a perceived legal wrong or to intimidate a rival group. Almost half of the urban homicides of 1632 involved young members of the Bolognese nobility.

For non-nobles, too, the city was a troubled place, although not on the scale of the wave of violence that swept the city in the 1640s and 1650s. Killings among the city's non-nobles showed a disregard for traditional relationships of support and comfort, such as within families, friendships and business associations. Even the church's power to engender respect was destroyed, as the brazen night-time robbery of San Salvatore shows.

Botteghe became loci of violent dispute in which intensely personal relationships and conflicts were resolved with deadly force. Significant to the
idea that killings in 1632 destructured stable hierarchies is the fact that a
firearm was used as the primary weapon in only one case, even though
men with guns were part of the crowd that assaulted and killed Orazio
Donati. Killing with blades and other close weapons was characteristic of
homicides in which long-established relationships formed the basis of the
bad blood, and where the killing was very much an act of personal
communication. The repressive measures designed to protect against
the plague created conditions under which factional violence blossomed
alongside robbery, revenge and romance killings.

Elite Feuding and Common Struggles: Case Studies from the War

The Pungelli affair stands out in *Torrone* documentation because of the
egregious nature of the Barbazza attack on the court's authority and its
directly rebellious overtones. It was a brutal public assault on an officer of
the court that could not be tolerated without major court action; nevertheless, it also demonstrated the court's relative inability to sanction and
reduce noble violence. The plot's leaders remained outside the court's
reach, due to the various witnesses' obfuscations and misdirections.
Although the court's conclusions pointed blame at Count Astorre Barbazza as a high-powered sponsor of the plot to kill the judge, only the rural
partisans, the Stefanini brothers, and their servant Francesco Vitale, were
hanged.[76] Political connections, the need to prevent further violence, and
a limited set of police resources all left elite nobility unscathed, if not
untouched, by the court's inquest into the public murder of Pungelli.
Other prominent political and revenge-based killings among the city's
elites resulted in similar *processi*, in which the henchmen and knife-bearers
of noble houses suffered the violent consequences of elite feuding, violence
that in these decades was overtly political and rebellious.

Assassination in Castel Bolognese

Of the manifold misdeeds of which nobility were habitually accused, we
have already seen that harbouring bandits was enough to draw the ire of
Torrone judges. Bandits often functioned as private henchmen for rural
nobles, preying on local populations and enforcing oft-illegal feudal

---

[76] ASBo, *Cronaci*, three executions of April 26, 1653.

obligations. Bandits were recognized for their capacity for violence. In the breakdown of civil order that followed the 1630 plague, they played a significant role in the violence-as-politics practiced by noble clans. Already by 1640, they reappeared in *Torrone* records as the agents of noble predation on rural settlements, even fortified towns.

On February 25, 1640, as reported by the bailiff of Castel Bolognese, a group of men entered the town of Castel Bolognese armed with arquebuses and launched an assault on Signore Don Antonio Maria Marcolini, a priest who had just finished eating dinner near the church of Santa Maria.[77] At least four men were involved, "the majority of whom were Capital Bandits, who are accustomed to committing murder," and they picked their target deliberately, launching their attack in public at an hour that guaranteed maximum exposure as the people of Castel Bolognese went about their evening tasks and sociality. After the priest finished his meal in the barbershop of Domenico Faschieri, he turned down the offer of a shave, and got up to leave, "without arms of any sort." The bandits waited for him to go outside and "immediately started shooting without saying any words."[78] The twenty-five-year-old priest, his companion Marco Contoli, and one of the attackers, an unknown bandit, were all hit in the crossfire. As the smoke cleared, the bailiff of Castel Bolognese grabbed a gun from the unknown shooter, who had died on scene, ran to ring the tocsin and summon the townspeople, and gave chase to the bandits. Unfortunately, the bandits had "immediately escaped outside of the Castello after the deed."[79] Two companions of the priest died immediately amid the gunfire, and the priest himself succumbed to his wounds en route to Bologna for medical help.

The killing was immediately recognized as significant: fearing that the bandits would return to desecrate the bodies, the bailiff put the corpses in the castle's *Hospitale di S.ta Maria* and posted extra guards on the doorways.[80] Seeking to identify the priest's unknown companion, he posted clothing and goods near the site of the shooting for three days in the hopes that someone would recognize them and be inspired to provide some information about the killing.[81] In an attempt to preserve the integrity of the evidence, he put the recovered murder weapon, an arquebus whose powder-pan he had dropped in the initial chaos, into the safekeeping of Ercole Marcolini, the priest's brother.[82] As one of the

---

[77] ASBo, *Torrone*, 6262, f. 404r.   [78] Ibid., f. 404v–405r.   [79] Ibid., 406v.
[80] Ibid., 407r.   [81] Ibid., 418v.
[82] Ibid., 420v. The echoes of accusatory justice still rang in the halls of the *Torrone*, as victims' families often played significant roles in the investigation and prosecution of killings.

larger towns in the Bolognese state, Castel Bolognese witnessed its share of violence over the century. The brazen triple homicide in an attack against a local elite warranted a significant (about 300 folios) *processo* to investigate and remedy the attack on the Marcolini family.

Public knowledge, along with the sharp ears of the bailiff, identified the killers as a group of bandits headed up by the noble military man Signore Capitano Gioanni Balducci, a member of an old lineage of rural feudatories whose patrimony lay in the lands around Castel Bolognese.[83] Commanded by locals, the men themselves were strangers: a bandit from La Massa, a bandit known as "The Venetian," and a bandit from Imola. The Balducci family (which included Gioanni, his *capitano* brother Filippo and his nephew Antonio Maria) reputedly harboured these bandits in their holdings in La Massa.[84] The Balducci were also known to keep these men protected in their home, a fact that was "daily observed" by the inhabitants of Castel Bolognese. The Balducci continued to practice intimidation and thuggery as the measure of their local power in their hereditary seat, despite the efforts of Bologna's central authority to reduce the privileges and violent governance of feudal elites in both city and *contado*. In that view, the killing of Don Marcolini marked an episode of noble revenge-as-politics; the complicated intertwining of personal and political motivations in this murder elaborates the noble mentality that produced the violent homicides and atmosphere of social distrust that permeated mid-century Bologna.

The Balducci attack was clearly a targeted killing, and the Marcolini recognized it as part of a pattern of enmity. As was common in all homicide investigations, after interviewing the bailiff of Castel Bolognese and witnessing what must have been a nauseating series of nine body inspections, the notary looked to the victim's relatives to shed light on the assault. Don Marcolini's brother Ercole was the first to be interviewed; he identified "The Venetian" as a thirty-year-old named Vincenzo and another of the bandits as Giulio Mazzini, banned from Ferrarese territories but happily ensconced in Castel Bolognese.[85] Ercole was free with information that painted the Balducci as murderous aggressors. He couldn't say why his brother was killed, because "I've not heard that they had any argument between them, but these men of Balducci threw themselves at my brother's life ... without being provoked by anyone."[86] Ercole described how his suspicion formed that the attack was ordered by Filippo Balducci, who held a public hatred against the Marcolini. After the shooting, as the bandits fled the town, Ercole had rushed toward the

---

[83] Ibid.   [84] Ibid., 405r.   [85] Ibid., 424rv.   [86] Ibid., 425v.

commotion and was passed the other way by Filippo Balducci's young son Antonio Maria, running toward his father's house.[87] His suspicions piqued, Ercole followed the boy to the Casa Balducci where, after the boy rushed in, Filippo Balducci and his father Gioanni Balducci emerged and headed toward the piazza. When they saw Ercole, they advanced toward him; when Ercole's father arrived wailing over his son's injury, they retreated into their own home.[88] That was enough for Ercole to pin the blame on the Balducci, and he was willing to expound on the history of conflict that made him so sure.

The conflict he described aptly illustrates the continued dominance of kinship and family ties over obligations to maintain order within the state. During Carnival in 1639, Balducci's young son Antonio Maria quarrelled with the son of Captain Signore Giovanni Francesco Mezzamici, a friend of the Marcolini family.[89] The original quarrel took place over a jousting disagreement between the boys; nevertheless, the insults were grave enough that this carnival-game argument prompted the Mezzamici family to call together a posse that included the Marcolini brothers (incidentally, one of whom was himself a capital bandit for unmentioned crimes) and to march in arms against the Balducci faction in Castel Bolognese. In the peace process that followed – in which each side wrote petitions, swore peace and publicly reconciled their differences – the Balducci, according to Ercole Marcolini, had continually cast "evil eyes" in the direction of Don Antonio and his soon-to-be-slain companion Marco Contali, who bore the Balducci's particular ire.[90] Since that summertime peace ceremony in the Basilica di San Petronio in Bologna, the Balducci had continually harassed Don Antonio, including earlier in Carnival when "The Venetian" had jumped him on the road home from Imola.[91] To Ercole, the latest assault was undoubtedly a direct upshot of the quarrel between youths in Carnival one year previous. The urge to avenge offence was not moderated by the state- and church-imposed peace, which was backed with legal power and whose breaking was justification for the execution of even elite *bolognesi*.

Revenge here was also a young man's urge. Don Antonio Marcolini died at age twenty-five, according to the inspections of his corpse and the men who knew him well; so too did Marco Contali. Recall that the average age of homicide victims across the century was in the early thirties; as such, these two men appear unusual – not extremely so, but certainly younger than one might expect for high-ranking rural elites. The homicides that constituted the "civil war" Bologna experienced in

[87] Ibid., 427r.   [88] Ibid., 427v.   [89] Ibid. 427v–428v.   [90] Ibid., 429r.   [91] Ibid.

the mid-seventeenth century were overwhelmingly committed by younger men and involved younger men, more so than in other sampled years on either side of this wave. The predominance of youth in these murders was not atypical nor unexpected but bears comment in this context.

The young men who grew up in the generation after the plague did so in a demographic bottleneck that left many of them without fathers, uncles or other senior male family. With mortality rates in the range of 300–500, the 1630 plague did not discriminate based on wealth; but it did discriminate by age, attacking the working-age, adult population and creating significant labour shortages across all of Northern Italy. The dead Marcolini had a father, who gave a statement to the *Torrone*, but in all the listings of the Balducci clan given by various witnesses, only the two brothers and Filippo's "young son" were named. In his statement, Ercole Marcolini noted that the argument in 1639 had begun between the two young boys.[92] Initial witnesses put the ages of the hired killers, habitual companions of the Balducci brothers, between twenty-five and thirty.[93] Don Antonio Maria was fifteen in 1640 and on the cusp of adult life. We can thus conclude that the principals in this conflict – the Balducci brothers Filippo and Gioanni, and the Marcolini brothers Ercole and Don Antonio Maria – were the young generation that survived the 1630 plague. Filippo and Gioanni assumed control of their father's land and began their careers as military officers.

The absence of an adult generation in this period is significant because, by 1652 and 1660, the children and teenagers of the plague were *padroni* and patriarchs of their own families, and they lacked the counsel of seasoned relatives. Countless studies have shown that men generally become less violent over time and that middle-aged adults can quell the violence of the young in strongly bound kinship groups.[94] As demonstrated by Chapter 3's Ronchetta–Tozzi affair and its generally peripheral violence, strong age-based hierarchies of authority protected leading members of factions and kept violence at tolerable levels. After the plague, the noble factions were dominated by young men for whom violence remained a useful skill and mode of social conflict. The violence committed by these factions was a result of the destabilization of social, judicial and political authority among these young men. The open attack on the Marcolini, in public view with the local bailiff present and the victim's relatives nearby, was planned as a deliberate challenge both to a

---

[92] ASBo, *Torrone*, 6262, f. 425v.   [93] Ibid., f. 405v.
[94] For an overview of past and recent research, cf. Daly and Wilson, *Homicide*; Spierenburg, "Faces of Violence"; Roth, *American Homicide*.

rival and to the judicial regime that attempted to prevent such violence. Similar influences were at work in 1639, when the Marcolini and their allies the Mezz'Amici rode in force against the Balducci over a disagreement between boys playing at joust. Young men, more likely to respond to perceived insults with violence, dominated the elite factions of mid-century Bologna; this fact helps to explain the qualitatively and quantitatively different violence in the years 1640, 1652 and 1660.

Community violence was a community affair, and the *Torrone* went to the community for help in resolving this homicide. In the tightly knit lives of rural Bolognese communities, reputations and public appearance mattered.[95] Notaries did not entirely trust the families of victims to give complete facts. In this case, the notary Bartolomeo Carelli spoke first to the victim's brother and father, but he also asked them who else had been present who might provide more information. Ercole told Carelli that if he wanted proof of the Balducci's involvement in the murder, "particularly the women of this neighbourhood" would enlighten him.[96] By directing the notary to the local networks of women, Ercole demonstrated that in Bologna, as elsewhere in North Italy, community networks could be underpinned as much by female solidarities as by masculine sodalities.[97] Particularly in rural homicide cases in Bologna, across the century, women acted as contextual witnesses who provided local information, often couched in the terms of public gossip, which fit homicide narratives into local schemas of worth, repute and public comportment. In the mid-century, as judicial and institutional authority came under attack from various elite networks, we see once again how neighbourhood and kinship identities were more important in the management of violence than was state action. Indeed, the court's ability to intervene in rural feuds had seemingly decreased since the heady days of the 1600 Ronchetta–Tozzi peace conference.

The court duly called in as many witnesses as would respond to citations, banning the Balducci and retainers who failed to attend. The first crop of citations went to twenty-nine individuals, beginning with the Mezz'Amici, who were at the heart of the conflict as outlined by Ercole Marcolini and his father. Once again, the rural elites of Castel Bolognese refused to participate on the court's terms. Capitano Giovanni Francesco Mezz'Amici denied his family's involvement in the conflict and blamed

---

[95] Cf. D. Smail and T. Fenster, eds., *Fama: The Politics of Talk and Reputation in Medieval Europe* (Ithaca, NY: Cornell University Press, 2003).

[96] ASBo, *Torrone*, 6262, f. 428v.

[97] On the roles of women in judicial and political arenas, cf. Ferraro, *Marriage Wars in Late Renaissance Venice*; Ferraro, *Nefarious Crimes, Contested Justice*; Astarita, *Village Justice*; Cohen, "Honor and Gender in the Streets of Early Modern Rome."

the victim's failure to properly salute his social equals as they passed; when pressed, he denied that the attack was targeted at the noble, saying that the intended victim was the one who had died immediately, the *socio* Marco Contali.[98] He admitted to having argued with the Balducci the year before when, as judge of the youth joust during Carnival, he had awarded in favour of his own son.[99] He also emphasized that the families had come together in San Petronio and, under the benediction of a priest, had spoken "four words of peace" and reconciled their argument. Mezz'Amici minimized the role of family conflicts in this killing, attempting to reduce it to an individual act of masculine honour and avoid the court's involvement in his clan's conflicts.

The local women told a different tale. A certain Camilla told how Balducci had been accustomed to parading through the Castello in recent weeks, with four or sometimes eight armed men displaying their guns and threatening the retainers of the Mezz'Amici.[100] She and two other witnesses also mentioned a deeper root to the conflict: the past parricide of Battista Contali by his wife, who had taken shelter with the Balducci men. Since none of the women could properly remember the wife's name, this murder appears to have been far removed from the daylight attack in the Castello. Throughout the case, elite witnesses tried to avoid giving complete stories, while local stakeholders and artisans were more likely to describe the conflict as they understood it best: a public danger to peace and the practice of open conflict between hereditary social elites.

The murder of Antonio Maria Marcolini and Marco Contali by armed thugs under the employ of Capitano Gioanni Balducci encapsulated the situation that deteriorated into the civil war of the mid-seventeenth century. Although technically the legitimate court of criminal authority and backed by an entrenched papal regime, the *Torrone* nevertheless lost the allegiance of rural elites following the 1630 plague, the loss of a mature generation of faction leaders, and the disruption of the law-and-order programs of the early century that had channelled noble violence toward the elimination of banditry and other social ills.[101] Following the disruption to demographic and economic structures wrought by the massive mortality of 1630, factions of the remnant nobility abandoned their participation in papal civility and returned to vendetta and revenge as politics. The *Torrone* became embroiled as a faction of its own,

---

[98] ASBo, *Torrone*, 6262, *in fine*, fasc. 2.5.   [99] Ibid.   [100] Ibid.
[101] On similar processes in early modern Germany, cf. B. Ann Tlusty, *The Martial Ethic in Early Modern Germany: Civic Duty and the Right of Arms* (New York: Palgrave Macmillan, 2011).

becoming a participant in, rather than an adjudicator of, the factional civil war that tore at Bologna in the mid-century. The war began in the *contado* with killings like Marcolini's and moved into the city in a general outbreak of violence by 1660.

With elite violence in the hinterland came a breakdown of order in the towns and fields. In 1640, repeated cases of homicide occurred on noble-owned lands during the harvest, and several labourers killed the retainers hired by nobles to supervise their work.[102] Revenge killings took on a renewed importance as the *Torrone*'s penetration into the villages was reduced by elites' non-cooperation in its policies. Ordinary farmers and villagers killed each other and sometimes their families as society recovered from the plague less than a decade previous. Bologna's situation in mid-century demonstrates a critical weakness of the civilizing process theory of violence: the theory relies upon a unity of purpose between governing authority and elite networks in controlling and disciplining a population. In Bologna, the nobility defiantly rejected that unity and upheld violence as the expression of republican liberty, in deeds if not in words. The result was a general increase in homicides during these years.

The War Comes to Bologna: The Murder of Paris Maria de' Grassi

Twelve years after the assassination of Antonio Maria Marcolini in Castel Bolognese, the urban authorities of Bologna faced a similar dissolution of order in the city as had occurred in the countryside. The tensions that emerged among the city's governing institutions and its hereditary native elite classes did not dissipate by 1652 but rather increased. The court's attempts to police and control the rural nobility's behaviour led to outbreaks of violence such as the killing of the *Torrone* judge Pungelli in broad daylight. Moreover, the Pungelli killing was neither the only high-profile, politically motivated murder in 1652, nor was it the most dramatic. Pungelli's killing showed the powerful animus between the city's elite clans, particularly the Barbazza, and the judicial institutions such as the *Torrone* that represented centralized papal authority and the reduction of noble privilege. But the factional conflicts of Bologna were the products of long-standing, oft-mutating rivalries and enmities between various noble clans, and went deeper than comparatively tame anti-papal agitation.[103]

---

[102] ASBo, *Torrone*, 5946, *in fine*; 5606, *in fine*; 6231, *in fine*.
[103] On Bolognese family alliances in the *quattrocento*, cf. E. L. Bernhardt, "Behind the Scenes of Fifteenth-Century Marriage Schemes: Forced Marriages, Family Alliances

In many ways, the prosecution of these rivalries functioned as politics in Bologna's medieval and renaissance periods.[104] Elite families formed violent oligarchies that dominated the city, with posts in communal government and local benefices distributed to the clients of dominant families such as the Bentivoglio and the Pepoli. Under papal rule, the deep hatreds that undergirded Bolognese politics were not completely assuaged, but simply quieted and redirected for long periods of time. As I have argued, they reemerged in the wake of the Great Plague of 1630. First in the country (as we saw in Castel Bolognese) and then in Bologna, noble gangs killed each other in brazen public assaults that both reignited feud-type conflict and rejected the pretences of centralized, institutional justice in the hands of the popes and the *Torrone*. The murder of Paris Maria de' Grassi in 1652 illustrates this theme well.

Paris Maria de' Grassi was forty-five in 1652, a senior member of one of Bologna's oldest and most esteemed households.[105] According to the investigation into his homicide, he had fought in Dalmatia, presumably during the Thirty Years' War. He has appeared in this chapter previously, when in 1632, he and a group of companions got into a brawl with some Spanish students over matters of precedence. No longer a young man, in 1652 his death demonstrates how the violence of mid-century Bologna was not simply the preserve of young gangs of nobles like those involved in the assault on Castel Bolognese – the civil war in Bologna claimed the lives of senior family members as well. Paris died during a planned attack against his household perpetrated by senior members of the Lignani and Scotti lineages, including the Marchese Antonio Lignani. The attack occurred around midnight on February 9, 1652. Eleven men in total assaulted de' Grassi and his retinue outside the church of San Martino, and de' Grassi was killed in the firefight; one of his retainers managed to kill the shooter with his sword, and several of de' Grassi's retinue was injured.[106] After de' Grassi died, the killers fled the city by scaling the nearby wall with ropes and tackle; the ropes and hooks were later discovered by the *Torrone*'s *sbirri* and notaries. This was not the only murder committed by high-ranking members of Emilian noble houses in 1652; it was not even the only murder committed by leaders of the

---

and Power Politics in Bentivoglio Bologna," in Terpstra et al., *Bologna, Cultural Crossroads*, pp. 161–72.
[104] On the deep embedding of these rivalries within Bologna's poltical and judicial systems, cf. S. Blanshei, *Politics and Justice in Late Medieval Bologna* (Leiden: Brill, 2010), pp. 313–497.
[105] ASBo, *Torrone*, 6662, *in fine*.
[106] Ibid., denunciation by Ludovico Brunetti, *baroncello*, f. 1.

Lignani family.[107] Among the other homicides committed by senior nobility in 1652, the murder of Paris Maria de' Grassi demonstrates how the civil war grew to threaten the apex of social hierarchies.

A witness, called only after the basic facts of the assault were established by questioning local witnesses and de' Grassi's retinue, said that he had heard it publicly that the Marchese Lignani had ordered de' Grassi's death in response to de' Grassi's involvement in an earlier shootout in the neighbourhood of San Mammolo.[108] The notary of the *Torrone*, Angelo Pioda, followed this line of inquiry through the remainder of the investigation, teasing out the degree to which the Marchese was responsible: the *Torrone* developed the case that the Marchese had hired two Ferrarese soldiers, the Barbieri brothers, to kill de' Grassi in exchange for protection from Ferrarese justice; they had been condemned for raping a farm girl in September 1651.[109] The investigation drew in high-ranking members of nobility, who participated in varying degrees, from refusal to show up for interrogation to a full accounting of the rivalries between the Grassi and the Lignani.[110] Interestingly, the judge presiding over this investigation was none other than Giacinto Pungelli, whose death set the scene for this chapter. Pungelli's involvement in precisely these types of homicide investigations made him a target for violence as resurging factionalism among the nobility's oligarchic and republican branches directed violence not only against the noble class but also against the officers of the *Torrone*, who collectively represented papal claims to absolute criminal jurisdiction over violence.

Prosecuting noble violence was a pillar of those claims to a judicial monopoly on violence. The trial against Marchese Antonio Lignani, and others, shows how papal policy toward nobility still relied more on a soft touch that left Bologna's powerful elite networks largely unbloodied. At the end of the trial, the only killer executed was the soldier Alessandro Barbieri, whose brother Giovanni had died during the attack on de' Grassi. The remaining conspirators escaped with their lives, though not their freedom: the Marchese Lignani and noblemen Marc'Antonio Scotti and Giuseffe Vetturi were condemned to exile. The Marchese Lignani decamped to Tuscany, whence he wrote a petition in 1656 that asked for

---

[107] Cf. ASBo, *Torrone*, 6613, *in fine*, trial of Count Gabrielle Legnani, the Marchese's son, for homicide of Andrea Vernizzi; 6594, *fasc.* 1, trial of Count Giacopo Ercolani for homicide of Gioseffe Pachioni.

[108] ASBo, *Torrone*, 6662, f. 34rv.

[109] Ibid., f. 20rv, petition of Alessandro and Giovanni de Barbieri.

[110] Ibid., f. 77r–78v, interrogation of Francesco di Filippo Landi; f. 93r–5v, interrogation and supplication of Pietro Maria Landi, f. 108r–117v.

pardon and permission to return to Bologna.[111] It was sponsored by the Grand Duke of Tuscany, and although it does not appear to have been granted, Giuseffe Vetturi was nevertheless pardoned for his role in the conspiracy and returned to Bologna after he wrote a similar petition in July 1655. Still, the legatine government of Bologna and the officers of the *Torrone* found themselves unable to execute Marc'Antonio Lignani, the Marchese at the apex of the conspiracy, who remained protected by his connections to the broader nobility of Italy.

Conclusion

A similar pattern, on a larger scale, existed in 1660. The sixty-six homicides that occurred within the city walls collectively show the city suffering from social instability brought on by the revival of factionalism and vendetta-based killing among sectors of the city's elite population. Gangs of liverymen killed the servants of jurists and other nobles.[112] High-ranking noblemen practiced petty violence to dominate and terrorize subjects, and they were not above killing artisans and peasants to demonstrate their elite social status.[113] Some of the more senior members of noble houses continued to practice violence in the streets and maintained large retinues who provided protection and intimidation.[114] The best way to describe the quantity and quality of violence in the city and province of Bologna in the judicial records of 1652 and 1660 is as a civil war in which the factions were not always clear, loyalties shifted within and among elite families, and the legatine government was left largely unable to control order within Bologna. In short, mid-seventeenth-century Bologna demonstrated a failed civilizing process.

Despite efforts by both the legatine government and *Torrone* officials to legislate factionalism through sumptuary laws, public-order laws and firearms regulation, remnants of the pro-Bentivoglio factions that had struggled against the Papacy in the sixteenth century revived violent opposition to centralized papal bureaucracies. In particular, these radical oligarchs sought to retain feudal judicial privileges – this included a large degree of freedom from censure and punishment by the central court and

---

[111] ASBo, *Torrone*, 6662, copy of Marchese Lignani's petition of November 7, 1656.

[112] ASBo, *Torrone*, 6789, *in fine*, investigation into death of Pietro Laghi; 6789, trial of Antonio Maria Bertocchi for homicide of Giuseffe Palmierani.

[113] ASBo, *Torrone*, 6788, fasc. 3, trial of Count Fontana and retainers for homicide of Bartolomeo Filippino; 6787, trial of Count Francesco Zambeccari for homicide of Simone Santini; 6787, *in fine*, trial of Doctor Giulio Cesare Claudini for homicide of Giacomo Scandellata, a carter.

[114] ASBo, *Torrone*, 6787, *in fine*, trial of *Marchese* Albergati and his retainer Giuseffe Peri.

the right to adjudicate conflicts (and collect fees for doing so) on their rural lands, rights that were granted in the sixteenth century to appease their ancestors.[115] Their renewed agitation against the centralizing drives of papal government and justice included a great deal of violence committed by nobles and their retainers. This created a dangerously uncertain atmosphere in the city of Bologna, under which circumstances artisan and labouring communities continued the types of violence spurred on by plague in 1630. Servants killed masters, and vice versa, in the city's *botteghe*, and young men killed each other in arguments over the city's prostitutes.[116] In the decade 1650–60, the *Torrone* executed only forty-five individuals, showing that it was not at the time using the threat of punitive or retaliatory violence as a means to control these violent populations.[117] Despite the gains in peace made in the late sixteenth and early seventeenth centuries, under the socioeconomic strain of plague, stagnation and regional war, homicides increased in frequency in the middle years of the century. Moreover, the homicides that occurred were more characteristic of the revenge and political homicides that are present in societies where deep structures of social trust, such as social and political authority and hierarchy, have crumbled.

Nobles were not solely responsible for the mid-century violence that occurred in Bologna. The homicides analyzed here make clear that labourers and artisans also killed in ways that distinguish 1632 from sampled years on either side. While the immediate causes surrounding homicide were not unique – arguments over women, robberies, business disputes are all familiar – the relationships of the victims and killers were unusual for their social classes. Romantic rivalries crossed social lines, as in the case of the shopkeeper's son who murdered his father's employee after the man married the wrong woman. Robbers were desperate, a fact reflected in the victims they chose: a sleeping priest, or the elderly innkeeper who habitually put his killer up for the night. Economic pressures could rend families violently, as seen in the death of the pigeon breeder at the hands of his brother-in-law. These types of homicides were prevalent among the lower orders of Bologna in the years after the plague.

The failure of the legatine governments and the judges of the *Torrone* to effectively pacify Bologna shows how civilizing processes, if they are to retain their heuristic power, should not be reified as monolithic, led by elites and progressive in an unstoppable linear fashion. What appeared to

---

[115] Gardi, "Lineamenti," in Prosperi, *Storia di Bologna*, 13–25.

[116] ASBo, *Torrone*, 6787, fasc. 26, trial of Bartolomeo Pazzini and others for homicide of Giacopo Andrea Marescalchi.

[117] ASBo, *Cronaci delle giustizie seguite in Bologna del 1030 al 1750*.

have been successful in convincing large swaths of the nobility to submit to papal authority in the sixteenth century – limited participation in the Senate, small land grants in strategic locations to buttress the ambitions of valuable families, and access to the Papacy's wide network of Italian nobility bound through marriage, alliance and economic interdependence – seemingly lost its power in the seventeenth. At that point, dissolution of Bologna's urban and rural economies under the repeated pressures of famine, plague and war created resentment and violent anger among radical elements of both republican and oligarchic factions. Territorial, resource-based vendettas resumed between these factions, and, in attempting to police and punish public violence in the state, the *Torrone* judges became parties to the cycle of revenge: when they condemned noblemen or their retainers, they made themselves targets for vengeance. A monolithic state, with secular, centralized institutions unbeholden to local interests, was not a sufficient precondition for a "civilizing process" in this ambiance. Rather, if Bologna were to achieve public order and a widespread decline in interpersonal violence, it required the participation of all sectors of society, particularly the elites whose public violence could be the most destructive to state aims. With large sectors of the nobility unwilling to participate in the system of centralized judicial authority, vendetta-based violence retained its outsized political role, and grew in mid-century to encompass even the apex of the judicial hierarchy.

7   Conclusion

With a claimed and enforced monopoly on criminal justice, the apparatus of centralized government failed to maintain the fragile social and political accords that Bolognese legates had made with the city's elite population in the late sixteenth century. Those accords themselves had reforged a measure of peace and stability among the *legato*'s fractious and vendetta-prone nobility that had been broken by Julius II's conquest of the city in 1506. Moreover, Julius II had conquered the city in part to quell the tyrannous violence with which Bolognese oligarchs under the Bentivoglio regime had ruled the northern papal states. The Bentivoglio tyranny had emerged from fourteenth- and fifteenth-century struggles between republican and oligarchic factions of nobility, whose vendettas characterized Bolognese government. They governed as lords in their rural domains and manipulated city institutions, such as criminal justice or the Senate, to advance their urban political ambitions. During each of these transitionary phases, successive generations of Bolognese elites renegotiated and reestablished the conditions under which they would accommodate the rule of an opposing faction or, as of 1506, a foreign ruler – the Pope in Rome, and his legates.

The breakdown of that social peace in the seventeenth century in many ways continued this Bolognese tradition of violent renegotiation of its terms of governance. The peace had been established through the expansion of the Senate to allow greater noble participation in legatine government, through a reform of criminal justice designed to improve the *Torrone*'s appearance of transparency and impartiality, and through a redirection of noble energies toward banditry in the borderlands. In the early decades of the century, regional warfare and a series of economic and environmental crises, culminating in the Great Plague of 1630, brought government authority low and ruined the ability of Bolognese institutions and their officers to credibly maintain order. Whereas homicide rates had previously remained stable at levels comparable to Northern European states, in the plague's immediate aftermath, violence swept the countryside as landowners and peasants fought among themselves to

223

protect their fragile resources or to increase their holdings. Beginning with a series of 1632 attacks on law-men and other figures of authority, homicides in the wake of the plague illustrate the fragility of Bolognese social trust and the long-term consequences of its diminution. The breakdown of social stability and trust manifested in a civil war, fought primarily in the streets of Bologna's urban core and visible in the prosecution of homicides by the city's autocratic criminal court, the *Tribunale del Torrone*. This book has analyzed the failure and reestablishment of the fragile accords that propped up Bolognese civil society, over the course of the century, in eleven sampled years.

That analysis contributes to a broader European understanding of the role of violence in *ancien régime* society, and the sociocultural and political means by which European states pacified professionally violent nobility and the less-practiced, though no less vital, violence of artisan and labouring communities. It demonstrates how the weight of accumulated numbers in homicide studies must be balanced with a thorough qualitative understanding of the socioeconomic and political contexts in which the records of homicide are produced. Foremost among those qualitative interpretations in European history has been the "civilizing process" theory of violence elaborated by Pieter Spierenburg and others. Whereas the centralizing Northern states witnessed dramatic declines in homicide rates during the seventeenth century, Bologna, equipped with all of the institutional machinery of centralized, civilized government, suffered the reverse, with a sharp increase in violence in mid-century. The critical difference between Bologna's experience and that of Scandinavia was the refusal by Bolognese nobility to acquiesce entirely to that centralizing machinery. Even when actively participating in legatine government, as the Pepoli did, Bolognese nobility continued to openly practice private warfare, as Odoardo Pepoli did, riding against the Bevilacqua in 1640. Meanwhile, urban and rural artisans and peasants increasingly brought denunciations and complaints to the centralized criminal court rather than to a local *padrone*, further heightening tensions between republican, oligarchic and papal factions within the city. All were in competition for power over Bologna's population, and the legates were confronted with elements of the nobility who worked both within the system of centralized government and through the continued practice of violence to challenge papal authority.

Shrewd manipulation of institutional structures and violence by Bolognese elites lends itself to functional and ritual analyses of the character of homicide in Bologna. Both the *Torrone*'s original development and its subsequent reform were done pragmatically, taking a realist approach to the source of the court's authority: not terror, but justice.

The structure and procedure of the *Torrone*, governed by a permanent judge and a staff of elite notaries, projected the image of impartiality to attract users to its officers' services. Moreover, inquisitorial procedure's emphasis on determining the "truth" made the *Torrone* preferable for many court users to the heavily partisan arbitration of local elites and landowners. In a series of reforms from the mid-sixteenth century onward, legates, Senate officials and *Torrone* judges worked to improve the court's image in the eyes of Bolognese subjects, moderating and standardizing judicial fees and penalty schemes, and ensuring multiple levels of notarial oversight. Much of that reform was simultaneously pragmatic and symbolic, speaking as much to the court's ideal, ritualized version of justice as it did to its actual operation.

In their approach to capital punishment, *Torrone* judges displayed a similar pragmatic approach: the most theatrical and violent executions were reserved for criminals whose crimes significantly threatened the state's authority, such as counterfeiters and the men who murdered a *Torrone* judge in 1652. At the same time, *Torrone* judges took a lenient approach to the everyday violence of the population. For the most part, killers escaped the *legato* in contumacy, incurring a theoretical penalty of death; they could return home after a period of exile and the public, notarized reestablishment of peace between killers and their victims' kin. The peace was heavily ritualized and the leniency practical: the *Torrone* possessed neither the manpower nor the will to apprehend and execute every killer in the *legato*. Moreover, *Torrone* judges recognized that in the murky and unstable politics of *ancien régime* Bologna, court action to censure a murderer on behalf of a victim made the court party to the vendetta, and, as demonstrated by the civil war that erupted in mid-century, made court officers into targets of noble revenge violence.

The resurgence of noble violence in mid-century belies a strictly functionalist interpretation of noble violence as political strategy, however. Republicanism and the return of communal rule in Bologna was a dead letter by the seventeenth century, and so too was the Bentivoglio oligarchy. Papal authority not only was entrenched in Bologna, but after the conquest of Ferrara in 1598, encompassed the Romagna and a large part of Emilia.[1] The outburst of noble violence in Bologna before the late seventeenth century and the ensuing reestablishment of a fragile social peace did not advance the interests of the violent factions of either republican or oligarchic nobility; it instead bred distrust between various sectors of the ruling class and ultimately tightened the noose of papal

---

[1] A. Gardi, "Lineamenti della storia politica di Bologna: da Giulio II a Innocenzo X," in Prosperi, *Storia di Bologna*, 27–30.

governance around the *legato*. It can be read, however, as an expression of identity from a threatened nobility, whose historical skill at violence no longer fit the expected qualities of European elites. Indeed, it appears to have surfaced again late in the century, when the Pepoli and de' Grassi feuded again from 1695 to 1698.[2] In cultures of violence such as the warrior nobility of early modern Italy, violence did not necessarily need to achieve any pragmatic goals, and the language of anger, honour and dissatisfaction that early modern violence communicated was as valuable an end as any practical achievement.

Although deeply concerned by the culture of violence operating among recalcitrant elements of elite nobility, the officers of the *Torrone* remained relatively untroubled by a culture of violence against women, if limited numbers of investigations into uxoricide indeed reflect the inability or unwillingness of court officers to pierce the domestic veil. Men who killed their wives during domestic arguments or in fits of sexual jealousy generally received lenient sentences from the court, if they were condemned at all. The city's sex workers remained vulnerable to homicide by clients who fought among themselves in brothels and who killed *meretrici* on the streets and in their homes. The confluence of marriage and sex work was a potent mixture for violence, and a husband's suspicion or knowledge that his wife engaged in sex work drove multiple Bolognese men to kill their wives. The *Torrone*'s access to these crimes was often not through official channels or a neighbourhood outcry, but through the networks of local women who intervened in incidents of domestic violence and reported murderous husbands.

The lax attitude of judicial officials toward uxoricide and other killings of women did not extend to homicides committed by women. Notaries and judges of the *Torrone* pursued patricides and infanticides with vigour, following medieval stereotypes of poisonous wives and amoral young women abandoning babies in shame and secrecy. Both these stereotypes were exaggerated in the record, with a near parity of men being prosecuted for similar crimes, though the women received harsher punishments in comparison to male baby-killers and poisoners. The limited sample of killings of and by women limits the available analysis of these categories of homicide; nevertheless, the continued appearance of a judicial regime widely tolerant of violence against women and fearful of the spectre of women's violence was characteristic of a society that had

---

[2] Giancarlo Angelozzi and Cesarina Casanova, *La nobiltà disciplinata: violenza nobiliare, procedure di giustizia e scienza cavalleresca a Bologna nel 17. secolo* (Bologna: CLUEB, 2003), 322–40.

not achieved the reduction in public cultures of violence and misogyny indicative of a successful "civilizing process."

It was male violence, public and peace-disturbing, that most occupied the judiciary of early modern Bologna. That violence was a problem that was not easily ignored or resolved. Indeed, despite the declining numbers of homicides in the late seventeenth century, Bolognese elites and ordinary people continued to kill one another in high numbers into the eighteenth century, and the *Torrone* continued to adapt and reform itself to try to assuage that violence.[3] This book therefore analyzed an incomplete and ongoing process of both social trust-building and state-making. The elite men of Bologna continued to practice an ethos of violent individualism, paradoxically aided by the development of social codes that ostensibly sought to curb that violence.[4] Both they and ordinary *bolognesi* continued to distrust legatine authority and to complain about judicial venality. Whether the reforms imposed upon the *Torrone* in the eighteenth century to combat those complaints succeeded in reducing violence among the population as well remains to be tested in the criminal archive; certainly the prevailing thought among judicial authorities was that male violence continued to plague the city and its territories.

The combined crises of war, economic decline, famine and the crushing trauma of the 1630 plague interrupted the achievements made by papal legates and *Torrone* judges in the late sixteenth century to reduce local instability. In other words, the process of state-building in Bologna failed. Demographic disaster and endemic poverty made the city's countryside a dangerous and violent land, where peasants and artisans killed each other in conflicts over resources, romance, robbery and revenge: the pressures of profound agricultural poverty led people to violence for many reasons. The countryside also hosted significant feudal domains, and from these bases, recalcitrant sectors of nobility launched an assault on central authority in the mid-century. Powerful interest groups among the city's elite were at odds with papal judicial policy and the reduction of their hereditary privileges, and they murdered judicial officers, law-men and each other in flagrant public killings.

This book has rested upon qualitative analysis of a nominal body count of homicides in Bologna across the seventeenth century. That analysis reveals that, contrary to the predictions of a "civilizing process" approach

---

[3] Giancarlo Angelozzi and Cesarina Casanova, *La giustizia criminale a Bologna nel XVIII secolo e le riforme di Benedetto XIV* (Bologna: CLUEB, 2010), 34–39.
[4] Stuart Carroll, "Revenge and Reconciliation in Early Modern Italy," *Past & Present* 233, no. 1 (November 1, 2016): 101–42.

to violence, the imposition of centralized rule and justice did not reduce interpersonal homicides in a dramatic fashion during the seventeenth century. Revenge and vendetta violence retained their place in the social arsenal of *bolognesi* at all social levels; only slowly did the *Tribunale del Torrone* and its judges make meaningful progress in reducing violence across the *legato*. Still, the court's growing power attracted a larger base of users from all walks of life; artisans and rural labourers began to view the *Torrone* as a better forum for justice and conflict resolution than the unreliable adjudication of disputes offered by local nobility. Those nobility retained and strongly guarded their rights to violence, even when members of their families were cooperating in government bodies to advance family interests peacefully. The continued antagonism among republican, oligarchic and papal factions within the city's elite destroyed the city's thin atmosphere of social trust. These tensions created a society in which violence retained a strong presence, and homicide remained a frequent means for neighbours and nobles to resolve their disputes.

Bibliography

Primary Sources

Archivio di Stato di Bologna, *Assunteria de liti e paci, Atti dell'Assunteria e di Paci, 1658–72.*

Archivio di Stato di Bologna, *Assunteria del Torrone,* 3a, *Constitutiones Turroni Bandi e Stampe.*

Archivio di Stato di Bologna, *Assunteria del Torrone,* 3c, *Constitutioni e bolle del Torrone,* 1488–1623.

Archivio di Stato di Bologna, *Bandi e Notificazione,* Serie I.

Archivio di Stato di Bologna, *Cronaci delle Giustizie seguite in Bologna del 1030 al 1750.*

Archivio di Stato di Bologna, *Tribunale del Torrone, Atti e Processi,* 3171-7352.

Ghiselli, Francesco Antonio, *Memorie antiche manuscritte di Bologna raccolte et accresciute sino a'tempi presenti,* Biblioteca Universitario di Bologna, Ms. 770, v. 30–34.

Spada, Bernardino, *I Bandi di Bernardino Spada durante la peste del 1630 in Bologna,* ed. Pietro Malpezzi. Faenza (Ravenna): Casanova, 2008.

Secondary Sources

Acton, Harold. *The Pazzi Conspiracy: The Plot against the Medici.* London: Thames and Hudson, 1979.

Alfani, Guido. "The Effects of Plague on the Distribution of Property: Ivrea, Northern Italy 1630." *Population Studies* 64, no. 1 (March 1, 2010): 61–75.

"Population and Environment in Northern Italy during the Sixteenth Century." *Population (English Edition, 2002–)* 62, no. 4 (January 1, 2007): 559–95.

Alfani, Guido and Marco Percoco. "Plague and Long-Term Development: The Lasting Effects of the 1629–30 Epidemic on the Italian Cities." Working Paper. IGIER (Innocenzo Gasparini Institute for Economic Research), Bocconi University, 2014. http://ideas.repec.org/p/igi/igierp/508.html.

Altpeter-Jones, Katja. "Inscribing Gender on the Early Modern Body: Marital Violence in German Texts of the Fifteenth and Sixteenth Century." *Early Modern Women* 3 (2008): 27–60.

Amussen, Susan Dwyer. "Punishment, Discipline, and Power: The Social Meanings of Violence in Early Modern England." *Journal of British Studies* 34, no. 1 (January 1, 1995): 1–34.

Anderson, Barbara A. and Brian D. Silver. "Ethnic Differences in Fertility and Sex Ratios at Birth in China: Evidence from Xinjiang." *Population Studies* 49, no. 2 (1995): 211–26.

Angelozzi, Giancarlo and Cesarina Casanova. *Donne criminali: il genere nella storia della giustizia*. Bologna: Pàtron, 2014.

La giustizia criminale a Bologna nel XVIII secolo e le riforme di Benedetto XIV. Bologna: CLUEB, 2010.

La giustizia criminale in una città di antico regime: il tribunale del Torrone di Bologna, secc. XVI–XVII. Bologna: CLUEB, 2008.

La nobiltà disciplinata: violenza nobiliare, procedure di giustizia e scienza cavalleresca a Bologna nel 17. secolo. Bologna: CLUEB, 2003.

Appleby, Andrew B. "Epidemics and Famine in the Little Ice Age." *The Journal of Interdisciplinary History* 10, no. 4 (April 1, 1980): 643–63.

Armit, Ian. "Violence and Society in the Deep Human Past." *British Journal of Criminology* 51, no. 3 (May 1, 2011): 499–517.

Astarita, Tommaso. *Village Justice: Community, Family, and Popular Culture in Early Modern Italy*. Baltimore, MD: Johns Hopkins University Press, 1999.

Auerbach, Carl F. *Qualitative Data: An Introduction to Coding and Analysis*. New York: New York University Press, 2003.

Baernstein, Renée. P. and J. Christopoulos. "Interpreting the Body in Early Modern Italy: Pregnancy, Abortion and Adulthood." *Past & Present* 223, no. 1 (May 1, 2014): 41–75.

Beam, Sara. *Laughing Matters: Farce and the Making of Absolutism in France*. Ithaca, NY: Cornell University Press, 2007.

Beattie, John M. *Crime and the Courts in England, 1660–1800*. Princeton, NJ: Princeton University Press, 1986.

Beattie, John M. "The Pattern of Crime in England 1660–1800." *Past & Present*, no. 62 (February 1, 1974): 47–95.

Bellettini, Athos. *La popolazione di Bologna dal secolo 15 all'unificazione italiana*. Bologna: Zanichelli, 1961.

Benedictis, Angela De. *Una guerra d'Italia, una resistenza di popolo: Bologna 1506*. Bologna: Società editrice Il Mulino, 2004.

Benedictow, O. J. "Morbidity in Historical Plague Epidemics." *Population Studies* 41, no. 3 (November 1, 1987): 401–31.

Bessel, Richard. "Assessing Violence in the Modern World." *Historical Reflections/Réflexions Historiques* 44, no. 1 (March 1, 2018): 66–77.

Black, Christopher F. "The Development of Confraternity Studies over the Past Thirty Years." In *The Politics of Ritual Kinship*, ed. N. Terpstra. Cambridge Studies in Italian History and Culture. Cambridge: Cambridge University Press, 1999.

Early Modern Italy: A Social History. London: Routledge, 2001.

Blanshei, Sarah Rubin. *Politics and Justice in Late Medieval Bologna*. Boston, MA: Brill, 2010.

ed. *Violence and Justice in Bologna: 1250–1700*. Lanham, MD: Lexington Books, 2018.

Blastenbrei, Peter. "Violence, Arms and Criminal Justice in Papal Rome, 1560–1600." *Renaissance Studies* 20, no. 1 (February 2006): 68–87.

Blok, Anton. *Honour and Violence*. Malden, MA: Polity Press, 2001.

Body-Gendrot, Sophie and Pieter Spierenburg, eds. *Violence in Europe: Historical and Contemporary Perspectives*. New York: Springer, 2008.

Bornstein, Daniel. "The Bounds of Community: Commune, Parish, Confraternity, and Charity at the Dawn of a New Era in Cortona." In *The Politics of Ritual Kinship*, ed. N. Terpstra. Cambridge Studies in Italian History and Culture. Cambridge, UK: Cambridge University Press, 1999.

Bossy, John, ed. *Disputes and Settlements: Law and Human Relations in the West*. New York: Cambridge University Press, 1983.

Bourke, Joanna. "The Rise and Rise of Sexual Violence." *Historical Reflections/Réflexions Historiques* 44, no. 1 (March 1, 2018): 104–16.

Brackett, John K. *Criminal Justice and Crime in Late Renaissance Florence, 1537–1609*. Cambridge, UK: Cambridge University Press, 1992.

Braun, Theodore and John B. Radner, eds. *The Lisbon Earthquake of 1755: Representations and Reactions*. Oxford: Voltaire Foundation, 2005.

Butler, Sara M. "A Case of Indifference?: Child Murder in Later Medieval England." *Journal of Women's History* 19, no. 4 (2007): 59–82.

"Getting Medieval on Steven Pinker: Violence and Medieval England." *Historical Reflections/Réflexions Historiques* 44, no. 1 (March 1, 2018): 29–40. https://doi.org/10.3167/hrrh.2018.440105.

Carboni, Mauro. *Il debito della città: mercato del credito, fisco e società a Bologna fra cinque e seicento*. Bologna: Il mulino, 1995.

"Public Debt, Guarantees and Local Elites in the Papal States (XVI–XVIII Centuries)." *The Journal of European Economic History* 38, no. 1 (Spring 2009): 149–74.

Carroll, Stuart. *Blood and Violence in Early Modern France*. New York: Oxford University Press, 2006.

Carroll, Stuart, ed. *Cultures of Violence: Interpersonal Violence in Historical Perspective*. Houndmills: Palgrave Macmillan, 2007.

"The Peace in the Feud in Sixteenth- and Seventeenth-Century France." *Past & Present* 178, no. 1 (February 1, 2003): 74–115.

"Revenge and Reconciliation in Early Modern Italy." *Past & Present* 233, no. 1 (November 1, 2016): 101–42.

Casagrande, Giovanna. "Confraternities and Lay Female Religiosity in Late Medieval and Renaissance Umbria." In *The Politics of Ritual Kinship*, ed. N. Terpstra. Cambridge Studies in Italian History and Culture. Cambridge, UK: Cambridge University Press, 1999.

Castan, Nicole. *Les criminels de Languedoc: les exigences d'ordre et les voies du ressentiment dans une société pré-révolutionnaire, 1750–1790*. Toulouse: Association des publications de l'Université de Toulouse-Le Mirail, 1980.

Justice et répression en Languedoc à l'époque des lumières. Montreal: Flammarion, 1980.

Vivre ensemble: ordre et désordre en Languedoc au XVIIIe siècle. [Paris]: Gallimard/Julliard, 1981.

Cavina, Marco. *Nozze di sangue: storia della violenza coniugale*. Rome: Laterza, 2011.

Il sangue dell'onore: storia del duello. Bari: GLF editori Laterza, 2005.

Cesco, Valentina. "Female Abduction, Family Honor, and Women's Agency in Early Modern Venetian Istria." *Journal of Early Modern History* 15, no. 4 (2011): 349–66.

Chambers, David. *Clean Hands and Rough Justice: An Investigating Magistrate in Renaissance Italy*. Ann Arbor: University of Michigan Press, 1997.

Christopoulos, John. "Abortion and the Confessional in Counter-Reformation Italy." *Renaissance Quarterly* 65, no. 2 (June 1, 2012): 443–84.

"Nonelite Male Perspectives on Procured Abortion, Rome circa 1600." *I Tatti Studies in the Italian Renaissance* 17, no. 1 (2014): 155–74.

Cipolla, Carlo M. *Fighting the Plague in Seventeenth-Century Italy*. Madison: University of Wisconsin Press, 1981.

Cochrane, Eric. *The Late Italian Renaissance, 1525–1630*. New York: Harper & Row, 1970.

Cockburn, J. S., ed. *Crime in England, 1550–1800*. Princeton, NJ: Princeton University Press, 1977.

Cockburn, J. S. "Patterns of Violence in English Society: Homicide in Kent 1560–1985." *Past & Present*, no. 130 (February 1, 1991): 70–106.

Cohen, Elizabeth S. "Honor and Gender in the Streets of Early Modern Rome." *The Journal of Interdisciplinary History* 22, no. 4 (April 1, 1992): 597–625.

"Open City: An Introduction to Gender in Early Modern Rome." *I Tatti Studies in the Italian Renaissance* 17, no. 1 (2014): 35–54.

"The Trials of Artemisia Gentileschi: A Rape as History." *The Sixteenth Century Journal* 31, no. 1 (2000): 47–75.

Cohen, Thomas V. "The Case of the Mysterious Coil of Rope: Street Life and Jewish Persona in Rome in the Middle of the Sixteenth Century." *The Sixteenth Century Journal* 19, no. 2 (July 1, 1988): 209–21.

"The Lay Liturgy of Affront in Sixteenth-Century Italy." *Journal of Social History* 25, no. 4 (July 1, 1992): 857–77.

Cohen, Thomas V. and Elizabeth S. Cohen. *Words and Deeds in Renaissance Rome: Trials before the Papal Magistrates*. Toronto: University of Toronto Press, 1993.

Cohn, Samuel K., Jr. and Guido Alfani. "Households and Plague in Early Modern Italy." *The Journal of Interdisciplinary History* 38, no. 2 (October 1, 2007): 177–205.

Cummins, Stephen and Laura Kounine, eds. *Cultures of Conflict Resolution in Early Modern Europe*. Farnham: Ashgate, 2016.

Daly, Martin and Margo Wilson. *Homicide*. New York: A. de Gruyter, 1988.

Dani, Alessandro. *Il processo per danni dati nello Stato della Chiesa (secoli XVI–XVIII)*. Milan: Monduzzi, 2006.

Darnton, Robert. *The Great Cat Massacre and Other Episodes in French Cultural History*. New York: Vintage Books, 1985.

Davies, Jonathan, ed. *Aspects of Violence in Renaissance Europe*. Farnham: Ashgate, 2013.

Davis, Diana K. *Resurrecting the Granary of Rome: Environmental History and French Colonial Expansion in North Africa*. Athens: Ohio University Press, 2007.

Davis, Natalie Zemon. *Fiction in the Archives: Pardon Tales and Their Tellers in Sixteenth-Century France*. Stanford, CA: Stanford University Press, 1987.

Society and Culture in Early Modern France: Eight Essays. Stanford, CA: Stanford University Press, 1975.

Davis, Natalie Zemon, Andrew Spicer, Penny Roberts and Graeme Murdock. *Ritual and Violence*. Vol. [new series] 7. *Past & Present* Supplements. Oxford: Oxford University Press, 2012.

Davis, Robert. "Say It with Stones: The Language of Rock-Throwing in Early Modern Italy." *Ludica* 10 (2004): 113–28.

The War of the Fists: Popular Culture and Public Violence in Late Renaissance Venice. Oxford: Oxford University Press, 1994.

Dean, Trevor. *Crime and Justice in Late Medieval Italy*. Cambridge: Cambridge University Press, 2007.

Dean, Trevor and K. J. P. Lowe. *Murder in Renaissance Italy*. Cambridge: Cambridge University Press, 2017.

Di Simplicio, Oscar. *Peccato, penitenza, perdono: Siena 1575–1800: la formazione della coscienza nell'Italia moderna*. Milan: FrancoAngeli, 1994.

Di Zio, Tiziana. "Il tribunale del Torrone." *Atti E Memorie (Romagna)* 43 (1992): 333–48.

Duby, Georges. *The Chivalrous Society*. London: Arnold, 1977.

Dwyer, Philip. "Whitewashing History: Pinker's (Mis)Representation of the Enlightenment and Violence." *Historical Reflections/Réflexions Historiques* 44, no. 1 (March 1, 2018): 54–65.

Eckstein, Nicholas and Nicholas Terpstra, eds. *Sociability and Its Discontents: Civil Society, Social Capital, and Their Alternatives in Late Medieval and Early Modern Europe*. Turnhout: Brepols, 2009.

Eisenbichler, Konrad, ed. *The Premodern Teenager: Youth in Society, 1150–1650*. Toronto: Centre for Reformation and Renaissance Studies, 2002.

Eisner, Manuel. "Human Evolution, History and Violence: An Introduction." *British Journal of Criminology* 51, no. 3 (May 1, 2011): 473–78.

"Killing Kings: Patterns of Regicide in Europe, AD 600–1800." *British Journal of Criminology* 51, no. 3 (May 1, 2011): 556–77.

"Long-Term Historical Trends in Violent Crime." *Crime and Justice* 30 (January 1, 2003): 83–142.

Elias, Norbert. *The Civilizing Process*. New York: Pantheon Books, 1978.

Elkins, Caroline. "The 'Moral Effect' of Legalized Lawlessness: Violence in Britain's Twentieth-Century Empire." *Historical Reflections/Réflexions Historiques* 44, no. 1 (March 1, 2018): 78–90.

Ewan, Elizabeth. "Disorderly Damsels? Women and Interpersonal Violence in Pre-Reformation Scotland." *The Scottish Historical Review* 89, no. 228 (2010): 153–71.

Fagan, Brian M. *The Little Ice Age: How Climate Made History, 1300–1850*. New York: Basic Books, 2000.

Ferraro, Joanne M. "The Power to Decide: Battered Wives in Early Modern Venice." *Renaissance Quarterly* 48, no. 3 (October 1, 1995): 492–512.

Ferraro, Joanne Marie. *Marriage Wars in Late Renaissance Venice.* New York: Oxford University Press, 2001.

Nefarious Crimes, Contested Justice: Illicit Sex and Infanticide in the Republic of Venice, 1557–1789. Baltimore, MD: Johns Hopkins University Press, 2008.

Fibiger, Linda. "The Past as a Foreign Country: Bioarchaeological Perspectives on Pinker's 'Prehistoric Anarchy.'" *Historical Reflections/Réflexions Historiques* 44, no. 1 (March 1, 2018): 6–16.

Finn, Sarah and Susan Broomhall, eds. *Violence and Emotions in Early Modern Europe.* Abingdon: Routledge, 2016.

Fosi, Irene. *La giustizia del papa: sudditi e tribunali nello stato pontificio in età moderna.* Rome: GLF editori Laterza, 2007.

Foucault, Michel. *Discipline and Punish: The Birth of the Prison.* New York: Vintage Books, 1995.

Gallant, Thomas W. "Honor, Masculinity, and Ritual Knife Fighting in Nineteenth-Century Greece." *The American Historical Review* 105, no. 2 (April 1, 2000): 359–82.

Gardi, Andrea. *Lo stato in provincia: L'amministrazione pella legazione di Bologna durante il regno di Sisto V: 1585–1590.* Bologna: Istituto per la storia di Bologna, 1994.

Garnham, Neal. "How Violent Was Eighteenth-Century Ireland?" *Irish Historical Studies* 30, no. 119 (May 1, 1997): 377–92.

Gaskill, Malcolm. *Crime and Mentalities in Early Modern England.* New York: Cambridge University Press, 2000.

"Reporting Murder: Fiction in the Archives in Early Modern England." *Social History* 23, no. 1 (January 1, 1998): 1–30.

Gauvard, Claude. *De grace especial: crime, etat et société en France à la fin du moyen age.* Paris: Publications de la Sorbonne, 1991.

Geertz, Clifford. "Deep Play: Notes on the Balinese Cockfight." *Daedalus* 101, no. 1 (1972): 1–37.

Given, James Buchanan. *Society and Homicide in Thirteenth-Century England.* Stanford, CA: Stanford University Press, 1977.

Gluckman, Max. "The Peace in the Feud." *Past & Present*, no. 8 (November 1, 1955): 1–14.

Gouwens, Kenneth. "Meanings of Masculinity in Paolo Giovio's 'Ischian' Dialogues." *I Tatti Studies in the Italian Renaissance* 17, no. 1 (2014): 79–101.

Grech, Victor, Charles Savona-Ventura and P. Vassallo-Agius. "Research Pointers: Unexplained Differences in Sex Ratios at Birth in Europe and North America." *BMJ: British Medical Journal* 324, no. 7344 (2002): 1010–11.

Greene, Robin D. "Mountain Peasants in an Age of Global Cooling." MA thesis, Dalhousie University, 2010.

Grossman, Lt. Col. Dave. *On Killing.* E-reads/E-rights, 2002.

Guilmoto, Christophe Z. "Skewed Sex Ratios at Birth and Future Marriage Squeeze in China and India, 2005–2100." *Demography* 49, no. 1 (2012): 77–100.

Gurr, Ted Robert. "Historical Trends in Violent Crime: A Critical Review of the Evidence." *Crime and Justice* 3 (January 1, 1981): 295–353.

Hale, J. R. *Renaissance Fortification: Art or Engineering?* [London]: Thames and Hudson, 1977.

Renaissance War Studies. London: Hambledon Press, 1983.

Hamoudi, Amar. "Exploring the Causal Machinery behind Sex Ratios at Birth: Does Hepatitis B Play a Role?" *Economic Development and Cultural Change* 59, no. 1 (2010): 1–21. https://doi.org/10.1086/655454.

Hanawalt, Barbara. *Crime and Conflict in English Communities, 1300–1348.* Cambridge, MA: Harvard University Press, 1979.

"Violent Death in Fourteenth- and Early Fifteenth-Century England." *Comparative Studies in Society and History* 18, no. 3 (July 1, 1976): 297–320.

The Ties That Bound: Peasant Families in Medieval England. New York: Oxford University Press, 1986.

Hanlon, Gregory. "The Decline of Violence in the West: From Cultural to Post-Cultural History." *The English Historical Review* 128, no. 531 (April 1, 2013): 367–400.

Early Modern Italy, 1550–1800: Three Seasons in European History. New York: St. Martin's Press, 2000.

The Hero of Italy: Odoardo Farnese, Duke of Parma, His Soldiers, and His Subjects in the Thirty Years' War. Oxford: Oxford University Press, 2014.

Human Nature in Rural Tuscany: An Early Modern History. New York: Palgrave Macmillan, 2007.

"l'infanticidio di coppie sposate in Toscana nella prima eta moderna." *Quaderni Storici* 38 (2003): 453–98.

Italy 1636: Cemetery of Armies. Oxford: Oxford University Press, 2015.

"Justice in the Age of Lordship: A Feudal Court in Tuscany during the Medici Era (1619–66)." *The Sixteenth Century Journal* 35, no. 4 (December 1, 2004): 1005–33.

Hardwick, Julie. "Early Modern Perspectives on the Long History of Domestic Violence: The Case of Seventeenth-Century France." *The Journal of Modern History* 78, no. 1 (2006): 1–36.

Harms, Roeland, Joad Raymond and Jeroen Salman. *Not Dead Things: The Dissemination of Popular Print in England and Wales, Italy, and the Low Countries, 1500–1820.* Leiden: Brill, 2013.

Hughes, Steven. "Fear and Loathing in Bologna and Rome the Papal Police in Perspective." *Journal of Social History* 21, no. 1 (October 1, 1987): 97–116.

Huizinga, Johan. *The Autumn of the Middle Ages.* Chicago, IL: University of Chicago Press, 1996.

Hunt, John M. "Carriages, Violence, and Masculinity in Early Modern Rome." *I Tatti Studies in the Italian Renaissance* 17, no. 1 (2014): 175–96.

Hurnard, Naomi D. *The King's Pardon for Homicide before A.D. 1307.* Oxford: Clarendon Press, 1969.

Hynes, Laura. "Routine Infanticide by Married Couples? An Assessment of Baptismal Records from Seventeenth Century Parma." *Journal of Early Modern History* 15, no. 6 (January 1, 2011): 507–30.

Jacobs, Adam, Martin Voracek, Maryanne L. Fisher, M. D. Shields, Bernadette O'Hare, J. Nelson, M. C. Stewart and P. Coyle. "Different Sex Ratios at Birth in Europe and North America." *BMJ: British Medical Journal* 325, no. 7359 (2002): 334–35.

Jacoby, Russell. *Bloodlust: On the Roots of Violence from Cain and Abel to the Present.* New York: Free Press, 2011.

James, William H. "Inconstancy of Human Sex Ratios at Birth." *Fertility and Sterility* 94, no. 3 (August 1, 2010): e53.

——— "Sex Ratios at Birth as Monitors of Endocrine Disruption." *Environmental Health Perspectives* 109, no. 6 (2001): A250–51.

——— "The Validity of Inferences of Sex-Selective Infanticide, Abortion and Neglect from Unusual Reported Sex Ratios at Birth." *European Journal of Population/ Revue Européenne de Démographie* 13, no. 2 (1997): 213–17.

Johnson, Eric A. "Criminal Justice, Coercion and Consent in 'Totalitarian' Society: The Case of National Socialist Germany." *British Journal of Criminology* 51, no. 3 (May 1, 2011): 599–615.

Johnson, Eric and Eric Monkkonen, eds. *The Civilization of Crime: Violence in Town and Country since the Middle Ages.* Urbana: University of Illinois Press, 1996.

Jurdjevic, Mark and Rolf Strom-Olsen, eds. *Rituals of Politics and Culture in Early Modern Europe: Essays in Honour of Edward Muir.* Toronto: Centre for Reformation and Renaissance Studies, 2016.

Karras, Ruth Mazo. *From Boys to Men: Formations of Masculinity in Late Medieval Europe.* Philadelphia: University of Pennsylvania Press, 2003.

Kermode, Jennifer and Garthine Walker, eds. *Women, Crime and the Courts in Early Modern England.* Chapel Hill: University of North Carolina Press, 1994.

Kesselring, K. J. "Bodies of Evidence: Sex and Murder (or Gender and Homicide) in Early Modern England, c. 1500–1680." *Gender & History* 27, no. 2 (August 2015): 245–62.

King, Peter. *Crime and Law in England, 1750–1840: Remaking Justice from the Margins.* Cambridge, UK: Cambridge University Press, 2006.

Kollmann, Nancy Shields. "The Complexity of History: Russia and Steven Pinker's Thesis." *Historical Reflections/Réflexions Historiques* 44, no. 1 (March 1, 2018): 41–53.

Lansing, Carol. *The Florentine Magnates: Lineage and Faction in a Medieval Commune.* Princeton, NJ: Princeton University Press, 1991.

Lloyd, Charles. *The Conspiracy of the Pazzi.* Cambridge: Chadwyck-Healey, 1994.

Lynch, Katherine A. *Individuals, Families and Communities in Europe, 1200–1800: The Urban Foundations of Western Society.* Cambridge, UK: Cambridge University Press, 2003.

Lynn, John A. *Women, Armies, and Warfare in Early Modern Europe.* Cambridge, UK: Cambridge University Press, 2008.

Martines, Lauro. *April Blood: Florence and the Plot against the Medici.* London: Jonathan Cape, 2003.

——— *Power and Imagination: City-States in Renaissance Italy.* New York: Knopf, 1979.

Martines, Lauro, ed. *Violence and Civil Disorder in Italian Cities, 1200–1500.* Berkeley: University of California Press, 1972.

Mauch, Christof and Chiristian Pfister. *Natural Disasters, Cultural Responses: Case Studies toward a Global Environmental History.* Lanham, MD: Lexington Books, 2009.

McCarthy, Vanessa Gillian. "Prostitution, Community, and Civic Regulation in Early Modern Bologna." PhD dissertation, University of Toronto, 2015.

Mendes Victor, L. A., ed. *The 1755 Lisbon Earthquake: Revisited.* [Dordrecht]: Springer, 2009.

Meyerson, M. and O. Falk, eds. *A History of Young People in the West.* Cambridge, MA: Belknap Press of Harvard University Press, 1997

Meyerson, Mark D. *A Jewish Renaissance in Fifteenth-Century Spain.* Princeton, NJ: Princeton University Press, 2004.

Meyerson, Mark D. and Edward D. English, eds. *Christians, Muslims, and Jews in Medieval and Early Modern Spain: Interaction and Cultural Change.* Notre Dame, IN: University of Notre Dame Press, 1999.

Micale, Mark S. "What Pinker Leaves Out." *Historical Reflections/Réflexions Historiques* 44, no. 1 (March 1, 2018): 128–39.

Micale, Mark S. and Philip Dwyer. "Introduction: History, Violence, and Stephen Pinker." *Historical Reflections/Réflexions Historiques* 44, no. 1 (March 1, 2018): 1–5.

Miller, William Ian. *Bloodtaking and Peacemaking: Feud, Law, and Society in Saga Iceland.* Chicago, IL: University of Chicago Press, 1990.

Humiliation: And Other Essays on Honor, Social Discomfort and Violence. Ithaca, NY: Cornell University Press, 1993.

Monkkonen, Eric H. *Crime, Justice, History.* Columbus: Ohio State University Press, 2002.

Monkkonen, Eric. "New Standards for Historical Homicide Research." *Crime, Histoire & Sociétés/Crime, History & Societies* 5, no. 2 (January 1, 2001): 5–26.

Muchembled, Robert. *Le temps des supplices: de l'obéissance sous les rois absolus, XVᵉ–XVIIIᵉ siècle.* Paris: A. Colin, 1992.

Muir, Edward. *Civic Ritual in Renaissance Venice.* Princeton, NJ: Princeton University Press, 1981.

The Culture Wars of the Late Renaissance: Skeptics, Libertines, and Opera. Cambridge, MA: Harvard University Press, 2009.

"Italy in the No Longer Forgotten Centuries." *I Tatti Studies in the Italian Renaissance* 16, nos. 1–2 (September 1, 2013): 5–11.

Mad Blood Stirring: Vendetta and Factions in Friuli during the Renaissance. Baltimore, MD: Johns Hopkins University Press, 1993.

"The Sources of Civil Society in Italy." *The Journal of Interdisciplinary History* 29, no. 3 (January 1, 1999): 379–406.

"The 2001 Josephine Waters Bennett Lecture: The Idea of Community in Renaissance Italy." *Renaissance Quarterly* 55, no. 1 (April 1, 2002): 1–18.

Muir, Edward and Guido Ruggiero, eds. *History from Crime.* Baltimore, MD: Johns Hopkins University Press, 1994.

Muravyeva, Marianna and Raisa Maria Toivo, eds. *Gender in Late Medieval and Early Modern Europe*. New York: Routledge, 2013.

Naphy, William G. *Plagues, Poisons, and Potions: Plague-Spreading Conspiracies in the Western Alps, c. 1530–1640*. New York: Palgrave, 2002.

Niccoli, Ottavia. *Il seme della violenza: putti, fanciulli e mammoli nell'Italia tra Cinque e Seicento*. Rome: Laterza, 1995.

——— *Storie di ogni giorno in una città del seicento*. Rome: GLF editori Laterza, 2000.

Nirenberg, David. *Communities of Violence: Persecution of Minorities in the Middle Ages*. Princeton, NJ: Princeton University Press, 1996.

——— "Mass Conversion and Genealogical Mentalities: Jews and Christians in Fifteenth-Century Spain." *Past & Present*, no. 174 (February 1, 2002): 3–41.

Nivette, Amy E. "Violence in Non-State Societies: A Review." *British Journal of Criminology* 51, no. 3 (May 1, 2011): 578–98.

Nussdorfer, Laurie. *Brokers of Public Trust: Notaries in Early Modern Rome*. Baltimore, MD: Johns Hopkins University Press, 2009.

——— "The Vacant See: Ritual and Protest in Early Modern Rome." *The Sixteenth Century Journal* 18, no. 2 (July 1, 1987): 173–89.

O'Connell, Monique. "The Sexual Politics of Empire: Civic Honor and Official Crime Outside Renaissance Venice." *Journal of Early Modern History* 15, no. 4 (2011): 331–48.

Parkin, Sally. "Witchcraft, Women's Honour and Customary Law in Early Modern Wales." *Social History* 31, no. 3 (2006): 295–318.

Parsons, Gerald. *Siena, Civil Religion, and the Sienese*. Burlington, VT: Ashgate, 2004.

Pastore, Alessandro. *Crimine e giustizia in tempo di peste nell'Europa moderna*. Rome: Laterza, 1991.

Pinker, Steven. *The Better Angels of Our Nature: Why Violence Has Declined*. New York: Viking, 2011.

Polverini Fosi, Irene. *Papal Justice: Subjects and Courts in the Papal State, 1500–1750*. Washington, DC: Catholic University of America Press, 2011.

Povolo, Claudio. *L'intrigo dell'onore: poteri e istituzioni nella Repubblica di Venezia tra cinque e seicento*. Verona: Cierre, 1997.

Povolo, Claudio, Claudia Andreato, Valentina Cesco and Michelangelo Marcarelli. *Il processo a Paolo Orgiano (1605–1607)*. Series Fonti per la storia della terraferma veneta 19. Rome: Viella, 2003.

Prosperi, Adriano. *Dare l'anima: storia di un infanticidio*. Turin: G. Einaudi, 2005.

——— *Infanticide, Secular Justice, and Religious Debate in Early Modern Europe*. Europa Sacra, volume 10. Turnhout: Brepols, 2016.

Prosperi, Adriano, ed. *Storia di Bologna, Vol. 3: Bologna nell'età moderna*, parts I and II. Bologna: Bononia University Press, 2005–2008.

Pullan, Brian S. *Crisis and Change in the Venetian Economy in the Sixteenth and Seventeenth Centuries*. London: Methuen, 1968.

Putnam, Robert D. *Bowling Alone: The Collapse and Revival of American Community*. New York: Simon & Schuster, 2000.

Raggio, Osvaldo. *Faide e parentele: lo stato genovese visto dalla Fontanabuona*. Turin: G. Einaudi, 1990.

Ricciardelli, Fabrizio and Samuel Cohn, eds. *The Culture of Violence in Renaissance Italy: Proceedings of the International Conference: Georgetown University at Villa Le Balze, 3–4 May, 2010*. Florence: Le lettere, 2012.

Robertson, Ian G. *Tyranny under the Mantle of St Peter: Pope Paul II and Bologna*. Turnhout: Brepols, 2002.

Rondeau, Jennifer Fisk. "Homosociality and Civic (Dis)order in Late Medieval Italian Confraternities." In *The Politics of Ritual Kinship*, ed. N. Terpstra. Cambridge Studies in Italian History and Culture. Cambridge, UK: Cambridge University Press, 1999.

Rose, Colin. "'To Be Remedied of Any Vendetta': Petitions and the Avoidance of Violence in Early Modern Parma." *Crime, Histoire & Sociétés/Crime, History & Societies* 16, no. 2 (2012): 5–27.

Rossiaud, Jacques. *Medieval Prostitution*. New York: Blackwell, 1988.

Roth, Randolph. *American Homicide*. Cambridge, MA: Belknap Press of Harvard University Press, 2009.

"Biology and the Deep History of Homicide." *British Journal of Criminology* 51, no. 3 (May 1, 2011): 535–55.

"Does Better Angels of Our Nature Hold Up as History?" *Historical Reflections/Réflexions Historiques* 44, no. 1 (March 1, 2018): 91–103.

"Yes We Can: Working Together toward a History of Homicide That Is Empirically, Mathematically, and Theoretically Sound." *Crime, Histoire & Sociétés/Crime, History & Societies* 15, no. 2 (January 1, 2011): 131–45.

Rousseaux, Xavier and Kevin Dwyer. "Crime, Justice and Society in Medieval and Early Modern Times: Thirty Years of Crime and Criminal Justice History: A Tribute to Herman Diederiks." *Crime, Histoire & Sociétés/Crime, History & Societies* 1, no. 1 (January 1, 1997): 87–118.

Ruggiero, Guido. *The Boundaries of Eros: Sex Crime and Sexuality in Renaissance Venice*. New York: Oxford University Press, 1985.

Violence in Early Renaissance Venice. New Brunswick, NJ: Rutgers University Press, 1980.

Sahlins, Peter. *Forest Rites: The War of the Demoiselles in Nineteenth-Century France*. Cambridge, MA: Harvard University Press, 1998.

Sassatelli, Giuseppe, et al., eds. *Storia di Bologna*. Bologna: Bononia University Press, 2005–2008.

Schaik, Carel P. van and Sarah Blaffer Hrdy. "Intensity of Local Resource Competition Shapes the Relationship between Maternal Rank and Sex Ratios at Birth in Cercopithecine Primates." *The American Naturalist* 138, no. 6 (1991): 1555–62.

Sella, Domenico. *Italy in the Seventeenth Century*. London: Longman, 1997.

Sharpe, J. A. "Quantification and the History of Crime in Early Modern England: Problems and Results." *Historical Social Research/Historische Sozialforschung* 15, no. 4 (January 1, 1990): 17–32.

Signoria, Gianvittorio and Maria Antonietta Visceglia, eds. *Court and Politics in Papal Rome, 1492–1700*. New York: Cambridge University Press, 2002.

Smail, Daniel Lord. "Common Violence: Vengeance and Inquisition in Fourteenth-Century Marseille." *Past & Present*, no. 151 (1996): 28–59.

The Consumption of Justice: Emotions, Publicity, and Legal Culture in Marseille, 1264–1423. Ithaca, NY: Cornell University Press, 2003.

"Factions and Vengeance in Renaissance Italy: A Review Article." *Comparative Studies in Society and History* 38, no. 4 (1996): 781–89.

"In the Grip of Sacred History." *The American Historical Review* 110, no. 5 (2005): 1337–61.

"The Inner Demons of the Better Angels of Our Nature." *Historical Reflections/ Réflexions Historiques* 44, no. 1 (March 1, 2018): 117–27.

"Neurohistory in Action: Hoarding and the Human Past." *Isis* 105, no. 1 (2014): 110–22.

"Neuroscience and the Dialectics of History." *Análise Social* 47, no. 205 (2012): 894–909.

On Deep History and the Brain. Berkeley: University of California Press, 2008.

"Violence and Predation in Late Medieval Mediterranean Europe." *Comparative Studies in Society and History* 54, no. 1 (January 1, 2012): 7–34.

Smail, Daniel Lord and T. Fenster, eds. *Fama: The Politics of Talk and Reputation in Medieval Europe*. Ithaca, NY: Cornell University Press, 2003.

Spierenburg, Pieter. "Democracy Came Too Early: A Tentative Explanation for the Problem of American Homicide." *The American Historical Review* 111, no. 1 (February 1, 2006): 104–14.

ed. *Men and Violence: Gender, Honor, and Rituals in Modern Europe and America*. Columbus: Ohio State University Press, 1998.

"American Homicide: What Does the Evidence Mean for Theories of Violence and Society?" *Crime, Histoire & Sociétés/Crime, History & Societies* 15, no. 2 (January 1, 2011): 123–29.

"Faces of Violence: Homicide Trends and Cultural Meanings: Amsterdam, 1431–1816." *Journal of Social History* 27, no. 4 (July 1, 1994): 701–16.

A History of Murder: Personal Violence in Europe from the Middle Ages to the Present. Malden, MA: Polity Press, 2008.

"Questions That Remain: Pieter Spierenburg's Reply to Randolph Roth." *Crime, Histoire & Sociétés/Crime, History & Societies* 15, no. 2 (December 1, 2011): 147–50.

The Spectacle of Suffering: Executions and the Evolution of Repression: From a Preindustrial Metropolis to the European Experience. New York: Cambridge University Press, 1984.

"Violence and the Civilizing Process: Does It Work?" *Crime, Histoire & Sociétés = Crime, History & Societies/International Association for the History of Crime and Criminal Justice* 5, no. 2 (2001): 87–105.

Violence and Punishment: Civilizing the Body through Time. Malden, MA: Polity, 2013.

Strocchia, Sharon T. *Nuns and Nunneries in Renaissance Florence*. Baltimore, MD: Johns Hopkins University Press, 2009.

"Women and Healthcare in Early Modern Europe." *Renaissance Studies* 28, no. 4 (2014): 496–514.

Sudha, S. and S. Irudaya Rajan. "Persistent Daughter Disadvantage: What Do Estimated Sex Ratios at Birth and Sex Ratios of Child Mortality Risk Reveal?" *Economic and Political Weekly* 38, no. 41 (2003): 4361–69.

Taylor, Scott K. "Women, Honor, and Violence in a Castilian Town, 1600–1650." *The Sixteenth Century Journal* 35, no. 4 (December 1, 2004): 1079–97.

Terpstra, Nicholas. "Competing Visions of the State and Social Welfare: The Medici Dukes, the Bigallo Magistrates, and Local Hospitals in Sixteenth-Century Tuscany." *Renaissance Quarterly* 54, no. 4 (December 1, 2001): 1319–55.

    Cultures of Charity: Women, Politics, and the Reform of Poor Relief in Renaissance Italy. Cambridge, MA: Harvard University Press, 2013.

    ed. *The Art of Executing Well: Rituals of Execution in Early Modern Italy.* Kirksville, MO: Truman State University Press, 2008.

    ed. *The Politics of Ritual Kinship: Confraternities and Social Order in Early Modern Italy.* Cambridge, UK: Cambridge University Press, 1999.

    et al., eds. *Bologna: Cultural Crossroads from the Medieval to the Baroque: Recent Anglo-American Scholarship.* Bologna: Bononia University Press, 2013.

Thompson, Edward P. "Rough Music Reconsidered." *Folklore* 103, no. 1 (1992): 3.

    "'Rough Music': Le Charivari Anglais." *Annales. Histoire, Sciences Sociales* 27, no. 2 (1972): 285–312.

Tlusty, B. Ann. *The Martial Ethic in Early Modern Germany: Civic Duty and the Right of Arms.* New York: Palgrave Macmillan, 2011.

Trundle, Matthew. "Were There Better Angels of a Classical Greek Nature?: Violence in Classical Athens." *Historical Reflections/Réflexions Historiques* 44, no. 1 (March 1, 2018): 17–28.

Tuten, Belle S. and Tracey L. Billado, eds. *Feud, Violence and Practice: Essays in Medieval Studies in Honor of Stephen D. White.* Burlington, VT: Ashgate, 2010.

Vallerani, Massimo. *La Giustizia Pubblica Medievale.* Bologna: Il mulino, 2005.

Walker, Charles F. *Shaky Colonialism: The 1746 Earthquake-Tsunami in Lima, Peru, and Its Long Aftermath.* Durham, NC: Duke University Press, 2008.

Waquet, Jean-Claude. *Corruption: Ethics and Power in Florence, 1600–1770.* University Park: Pennsylvania State University Press, 1992.

Watkins, Renee, ed. and trans. *Humanism and Liberty: Writings on Freedom from Fifteenth-Century Florence.* Columbia: University of South Carolina Press, 1978.

Weissman, Ronald F. E. *Ritual Brotherhood in Renaissance Florence.* New York: Academic Press, 1981.

White, Stephen D. *Feuding and Peace-Making in Eleventh-Century France.* Burlington, VT: Ashgate/Variorum, 2005.

    Re-thinking Kinship and Feudalism in Early Medieval Europe. Aldershot: Ashgate Variorum, 2005.

Wood, John Carter. "A Change of Perspective: Integrating Evolutionary Psychology into the Historiography of Violence." *British Journal of Criminology* 51, no. 3 (May 1, 2011): 479–98.

Zmora, Hillay. *The Feud in Early Modern Germany.* New York: Cambridge University Press, 2011.

Index